HARRY OF ENGLAND

HARRY OF ENGLAND

THE HISTORY OF EIGHT KINGS

TERESA COLE

AMBERLEY

First published 2022

Amberley Publishing
The Hill, Stroud
Gloucestershire, GL5 4EP

www.amberley-books.com

British Library Cataloguing in Publication Data.
A catalogue record for this book is available from the British Library.

ISBN 978 1 4456 9864 9 (hardback)
ISBN 978 1 4456 9865 6 (ebook)

1 2 3 4 5 6 7 8 9 10

Typesetting by SJmagic DESIGN SERVICES, India.
Printed in the UK.

Contents

Map

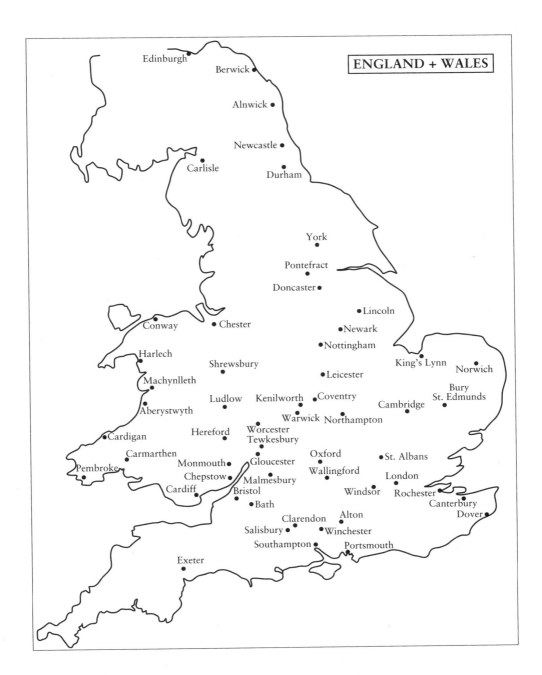

ENGLAND + WALES

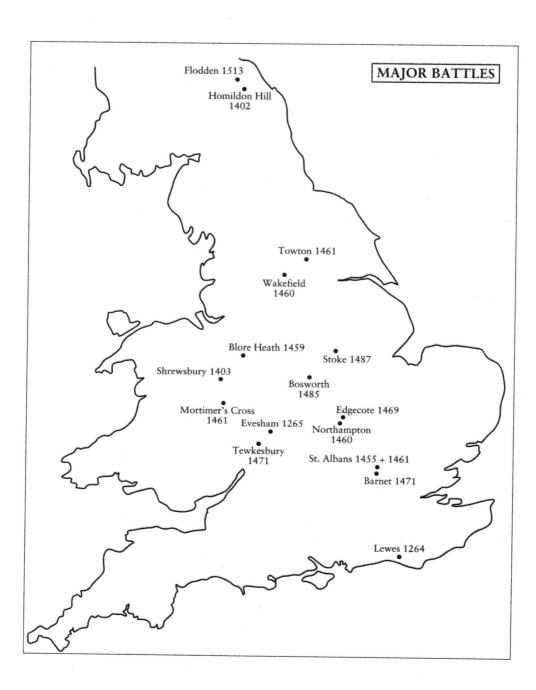

Flodden 1513

Homildon Hill
1402

MAJOR BATTLES

Towton 1461

Wakefield
1460

Blore Heath 1459

Stoke 1487

Shrewsbury 1403

Bosworth
1485

Mortimer's Cross
1461

Edgecote 1469

Evesham 1265

Northampton
1460

Tewkesbury
1471

St. Albans 1455 + 1461

Barnet 1471

Lewes 1264

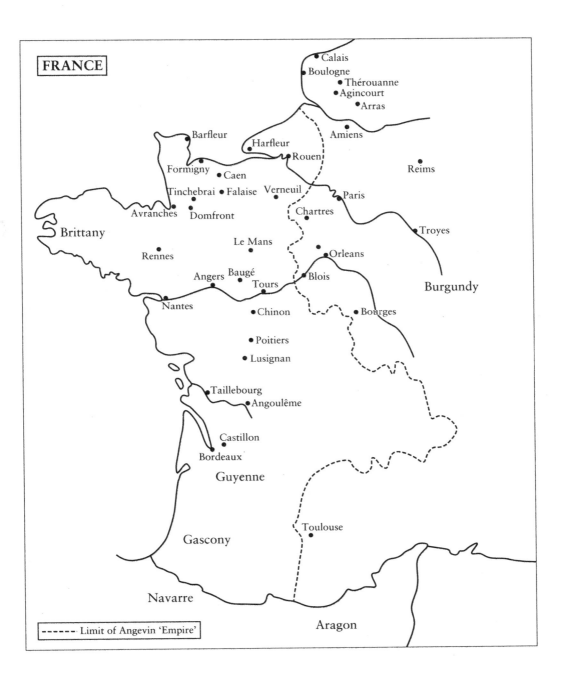

FRANCE

Calais
Boulogne
Thérouanne
Agincourt
Arras
Amiens
Barfleur
Harfleur
Rouen
Reims
Formigny
Caen
Tinchebrai • Falaise
Verneuil
Paris
Avranches
Domfront
Chartres
Brittany
Troyes
Le Mans
Rennes
Orleans
Angers Baugé
Blois
Tours
Burgundy
Nantes
Chinon
Bourges
Poitiers
Lusignan
Taillebourg
Angoulême
Castillon
Bordeaux
Guyenne
Toulouse
Gascony
Navarre
Aragon

------- Limit of Angevin 'Empire'

Family Trees

William the Conqueror = Matilda of Flanders

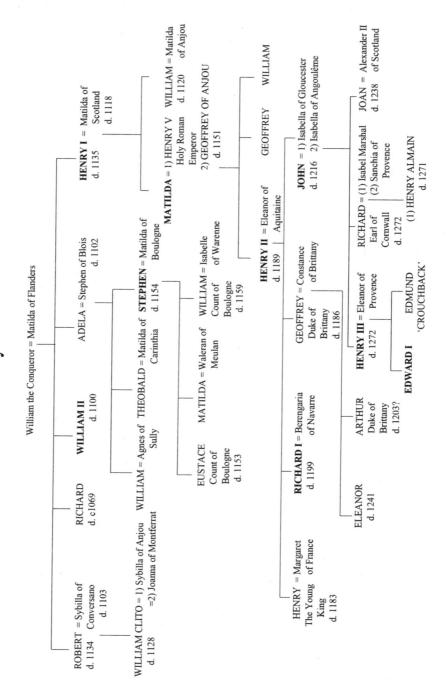

Selected descendants of William the Conqueror

SELECTED DESCENDANTS OF EDWARD III

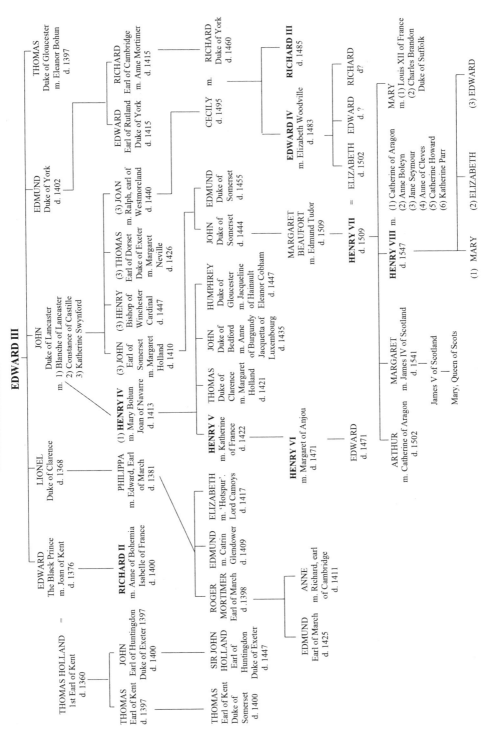

SELECTED CONNECTIONS OF THE FRENCH ROYAL FAMILY

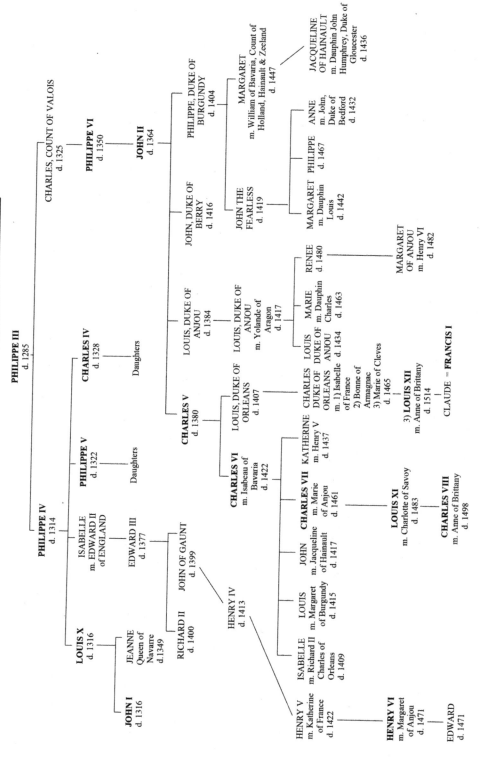

1

Henry I

'A good man he was, and there was much awe of him.'
— Anglo-Saxon Chronicle

Henry I, like so many of his namesakes, was not born to be a king. The fourth son and youngest child of William the Conqueror had no right to expect either the crown of England or the duchy of Normandy – and yet Henry ended up with both.

He was born at Selby in Yorkshire, probably in September 1068, the only one of the Conqueror's sons to be born on English soil. Yorkshire might seem an unusual birthplace for a Norman prince, but there is an easy explanation. A scant two years after the battle of Hastings, the conquest of England was by no means complete. 1068 produced a rash of defiant uprisings, led by a variety of Saxon figureheads, each of whom melted away at the approach of William and his army. The last of the uprisings centred on York in the late summer. Once again, the insurgents fled as William approached, the citizens of York came out to offer him the keys of the city and he entered peacefully.

William then spent some time in the area, raising a castle mound in York and negotiating a peace with the Scottish king, but whether Henry's birth at Selby took place by accident or design is not known. Possibly it symbolised the new dynasty putting down roots in English soil, in the same way as the later birth of Edward II at Carnarvon was to be symbolic of the conquest of Wales. We do know that very soon afterwards William founded an abbey at Selby, generously endowed with lands and privileges, a northern counterpart to his other English foundation, Battle Abbey near Hastings. If Battle commemorated the successful arrival of William in England, maybe Selby, in part at least, signified his determination to stay, a determination made visible by the birth of a son in that very place.

According to tradition, Henry was named by his mother, Matilda, after her uncle, Henry I of France, but little is known of his early childhood. All the nine children of William and Matilda, even the girls, were educated beyond the usual standards of the day, and it has been suggested that Henry received a better education than his brothers. Lanfranc, Archbishop of Canterbury and a man noted for his learning, is likely to have had a hand in this, and later Henry spent time in the household of Osmund, bishop of Salisbury. It may have been that a career in the church was intended, a common course for younger sons at the time, but if that was the plan it must have been abandoned quite early on. Certainly, there is nothing in Henry's later actions to suggest he would ever have willingly embraced such a life.

The result of this education was the ability to read and write, a fluency in Latin, and possibly a little English as well. This may not seem to us a remarkable level of achievement, but it was enough to win Henry a reputation for learning, and later the nickname that has stuck to him through history, 'Henry Beauclerc', sometimes translated as Henry the Learned. A later comment attributed to him – 'An illiterate king is a crowned ass' – suggests that Henry himself saw some value in education. He was undoubtedly shrewd enough in later life when it came to knowing what was good for him.

By the time Henry first appears in the chronicles, there were only three brothers left. The second son, Richard, died in a hunting accident in the New Forest – something that was to become almost a habit in this family. The oldest of the three, Robert, had the nickname 'Curthose', bestowed by his father, possibly translated as 'Shorty'. Presumably a good bit shorter than his father's 5´ 10˝, of all the brothers he seems to have inherited the least of his father's character and resolve.

The other brother, William, was certainly not lacking in resolve. Many of his actions might be put down to jealousy of Robert, whose martial upbringing as the son and heir he clearly envied. His ruddy complexion led to him being known as William Rufus, and it was surely he that led the young Henry into what might have been seen as a prank, but which would have long-lasting consequences.

In 1077, the chronicler Orderic Vitalis records 'a diabolical quarrel' between the brothers. While Robert and his friends were playing at dice, he declares, William and Henry climbed to the gallery above and tipped a full chamber pot over their heads. Robert was then around 23 years old and already nominally invested with both the Duchy of Normandy and the County of Maine, although allowed no actual power over either. Already chafing at this, he would have been in no mood to accept further insults from his siblings. The Conqueror's refusal to discipline the younger boys proved to be the final straw. Robert stormed off to make a tour of his father's enemies until he found one, the king of France, prepared to back him in rebellion. There was a reconciliation of sorts later, possibly instigated by Queen Matilda, following an incident at the siege of Gerboy when Robert inadvertently attacked and almost killed his father. The split between the two was never truly healed, however, and at the time of the Conqueror's death they were again at war.

On 9 September 1087, William the Conqueror died. Campaigning against Philip of France, he had been thrown violently against the high pommel of his saddle and suffered internal injuries. The campaign was instantly abandoned, and William returned to Rouen to prepare for the end. There were, however, notable absentees from his deathbed. Lanfranc was in England, acting as regent while the king was away, and Robert, as so often before, was with the king of France. William Rufus was there, though, the favourite and most loyal son, and Henry was there, along with a range of archbishops, bishops and abbots, assembled to offer prayers and advice for the division of the Conqueror's possessions.

Various accounts exist of this occasion, some complete with resounding speeches that owe more to the imagination of the chronicler than to reality. What they agree on is that William was only very reluctantly persuaded to confirm Robert as Duke of Normandy. The customs of Normandy demanded it and he had already received the homage of the Norman barons. England was a different matter.

Orderic Vitalis has William declaring that, since he won the land by conquest, he could leave it only to God, adding, however, that he hoped God would grant it to William Rufus. He then gave young William his ring and a letter commending him to Lanfranc as king designate. Another account suggests he gave crown, sceptre and sword as well, but it is undisputed that he told him to go at once and claim the kingdom. William duly departed and was at the coast, ready to embark for England, before he heard of his father's death.

Henry was left 'indescribable treasure' – in fact 5000 pounds of silver – and a prophecy that he would one day be master of both England and Normandy. This prophecy is first recorded some time after the event, so it probably owes more to hindsight than to any clairvoyant powers of the king, but the treasure was a fact, and we are told Henry went straightaway to have it weighed out, leaving his father to die deserted by all his family.

By the time of the funeral, in the Conqueror's Church of St Stephen in Caen, Henry had returned. There was an unseemly interruption to the ceremony when a man appeared claiming that his family had been wrongfully deprived of the land on which the church was built. Several accounts say it was Henry who took him aside and compensated him – in silver – in order that the funeral could proceed. No doubt he had some to spare.

The division of lands made by the Conqueror was never likely to lead to a peaceful settlement among the brothers. If they were fighting among themselves before, now they had something really contentious to quarrel about. The king's recommendation, and William Rufus's prompt action, led to the latter being anointed and crowned king of England, albeit reluctantly by Lanfranc, within three weeks of his father's death. When Robert returned to Normandy from the French court, he found a fait accompli. Nevertheless, it was not Robert but a prisoner released by the Conqueror on his deathbed who made the first challenge to William Rufus's rule.

Odo, bishop of Bayeux, half-brother to the Conqueror, had been imprisoned for treason in 1082, and was now only very reluctantly released in a general amnesty. His response was to rouse a number of barons in England into open rebellion, theoretically on behalf of Robert. The majority of noble families at the time held lands in both England and Normandy and in the impossible position of owing allegiance to two rival overlords, it is not surprising that they should take sides and support one against the other. Perhaps the rebels chose Robert as he was the elder brother, though inheritance by the first-born was by no means firmly established in England at the time. More likely, he had already proved himself to be a weaker master than the strong, decisive William Rufus. As was amply demonstrated later in Normandy, the pickings for powerful barons would be a great deal richer under Robert than under his younger brother.

Be that as it may, the rebellion proved short-lived. Robert hesitated, sent men, promised more, but never appeared in person, while William, making promises he never intended to keep, won the church and the English to his side. Odo and his fellows were besieged, defeated, exiled and worse, and Robert's reinforcements were annihilated before they could land.

And Henry? Henry's part in this was to sit on the side-lines in Normandy, and to advance to the perennially hard-up Robert £3,000 to pay for his fruitless expedition. In return he was given that part of Normandy known as the Cotentin peninsula. Some accounts say he bought it outright, others that it was only security for the repayment of the money. Either way, Henry took possession, and, as Count of the Cotentin, set about establishing himself in an area estimated to produce a third of the revenue of the entire Duchy of Normandy.

Though Odo's rebellion was only the first skirmish in the battle to unite England and Normandy, by 1088 matters between the brothers had been patched up enough for Henry to travel to the court of William Rufus, asking to be granted some of his mother's estates in England which he should have inherited. Initially the prospects seemed good. He did homage to his brother and was promised the estates.

Returning to Normandy, he and his travelling companion Robert de Bellème were promptly seized by Duke Robert as traitors and thrown into prison. They were only released when Bellème's father, Roger of Montgomery, 1st earl of Shrewsbury, persuaded Robert to do so, partly by force, partly by negotiation. Nevertheless, when in 1090 William Rufus invaded Normandy, Henry appeared once more on Robert's side.

Fighting and bribing his way across the duchy, William incited the citizens of Rouen, the Norman capital, to rebel against their duke. Robert appealed for help, and first on the scene was Henry. Possibly this was because, in the meantime, William had given away his English estates, or maybe simply that he was outraged that a royal duke should be challenged by mere citizens. We do know that, when victory was won, Henry claimed as his prisoner the leader of the rebels, a wealthy citizen called Conan. Then, despite pleas for mercy and the fact that Conan was willing and able to pay a large ransom in exchange for his life (as other prisoners were doing), he took him to the top of the tower of Rouen Castle and threw him to his death. With sturdy medieval humour, this place was known thereafter as 'Conan's Leap'.

Far from rewarding his brother for this service, when the following year Robert was brought to sue for peace with William Rufus, Henry was not even invited to the negotiations. Rufus by now had control over almost half the duchy of Normandy, and the provisions of the resulting Treaty of Rouen seemed specifically designed to keep the youngest brother in his place. Robert and William agreed, among other things, that each should be the other's heir (at the time neither was married), that William should keep the lands he had conquered in Normandy, and that, in exchange, he would help Robert recover other lands which had formerly belonged to the Conqueror. Within this broad definition fell the lands of the Cotentin – Henry's lands.

Refusing to go along with this cosy family arrangement, Henry became besieged at Mont St Michel, an eminently defensible fortress but for the lack of fresh water. One account suggests that Robert allowed Henry's garrison to fetch water, and even sent a barrel of wine for his brother, such an action no doubt infuriating the more ruthless William. Be that as it may, the siege lasted only 15 days before Henry decided it would be wiser to surrender.

Perhaps surprisingly, he was not imprisoned, though he was stripped of his lands on both sides of the Channel and for a while he disappears from the limelight. Orderic Vitalis, a monk in Normandy at the time, declares he was travelling in obscurity with only five companions. One of these, Roger le Poer, a priest from Avranches, would later become his most trusted administrator.

Henry next appears in the chronicles in 1092 at Domfront, a hilltop town on the southern edge of Normandy. This, along with other Norman lands, had been inherited by Robert de Bellème, his earlier companion in misfortune. Bellème was a skilled soldier and castle-builder, but also possessed one of the nastier reputations of the age, his particular hobbies being extortion and sadism. It was said that he would refuse to ransom captives, as was the custom at the time, in order to have the pleasure of torturing them to death.

His path would repeatedly cross Henry's, usually violently, but in 1092 Henry seems to have taken over Domfront unopposed, at the invitation of its citizens. Then having established a small foothold in Normandy, he set about consolidating and enlarging his influence by fire and sword, until, without the title of count, he had again become a substantial presence in the area. In the words of Vitalis, he had 'made reprisals for his own banishment'.

He had, though, given up on Robert Curthose. It was William Rufus who was now providing encouragement and assistance, and when open hostilities broke out again in 1094 between the English king and his elder brother, Henry was sent into the field on behalf of William, while the king's presence was required in England by an uprising of the Welsh.

In 1095, fortunes changed again. At the Council of Clermont in November of that year, Pope Urban II issued a decree calling for a crusade to drive the Seljuk Turks from the Holy Lands in the east. Robert, duke of Normandy, was one of many fired with the idea of re-taking Jerusalem for the Christian west, but Robert, as usual, was out of money. There was no chance of a loan from Henry this time, so instead he turned to William. A deal was made that Normandy would be pledged to William in exchange for 10,000 silver marks. Robert departed, and William, for a while at least, had control over both the lands ruled by his father. Whether he ever intended to give up Normandy we will never know, for on a fateful day in 1100, William went hunting in the New Forest.

On the afternoon of 2 August 1100, in the words of the *Anglo-Saxon Chronicle*, 'King William was shot with an arrow by his own men, as he was hunting, and he was carried to Winchester and buried there.' By all accounts the one who loosed the arrow was Walter Tirel, a French knight and one of the king's attendants. A later tradition says he was shooting at a stag and the arrow glanced off a tree and pierced the king's lung. The so-called 'Rufus Stone' marks the spot to this day. But was it accident or murder?

It appears that no such question was raised at the time. Hunting accidents were common. Not only did Henry's brother Richard die in that way, but the very year before, an illegitimate son of Robert had been killed while hunting in the New Forest. To modern eyes, though, many of the surrounding circumstances look highly suspicious. *Cui bono*? is the question that should be posed about any such 'accident'. 'Who benefits?' And the resounding answer in this case is Henry.

Henry, too, was hunting in the New Forest that day, some say with the king, some say in another area. Instead of taking charge of his brother's body, tending it properly and carrying it away for burial, Henry's immediate reaction to the death was to take horse and gallop to Winchester to seize control of the royal treasury, and thereby the crown.

He was not a moment too soon. Hot on his heels came William of Breteuil, a staunch supporter of Robert Curthose. A brief confrontation followed, with William asserting Robert's right to the throne as the elder brother. Henry replied with his English birth to parents who were at the time king and queen of England, while Robert's parents had been only duke and duchess of Normandy when he was born. To emphasise the point, according to Vitalis, he drew his sword and declared 'no foreigner should, on frivolous pretences lay hands on his father's sceptre.' The few nobles present, in particular the Beaumont brothers, Robert de Meulan and Henry, earl of Warwick, backed Henry's claim, the castle and treasury at Winchester were duly handed over, and thereafter Henry was accepted as king of England.

Walter Tirel fled to Normandy and later denied he had anything to do with the death of William Rufus. No action was ever taken against him. His property was not confiscated, and his connections, the Clare family, who may have connived at his escape, were well treated by the new king.

William died on a Thursday afternoon and, according to legend, his body was brought to Winchester on a peasant's cart. Centuries later, the Purkiss family from the area claimed it was their ancestor who had performed this deed (even claiming to possess a wheel from the cart) and so it is recorded on the Rufus Stone. The following day he was buried with the minimum of ceremony, and two days after that Henry was crowned and anointed king of England at Westminster Abbey.

That this was a hastily arranged ceremony may be judged by those present – or perhaps, more tellingly, by those who were not. The Archbishop of Canterbury, whose proper role it was to crown kings, was still living in exile after a dispute with William Rufus. The Archbishop of York was old and in poor health and Henry was not prepared to wait for him. In the absence of these senior clerics, the coronation was performed by Maurice, Bishop of London, in front of a few of Henry's supporters, but it achieved its purpose. Henry was now, by election, anointing and crowning, the king of England.

If the death of William Rufus was an accident it was a staggeringly well-timed one for Henry. Robert was already on his way back from the Holy Land, covered in glory. Moreover, he had married a rich wife on the way home, so his money troubles were likely to be at an end. Toppling an anointed king would be considerably harder than disposing of a rival claimant, and Henry, acting with lightning speed, had achieved that status with only a month to spare. And if the death was not an accident? Henry had certainly been very surefooted in his assumption of the crown, in just the right place, at just the right time. As to the truth of the matter, we are never likely to know.

Perhaps the easy acceptance of Henry owes more than a little to the character of the brother who preceded him as king. The *Anglo-Saxon Chronicle* tells us that William Rufus was 'hated by almost all his people and abhorred by God, as his end showeth.' We must remember that this description was written by a churchman and William's dealings with the church were notoriously bad. There may be some exaggeration involved, but his court is reputed to have attracted all the thugs of Europe, and his methods of raising money for his wars were imaginative and unscrupulous. There seemed very little to love about William Rufus and his passing was largely un-mourned.

Henry, though, would need more support than those few who had rallied to him for his election and coronation. The mighty nobles with lands on both sides of the Channel were once again presented with a choice of loyalties, and many had already returned to their own estates, either to await developments or to prepare to secure their own best advantage. There was, however, another untapped resource whose weight could prove decisive and whose support had never yet been seriously courted. The English!

It is just about possible that, because of his English birth, Henry felt some stirring of affinity with his fellow-countrymen, but far more likely that he had spotted their potential from afar and had seen how he could gain an advantage over his brother. Either way, it is entirely characteristic that he moved instantly to bind his new nation to himself, and he did this in a number of ways.

First, on the very day of his coronation he issued what has since been called his 'Charter of Liberties', abolishing the 'pernicious practices which had obtained during his brother's administration'. This contained something for everyone, clerics, nobles and English alike. For the clerics it declared that the holy church of God should be free, and that his brother's practice of keeping bishoprics vacant while he took their revenues should cease. For the nobles it stated that heirs should have their inheritance without being charged exorbitant sums for this, that permission for the marriages of daughters and widows would be given freely and without charge, and that these practices must also be followed by his barons in their dealings with those below them. For the English, it claimed to restore the laws of Edward the Confessor, subject to amendments made by his father, and further, that if any of his barons or men committed a crime they would no longer be able to buy their way out of justice, but must answer for it according to the law. 'I impose a strict peace upon my entire kingdom,' it concluded, 'And command that it be maintained henceforth.' There is, however, an interesting clause which forgives 'all murders committed before the day I was crowned,' and one has to wonder if he had a specific murder in mind.

It was not unknown at the time for kings to issue coronation charters. Henry's was based on earlier examples but is generally seen as going further than most. It was quoted in the time of his great-grandson, King John, and was taken as a model for Magna Carta, reluctantly accepted by that monarch and by others later.

In Henry's own time, it must be said, it was more followed in the spirit than in the letter, but it was nevertheless an important document. A copy was sent to every shire, addressed by 'Henry, king of the English,' to bishops, abbots, barons and faithful, 'both French and English', and had exactly the desired effect. Here, it proclaimed, was a king who might be of Norman descent but who was also English-born, and prepared to rule English people with English laws.

Among the witnesses to the charter were the Bishop of London who had just crowned the king, William, Bishop elect of Winchester – Bishop elect because Henry had just appointed him – and Robert Malet who had been with Henry in Normandy. Most of the others had been William's men, and some would go over to Robert's cause. Others, though, remained loyal to Henry, including Roger Bigod who had great estates in East Anglia, Eudo Dapifer (steward) and Robert Fitzhamon who had held office under William. The latter was said to have wept over the king's body in the New Forest and accompanied it to Winchester, and he was also the man to whom Henry's English estates had been given by William, yet he had contrived to remain on good terms with Henry and continued to serve him.

Henry's next step in consolidating his power was universally popular. Ranulf Flambard had been the chief administrator under his brother. Sometimes called treasurer, sometimes justiciar, sometimes chief justice, sometimes chaplain, Flambard fulfilled all these roles. He was an able, energetic man, responsible, among other things, for the building of the immense stone hall at Westminster and the first stone bridge over the Thames in London. In the minds of the English, however, he was chiefly associated with the constant levying of taxes to pay for the wars of William Rufus. Within two weeks of his coronation, Henry had him seized and imprisoned in the Tower of London – the new outer wall of which was another of Flambard's works. He was reputedly the first prisoner ever held there.

Recalling the saintly and well-loved Archbishop of Canterbury was Henry's next move towards pleasing his subjects. Anselm had been living in exile, first in Rome and later at Lyons, since 1097. Immediately after his coronation Henry wrote to him apologising that he had, by necessity, received the crown from another bishop, and inviting him to return and take up once more his rightful position in England. 'I commit myself and the people of the whole realm of England to your guidance and that of those who have the right to share with you in guiding me,' he wrote. To general rejoicing among the English church and people, Anselm duly returned on 23 September 1100.

Finally, Henry completed his design of binding himself to his English subjects by choosing for a wife Edith, daughter of the Scottish king Malcom Canmore and the saintly Margaret. Margaret was the niece of Edward the Confessor, and a grand-daughter of the Saxon king Edmund Ironside. No wife could have been more acceptable to the English people, or indeed the English church. Henry may even have heard the story of the death-bed prophecy of Edward the Confessor. In this Edward is said to have had a vision of a green tree being cut in half lengthways down its trunk. One half was carried three furlongs away, then later re-joined to the other half, whereupon the tree became whole again and produced leaves and fruit. This had been interpreted to foretell the coming of the Normans and the splitting away of the old royal line of English kings. Only when the old line was joined again to the new would England find peace and prosperity.

This marriage was undoubtedly a political move, and yet those writing at the time tell us that Edith was already known to Henry. Orderic Vitalis says he had 'been long attracted by her many graces and virtues', while William of Malmesbury, another contemporary chronicler, insists that Henry loved his wife, who was 'by no means despicable in point of beauty'. This may simply be the conventional wishful thinking on the part of two long-time clerics, but if there was genuine feeling between the two, it seems to have been an attraction of opposites.

Henry is noted not just for the number of mistresses he had, which was not unusual for the time, but for the number of illegitimate children he sired, acknowledged and provided for – twenty-two at least – which is a royal record. Edith, by contrast, had been educated at Romsey Abbey under the care of her aunt who was the abbess. There was even a suggestion that she might have taken vows as a nun, but this was firmly denied. She admitted that, at her aunt's insistence, she had worn the nun's costume on occasion, but solely to protect her from 'the lust of the Normans'. She declared that, as soon as her aunt was out of sight, she tore the veil from her head and stamped it underfoot.

The matter was investigated in order to decide whether or not she was free to marry. Anselm convened a council of the bishops to consider the point and witnesses were called who corroborated the story. Finally, it was declared that there was no evidence Edith had ever intended to become a nun, and the royal marriage was duly celebrated on 11 November 1100.

The English were delighted: the Normans rather less so. Despite Edith changing her name to the popular Norman name Matilda, the royal couple were for some time contemptuously referred to among the Norman barons by the Saxon nicknames Godric and Godgifu. Nevertheless, the new queen did what she was expected to do and produced first a daughter, another Matilda, in 1102, and then a son, William, in 1103. The two separate royal lines were thus successfully united in one legitimate, unchallengeable heir – something another Henry would achieve some four centuries later.

In September 1100, Robert Curthose returned to Normandy to great acclaim. His crusade was possibly the most successful undertaking of his life, and, though he had called himself king of England from the time news of his brother's death was brought to him in Salerno, he showed no great enthusiasm for making good his claim to the throne. This state of affairs might have continued indefinitely but for the escape of Ranulf Flambard from the Tower of London in February 1101. Flambard's friends, so the story goes, sent him a length of rope concealed in a cask of wine. The wine he used to make his gaolers drunk, and the rope to let himself down the wall of the fortress. From there he made his way to Normandy and immediately inspired Robert to assert himself to claim the English crown. An army was assembled and a fleet to carry it across the Channel. It was the first real challenge to Henry's rule.

He answered it swiftly, calling out the English fyrd, the militia of the time, levies of men due from each shire to fight for the king when required to do so. They responded immediately, and the chronicles say Henry took on their training himself, drilling some kind of military discipline into these very variable troops. The church, too, with Anselm at its head, was quick to back the anointed king. Only the Norman barons gave less than wholehearted support. A very few, those close to Henry, threw their weight behind him. Some others went over to Robert straight away, while a third, rather larger group, held back to see which way the wind of fortune would blow.

Pevensey was the usual area for invasions and by midsummer Henry was there in force. Robert, though, had different ideas. Some of Henry's sailors forsook him and went over to the enemy, as a result of which Robert's fleet was safely piloted into the shelter of Portsmouth harbour, landing unopposed on 20 July.

Now came Robert's chance to march on Winchester and seize the royal stronghold and treasury as Henry had done before him. Instead, he made straight for London. The two armies came together at Alton in Hampshire – not to fight, but to talk. 'The chief men interfered and made peace between them,' is how the *Anglo-Saxon Chronicle* expresses it.

By that point many of the Norman lords had gone over to Robert and his army heavily outweighed Henry's. It seems extraordinary he should give up this advantage when the prize was his for the taking. We can only guess whether it was bad advice he received, or treachery, or simple gullibility in the face of a smooth talker. All we know is that the meeting at Alton produced not a battle but a treaty, and a treaty heavily in Henry's favour at that.

Sealed by the oaths of twelve of the leading men on each side, it stated that Robert would recognise Henry's title as king of England. In return, Henry would give up all his lands in Normandy except his fortress at Domfront, and would assist his brother to recover the territory of Maine. In addition, he would pay him a sum of 3000 marks per year, and if either of them died without a legitimate heir, the other would inherit his lands. Finally, it was agreed that no action would be taken against those nobles who had supported Robert in his invasion, although punishment of 'wicked sowers of discord' was permitted.

It seems unlikely that Henry ever intended this to be a permanent arrangement, but it bought him out of a perilous situation a great deal more easily than he might have expected. Robert went back to Normandy, and Ranulf Flambard was forgiven and reinstated with his lands in England and his position as Bishop of Durham, spending his time thereafter trying and failing to win back favour with Henry.

Others, who were also apparently forgiven, were not so lucky. Orderic Vitalis declares that Henry now 'began gradually to wreak his vengeance on the traitors who had infamously deserted him in his time of need'. The way he did it seems entirely typical of the man. There were no sudden dawn raids, no arbitrary executions, no breaking of the Treaty of Alton. Instead, one by one, those who had opposed Henry found themselves charged before the king's court with a variety of breaches of the law, sometimes quite trivial matters. Found guilty, they were heavily fined, had their lands confiscated or were exiled.

One family in particular was to feel the strength of the king's wrath. The three Montgomery brothers, Robert de Bellème, Arnulf of Pembroke and Roger of Poitou, were the sons of Roger of Montgomery, Earl of Shrewsbury. Major landowners, with especially strong holdings in the borderlands between Wales and England, they had all backed the invasion of Robert Curthose, not for the rightness of his claim, but seeing more profit for themselves in backing a weak king in place of a strong one.

Robert de Bellême had inherited his father's title in 1098, and, given his evil reputation in Normandy, Henry foresaw further trouble in England and was determined to remove him. He spent a whole year collecting evidence against him, and in the end he was charged with forty-five offences, the last and most serious being the unauthorised building and occupation of Bridgnorth Castle. Summoned before the king's court in 1102, Robert asked for an adjournment to consider his response – and fled. His brothers were roused to his support, along with a number of Welsh princes. Castles were strengthened and provisioned, but he received no support from the other Norman lords.

When Henry, in turn, called up 'the whole military array of England,' not only the feudal levies but also the English fyrd, the end was never in doubt. One by one Robert's castles were picked off, until, threatened with a siege in Shrewsbury Castle, the brothers were forced to surrender. Exile followed, with all English and Welsh lands confiscated, and Arnulf and Roger drop out of the picture. Robert de Bellême, however taking out his fury on his lands in Normandy, was the unintentional catalyst for Henry's next and decisive advance. Over the following few years, his atrocities, committed against fellow magnates, the peasantry and even the church, sent victims scurrying to Henry pleading for his help. Robert Curthose made some attempt to rein in the man who was supposed to be his vassal, but completely without effect.

In fact, the weakness of Curthose at this time is neatly illustrated by the visit he made to England in 1103. Arriving uninvited with just a small escort, he was intercepted as soon as he landed by the king's men who informed him that Henry was displeased by this visit and by Robert's failure to deal with the king's enemies in Normandy. Having put himself in Henry's power, if he wanted to see his own lands again he needed to placate the king in some way. As a result, Robert 'voluntarily' gave up the annuity of £3,000 that Henry had agreed to pay him under the Treaty of Alton, this being thinly disguised as a gift from Robert to Queen Matilda.

In 1104, Henry made his first entrance onto the scene in Normandy. Again showing up the weakness of his brother, he visited and strengthened his base in Domfront without permission or challenge from the duke. He even summoned Robert to meet him and took him to task again over the state of affairs in Normandy. Taking stock of the allegiance of the Norman magnates and whether it could be won or bought over to his cause, he was, at this time, also forging alliances with all the surrounding powers of France, Flanders, Anjou, Maine and Brittany. When the time for action arrived, Robert would find no support there.

Then in Holy Week of 1105 Henry showed his hand. Landing at Barfleur, with an army made up of English and Normans, he was soon joined by men from Maine, Anjou and Brittany. Within a short time, Bayeux and Caen had fallen to him, and soon the entire area of the Cotentin was under his sway. At Falaise, however, the king suffered his first setback, not at the hands of Duke Robert but by a threat of excommunication from the pope.

For most of Western Europe in the early 12th century, Christianity was a given, though the state of the church institutions over a period of several hundred years had left a lot to be desired. Clergy, even popes, had been married, kept mistresses, had children and bought and sold their offices, while powerful families in Rome had installed and removed popes with something of the regularity of football managers today.

Towards the middle of the 11th century, however, a great reform movement had swept through the church, beginning at the monastery of Cluny in France. From there a new spirituality had begun to infiltrate the great offices, with assistance from the Holy Roman Emperor, who for a time assumed the right to appoint new popes. In 1073, Pope Gregory VII was elected to the Holy See by popular acclaim. Formerly Hildebrand, a monk of Cluny and advisor to four previous popes, he was determined to establish his own standards throughout the church. He decreed that clergy should be celibate, that only the church could appoint and remove bishops and other clergy, and even that the pope had power to depose and excommunicate kings and emperors who disobeyed his rulings, their subjects being released by the pope from their oaths of loyalty.

This was powerful stuff and almost certain to bring him into conflict with the rulers of the time, who had a fine sense of their own entitlements, and who had for some time been appointing their own bishops and archbishops. Royal power in these cases was shown by the king investing the new bishop with his ring and crozier, the symbols of his office, and the bishop paying homage to the king in return. This practice of 'Lay Investiture' was now forbidden by the pope, and some, particularly the Holy Roman Emperor, found this so hard to swallow that alternative 'antipopes' were appointed. For nearly 100 years there were rival popes claiming the allegiance of Christians throughout Europe and beyond.

In England this 'Lay Investiture Controversy' had had a particular twist to it. In 1066 William the Conqueror had sought the backing of Pope Alexander for his invasion of England. This had been granted, but with strings attached. William was to carry out reforms to the church and must acknowledge the pope's authority over the lands he conquered. William was happy to do the first, but when the new pope, Gregory VII, demanded he pay homage for his English lands, he was met with a polite but firm refusal. Similarly, William continued appointing and removing bishops and archbishops throughout his reign, and with the help of his friend Archbishop Lanfranc, the resolution of this issue was put off for decision at some future time.

William Rufus had had little of his father's zeal for church reform. Indeed, he and his advisor Ranulf Flambard (himself royally appointed as Bishop of Durham) turned lay investitures into a profitable business. Vacancies went unfilled for years at a time, while William took the revenues from their lands, and when a new incumbent was appointed he was charged a hefty 'relief', or fee for entering into possession of the church property, in the same way as the heir of a lord might be charged on his inheritance. While William no doubt regarded these as his rightful dues, to an outsider it looked very much as though the bishop was buying his office, a practice expressly forbidden by the pope.

The issue of lay investitures was the cause of Anselm's exile in the later years of Rufus's reign, and it was still outstanding when he returned at Henry's invitation. To the king's surprise, Anselm refused to pay homage in return for his church lands, nor would he receive his ring and staff of office from the king's hand or recognise the bishops Henry had appointed and invested since coming to the throne. When Henry pointed out that his right to appoint bishops had never been disputed in England, and that he was simply following the practice of his father, Anselm replied that the law of the church was against it. Furthermore, anyone who, without the church's authority, carried out such a lay investiture, or recognised a bishop so appointed and invested, was liable to a punishment of excommunication.

There were, of course, points on both sides. William the Conqueror had so far recognised the division between lay persons and clergy as to establish separate ecclesiastical courts for dealing with the latter. On the other hand, bishops and archbishops were major landowners at the time, and it was unthinkable to a Norman king that such power in the land should be held by a person not approved by himself, and not paying homage in return for such a landholding.

Henry took more after his father than his brother. He suggested the matter be referred to the pope, but negotiations dragged on for years with neither side prepared to move. In 1103, Anselm himself was directed by the king to go to Rome and try to obtain a satisfactory solution. Pope Paschal, however, instructed Anselm to stand firm on the issue, and, when heavy hints were dropped by Henry's envoy to the effect that Anselm would no longer be welcome in England, the archbishop entered a second exile in Lyons.

This was how matters stood when Paschal decided to force the issue, just as Henry was invading Normandy, ostensibly to come to the aid of the Norman church. First Robert de Meulan, the king's chief advisor, was excommunicated, along with all the bishops Henry had appointed and invested. Then the king himself was threatened with excommunication. His allies began to drift away, and the siege of Falaise had to be abandoned. Anselm himself was travelling north to deliver the excommunication personally, when Henry's favourite sister, Adela, intervened. She had been supportive of Anselm in his exile, and now set up a meeting between the king and the archbishop at L'Aigle in Normandy. There the former friendship between Henry and Anselm was renewed, negotiations began again in a more positive atmosphere, and a compromise was finally reached. Although this skirted around the main point of principle – the king's authority as against that of the pope – it satisfied both parties at the time. Henry agreed not to invest a new bishop with his staff and ring, but the bishop must pay homage to the king in exchange for the lands accompanying the office. In addition, Henry agreed to the free election of clergy by the church, though the election of bishops and archbishops would take place under his supervision.

This might seem an obvious compromise, especially as it dealt only with the formalities of clerical appointments. At the time, however, it represented quite a considerable change in the relationship between king and church. Previously it had been believed that God installed the king, with authority over church and state within his kingdom, hence the significance of the anointing with holy oils at his coronation. Now, in theory at least, rights over the church were reserved for the pope, and the papacy was seen as a new and rising power in Europe. It must be stated, however, that in England Henry ensured that the pope's instructions, by letter or by embassy, were filtered through him, and despite complaints from Rome this was the English practice throughout his reign. Nonetheless, the 'English compromise' paved the way for a similar arrangement for much of the rest of Western Europe in the Concordat of Worms, agreed between the pope and the Holy Roman Emperor in 1122.

When approved by Pope Paschal in 1106 – albeit seen as a temporary measure – it was enough to enable Henry to return to his campaigning in Normandy. This campaign, however, effectively began and ended with the siege of Tinchebrai, a stronghold of William of Mortain, one of the few Norman magnates still clinging to the cause of Robert Curthose. When Robert arrived at the siege, he rashly decided to end it by offering his brother a pitched battle, a rare occurrence at the time. Possibly he felt his experiences in the Holy Land would give him an advantage, but if so, he was wrong. The battle lasted less than an hour, a flanking attack by Henry's allies from Maine smashing the resistance of Robert's army and putting a final end to his rule in Normandy. Robert and William of Mortain were both taken prisoner. Robert de Bellème, in command of the rearguard of the army, fled at the first sign of the collapse, and the withdrawal of his troops was probably a decisive factor in Henry's total victory.

The chroniclers were quick to pick up on the date of the battle – 28 September, forty years to the day since the arrival of William the Conqueror in England. In 1066, they said, Normandy conquered England. In 1106 England conquered Normandy.

Robert Curthose and William of Mortain were sent to imprisonment in England. Robert at least, though, seems to have been treated well by his brother. Over the years there would be repeated pleas, from the pope among others, for his release, but Henry turned a deaf ear. Robert passed from the Tower to a comfortable imprisonment at Devizes Castle, under the control of Henry's chief administrator, Roger, Bishop of Salisbury. Eventually he ended his long life – he was reputedly around 80 years old when he died – at Cardiff Castle, where he had learned Welsh and written poetry to pass the time. He was buried with the full honours due to a crusader at St Peter's Abbey, Gloucester (later Gloucester Cathedral) where his effigy remains to this day.

If Henry made a mistake after Tinchebrai it was in failing to take control of his nephew, Robert's son William Clito. He had the six-year-old in his hands but was persuaded to entrust him to the safekeeping of Helias of Saint-Saens, who had married Robert's illegitimate daughter and was therefore the boy's brother-in-law. Helias would remain faithful to William's interests for the rest of his life.

Henry also erred in accepting the submission of Robert de Bellème, who, surprisingly, was restored to at least some of his Norman lands. Both Robert and William Clito would cause him further trouble in years to come, while possession of Normandy would entangle him in power struggles on the continent. All this was for the future, however. In the meantime, Henry was now master of two lands. Indeed, theoretically owing homage to the king of France for Normandy, he managed to avoid ever paying this homage.

England itself had now been at peace for a number of years and was to remain so throughout Henry's lengthy reign. Troubles, plots and rebellions might affect Normandy, and on occasion Wales and Scotland, but the government of England now entered on a time of quiet development. This was centred on the king's council, the *curia regis*, a body with two different aspects. When the king summoned the great landowners and clerics to advise him on major policies, it was the Magnum Conciliam – the Grand Council. For the rest of the time the curia was made up of officials appointed from among noblemen and church leaders, and officers of the royal court. More and more, the king selected his officials from the humbler ranks of the baronage. 'He raised them from the dust,' says Orderic Vitalis, and while this was not strictly true, service in the king's curia provided a first-class training in administration, and a career path that was likely to lead to much higher things. This curia, through which Henry governed the land, had both administrative and judicial powers, and contained within it the seeds that would eventually grow into the great departments of government, the law courts and even Parliament itself.

The curia regis, along with the numerous members of the king's household, naturally followed the king from place to place as he travelled round his lands, both in England and in Normandy. It is a measure of Henry's commitment to order that, from 1108 onwards, regulations were laid down as to allowances for food, drink and other necessities for every member of the court, and in a major break with tradition, such provisions were now bought instead of being requisitioned from the areas visited. While this travelling court was important in letting the king's power and majesty be seen around the land, it had disadvantages for some parts of the administration, in particular for receiving and accounting for the revenue due to the crown. As a result, the first specialist department of the curia, and the first to operate independently of the king, was the Exchequer.

Twice a year, at Easter and at Michaelmas, the king's representative in each county, the sheriff, had to account for all the royal revenue due from his area. This would come from a wide variety of sources. The geld was a tax based on landholding, originated by the Anglo-Saxons and taken over by the Norman kings. In addition, there would be income from royal landholdings, from royal manors, forests or other land let out 'at farm'; revenue from vacant estates and bishoprics; fees and fines from royal justice; various feudal incidents such as money paid in lieu of military service, or on inheriting an estate; and rents and tolls and, from time to time, 'aids' from royal boroughs. Over a period of time more and more of this would be paid in coin, thus providing the king with ready cash and enabling a more flexible approach to obtaining the services, particularly military services, that he required.

Traditionally the sheriffs would have travelled to wherever the king's court happened to be in order to deliver and account for this revenue. From the early years of Henry's reign, however, Roger of Salisbury is credited with revolutionising this procedure. At the appropriate time, officials from the curia would go to Winchester, where the royal treasury had been held since Anglo-Saxon times. There the sheriffs would bring their revenues and the money would be counted on a large table, 10 feet by 5 feet, covered with a checked cloth, rather like a chess board. The cloth operated as an abacus, making complicated sums possible at a time before Arabic numerals, including the zero, had been adopted in Europe. The name 'Exchequer' derives from this checked cloth and is still used for the department of finance today.

Frequently, the money would be weighed and assayed as well as counted, to assess the content of the silver coins. English kings had long controlled the coinage, and only licensed moneyers were allowed to issue coins. Tampering with the weight or silver content was common, however. Matters became so bad later in Henry's reign that in 1125, the *Anglo-Saxon Chronicle* declared that 'a man might have a pound, and yet not be able to spend one penny at a market.' All moneyers were then summoned to Winchester and those found guilty of issuing debased coins had their right hands cut off. The *Chronicle* stated that this was done 'with much justice because they had ruined this land with the great quantity of bad metal'.

When the money had been counted and assessed, royal officials noted down the amount, the source and other relevant details on long parchment sheets, which were then rolled up and stored. Resembling long pipes, these became known as Pipe Rolls. The earliest we have comes from 1130, but they had clearly been in existence for some time before then.

If the English moaned at the taxes imposed on them by Henry, they were probably more pleasantly surprised by his apparent regard for the law. He did, it is true, go back on many of the promises made in his Coronation Charter, but his justice was not arbitrary, as William Rufus's had been. In his reign the foundations were laid for almost the whole system of justice that we have today, and laid firmly enough to hold through all the challenges that would come, and to earn for Henry the title 'Lion of Justice'.

Sometime between 1115 and 1118 a clerk of the curia produced a manuscript entitled 'Leges Henrici Primi' – the Laws of Henry I – not new laws made by the king, but an attempt to state the law as it was applied in his reign, much of which derived from earlier times. It begins with a statement of Henry's Coronation Charter, which itself declared an intention to return to the laws of Edward the Confessor. Edward, in turn, had adopted much of the code of law laid down by the earlier King Cnut, who also claimed to be ruling by the laws of the still earlier King Edgar. It is not surprising then, to find a legal system with long established roots, albeit overlaid with developments derived from the Normans.

In the feudal state they had introduced, each lord held his own Manor court or Honour court, depending on the size of his landholding. There, disputes and matters relating to the management of the estate would be decided, and men punished for offences committed. This was profitable business for the lord as fines could be imposed for all manner of matters, including making accusations that could not be proved.

At the head of the system the king had his own court in which, traditionally, he would decide disputes and punish offences of his tenants in chief. Throughout his reign, though, Henry's inclination was to centralise justice in his own hands, in particular using pre-existing ideas relating to what we would call criminal law.

The 'Leges' listed a number of 'Pleas of the Crown', offences that could only be tried by the king or his officials. These included murder, rape, robbery, arson and some thefts. In addition, the concept of the 'King's Peace' was developed in a way that would enable the king to draw all criminal matters under his jurisdiction. In general, these cases would be tried in a Shire Court by the king's sheriff for that county, but increasingly royal officials would be commissioned to sit in the Shire Court and deal with such offences.

It was also the sheriff's duty to see that offenders were brought before the court, and he was helped in this by the 'frankpledge' system. Every man over the age of 15 was enrolled in a group called a 'tithing'. If a crime was committed by one of their number, it was their duty to produce him before the court, failing which they would themselves be fined.

Traditional methods of trial would be by ordeal, or by 'compurgation'. Both, in that highly religious age relied heavily on the judgement of God. The ordeal might be to carry a red-hot metal bar for a certain distance, with the healing or otherwise of the wound deciding guilt or innocence. Compurgation involved the swearing of oaths, the number prepared to swear, and thereby risk eternal damnation if they lied, varying according to the seriousness of the offence. To these methods the Normans had added trial by battle, where the accused or his champion fought to the death or until one yielded. Now, however, royal officials dealing with a case began to call upon 'jurors' – local people who could be expected to know the truth of the matter – and to base judgement upon their sworn testimony. These were not juries as we know them, but the beginning of a reliance on evidence, rather than God, in proving criminal cases.

In other matters, too, as royal justice began to extend its reach, evidence was becoming important. Any problem affecting the payment of dues to the crown would now be dealt with by the Exchequer itself, and soon a Court of Exchequer was recognised as a separate entity. Apart from this, the vast majority of disputes were about landholding, and increasingly the royal commissioners sent around the country were empowered to deal with these, requiring charters and other documents to be produced in order to establish the rights of the parties.

From 1111 onwards a feudal lord could only deal with his own tenants. Any dispute between freemen who were tenants of different lords had to be heard by the sheriff in the Shire Court. This brought a most important area of law within reach of royal justice, and a new procedure which came to be called the Writ of Right continued this centralisation. Now a person could appeal to the king that his lord was refusing or unreasonably delaying in giving a judgement in a case. The king would then issue a writ requiring the lord 'to do full right without delay', or the king would see that right was done, usually by his officials in the Shire Court. Although fees had to be paid for this, the procedures and outcomes of the royal courts were so superior that they quickly became established as the most popular form of justice.

Apart from increasing the profit to the Crown, the movement away from manorial courts into royal courts had a major effect on the development of law in England. Previously law had varied from area to area with local customs supplying most of the rules. Centralisation of justice allowed standardisation of rules across the country, though this would be a slow process only just begun in Henry's reign. Probably an increase in central control and the diversion of profit into his own treasury were Henry's motives, rather than the development of a new legal system. Nonetheless, were it not for his dedication to order and method, and his determination to run his country like a good landlord, the English legal system would probably look very different today.

Nor was Henry solely interested in legal and administrative reforms. Around the year 1100 a great movement began towards a more civilised society. Architecture, art, music and poetry all enjoyed a revival about this time, and in England this was encouraged by Henry's court, and in particular by his wife. The king himself kept a menagerie of exotic animals housed in a walled park at his favourite residence, Woodstock Palace.

The years 1106-1110 must be counted the high point of Henry's reign, when good government became established in both England and Normandy. From 1111 onwards, the almost constant rumble of continental conflicts increasingly required the king's attention, meaning that almost half his time was spent in Normandy. This left English affairs in the hands of regents, principally his wife Matilda and the great administrator Roger of Salisbury. These foreign conflicts acted as a drain on the resources of the kingdom, as was frequently mentioned in the chronicles, but may have benefitted the fledgling institutions of government and law, leaving them to develop themselves unhindered.

A new king in France from 1108 revived the ambitions of that country, and in particular the aim of subduing the land of Normandy into more than just a nominal homage to the French crown. The cause of William Clito was an obvious one to pursue, but Henry only seems to have woken up to this threat in 1110. Then his failed attempt to arrest the boy caused Clito and his guardian, Helias of Saint-Saens, to flee, seeking support wherever they could. Robert de Bellème, that serial thorn in the flesh, was the first to offer shelter and protection; then at his urging, the new king, Louis VI, invited William to the French court.

In 1111, war broke out between Henry and an alliance of France, Flanders and Anjou, with a number of renegade Norman barons joining themselves to the king's enemies. Soon after, however, the Count of Flanders was thrown from his horse and killed, and his forces withdrew from the contest. Even better, the following year Robert de Bellème appeared at Henry's court, apparently as an envoy from Louis of France. Having twice before pardoned the man, only to have him take up arms again as an enemy, the king was not about to let him go a third time. Disregarding any niceties about the status of an envoy, he promptly had him arrested, charged with a number of offences and imprisoned for life.

Henry frequently employed diplomacy as a weapon of war. Opening negotiations with Fulk, Count of Anjou at the end of 1112, by the following February he had secured a separate peace with him. By this agreement Henry recognised Fulk's right to Maine, which he was claiming through his wife. He insisted, however, that Fulk must do homage for it, a right which the Norman dukes had claimed with variable success back to the time of William the Conqueror. To seal the agreement, Henry's ten-year-old legitimate son, William, was betrothed to Fulk's daughter Matilda, then a two-year-old infant.

In the same year, with his main allies lost, Louis of France was also forced to settle with Henry, doing so from a position of weakness that forced him to acknowledge the English king's right, not only to Normandy, but also to overlordships of Brittany and Maine. Henry was thus freed to return across the Channel and deal with domestic matters, including the appointment of two archbishops, of Canterbury, and of York, the settlement of relationships with Scotland and Wales, and the gifting of the Honour of Eye, one of the largest in England, to Stephen of Blois, the younger son of his sister Adela. At this time, too, Henry followed the Norman fashion in having his son William formally acknowledged as heir, with homage paid to him by all the great lords of England and Normandy.

The year 1116, however, saw England and Normandy once again at war with the old alliance of France, Flanders and Anjou. Although aided by Stephen's brother Theobald, Count of Blois, for some time matters went against Henry. Normandy was invaded and many Norman lords deserted his cause in favour of William Clito. Gradually, however, the tide turned. Once again Flanders left the fight after the death of its count. And once again Anjou negotiated a separate peace, celebrated this time by the actual wedding, in June 1119, of the fifteen-year-old English heir William and his eight-year-old bride.

Two months later, Louis of France was decisively defeated at the Battle of Brémule. Entrusting his first division to William Clito, who then charged at the enemy with 'much courage but little sense', Louis was forced to flee the battlefield, and soon after decided on a change of tactics.

In October 1119 he laid his grievances and the claims of William Clito before the new Pope Calixtus II at a great church council in Rheims. At first, it seemed as though he would achieve all he wanted, but then Thurstan, the new Archbishop of York, who had many friends among the bishops and papal representatives, began to work on behalf of Henry. He was so persuasive that the pope agreed to meet Henry and hear his side of the case. Henry in turn convinced him that he only wanted peace with France and had no designs on that kingdom, but it took further negotiations through the agency of Thurstan, Adela of Blois and her son Theobald, and Cuno, a papal legate, before that peace was finally achieved in the spring of 1120.

Once again, Henry appeared to have come out on top. Now he was secure in England and, for the moment at least, in Normandy too, and had the overlordship of Brittany and Maine. The new count of Flanders was happy to make peace, and Fulk of Anjou had departed to the Holy Land. Furthermore, he had an acknowledged son and heir, who was already successfully married off and likely to produce heirs of his own in due course. And then, as if with malicious intent, fate played a hand.

In late November 1120 the court of Henry I was returning from Normandy to England. The king himself had already left when, on the evening of 25 November, young William, son and heir, set sail from Barfleur in the White Ship. With him were several illegitimate siblings and a great number of noblemen and members of the royal household, in all some 300 persons, seriously overloading the little vessel. Moreover, the entire company, passengers and crew were royally drunk. Leaving harbour with reckless haste, the ship struck a rock not far offshore, and in the cold darkness sank, drowning all but one, a butcher from Rouen called Berold. Efforts had been made to save William, but he too was drowned attempting to rescue his half-sister, the countess of Perche.

It took some time to carry the news to Henry, and when it reached him the king was devastated. On the personal side it was a tragedy; but for all his careful plans for the succession it was nothing less than a disaster. The record states, with maybe some exaggeration, that the king never smiled again. 'No ship,' says the chronicler William of Malmesbury, 'Ever brought so much misery to England.'

Henry was by now in his fifties, and despite his copious illegitimate offspring, had had only one legitimate male heir. His wife had died two years before, and his only legitimate daughter, another Matilda, was in Germany, the wife of the Holy Roman Emperor Henry V. She had been brought up in the German court from the age of eight, and married at the age of fourteen, and while there is no evidence she was ever formally crowned and anointed as empress by the pope, as tradition demanded, she assumed the title after her marriage and clung to it for the rest of her life. Now eighteen, she had already acted as regent for her husband in Italy and the only failure in her marriage was the lack of a child – a possible heir not only for her husband, but now also for her father.

The worst of the White Ship disaster was that it left William Clito, protégé of the French king, as the most obvious surviving legitimate male heir in direct line to the Conqueror. If Henry should die with the succession unresolved, it seemed likely he would claim not only Normandy but England as well, a prospect the king was determined to avoid at all costs.

There were several options open to him and, as usual, Henry went for the most practical first. Within three months of his son's death, he married Adeliza, daughter of Godfrey, Count of Louvain. Unlike her predecessor, who in later years had lived mainly at Westminster, the new queen travelled with her husband wherever he went, but no child was born of this marriage.

A second option would be to promote his eldest illegitimate son, Robert, who had already ably supported his father in the recent wars. There were precedents for this. The Conqueror himself had been illegitimate. Times were changing, however, and it was unlikely an illegitimate candidate would be supported if there were alternative legitimate claimants for the crown. Robert was, in fact, promoted to become Earl of Gloucester, but it is likely this was simply to enable him to support any new child that might be born to the king.

Aside from William Clito there were other legitimate male heirs, though these – Theobald of Blois and his brother Stephen – were descended through the female line. Both had aided Henry in his

French wars, and Stephen had already been favoured by the king, but there is no evidence that either was ever seriously considered as an heir.

While Henry pondered all these options, fate moved again to give him the chance of an heir from his own line. In 1125, the Emperor Henry V died. Matilda, now a childless widow in her twenties, was recalled to England by her father, and in January 1127 she was presented to the nobility of England and Normandy as Henry's heir. A female heir may have been harder for an Anglo-Norman lord to accept than an illegitimate male heir, but Henry insisted they all swore an oath to acknowledge her as future queen of England, and they all did so.

By this time a number of things had also changed on the continent, many of them to Henry's disadvantage. He had lost his alliance with Fulk of Anjou, returning Fulk's daughter but not her dowry when her husband was drowned. The count immediately married his other daughter, Sibylla, to William Clito, but Henry used his influence with the pope to get this marriage annulled on the grounds that the couple were too closely related – something that had not bothered him when his own son was the bridegroom, the relationship being exactly the same. Clito was promptly remarried to the sister-in-law of Louis of France, who took up his cause once again, granting him lands and fortresses in France, and backing his claim to become Count of Flanders.

Rebuilding relations with Anjou now became a priority for Henry, a task made easier by the fact that Fulk was about to marry the heiress to the kingdom of Jerusalem and was anxious to depart to the east. A new marriage agreement was made, this time between Fulk's fourteen-year-old son Geoffrey and Henry's daughter Matilda. Henry, of course, was hoping for heirs for his own lands, while bringing Anjou once more into alliance with the English crown. For Fulk, a major incentive was that his own descendants would become kings of England. Needless to say, the couple themselves were not consulted.

If the marriage was intended to neutralise the threat of William Clito, it was undermined by the death of that young man within a month of the ceremony. Nor was it a success in other ways, at least at first. Matilda herself regarded the match as demeaning. She was an empress and she was required to marry a mere count, and one, moreover, more than ten years her junior. Within a year she had left him and returned to Rouen.

According to the *Anglo-Saxon Chronicle* the marriage also 'displeased all the French and the English'. In particular there was a history of rivalry between Normandy and Anjou, which prejudiced many of the nobility against it. The idea that Geoffrey, now Count of Anjou, might claim the English crown was, so they later alleged, enough to free them from their oaths sworn to Matilda herself. William of Malmesbury, however, records a second oath, given in 1131, at around the time when – after a possibly forced reconciliation – Matilda was returned to her husband.

There still seemed to be little love lost between the couple, but eventually, in March 1133, a son was born to them. It was no surprise that he was named Henry. A second son, Geoffrey, followed in 1134, born in Rouen where the English king was spending a considerable amount of time with his daughter. This time, though, the birth was less straightforward, and Matilda nearly died. Thereafter relations with her father seemed to cool.

By this time Henry was in his mid-sixties. The succession seemed to be secure, but there had been no clear statement as to what Count Geoffrey's future role was to be, nor had the count received the castles in Normandy that had been promised as Matilda's dowry. When trouble erupted, however, it is perhaps surprising that Matilda took the part of her husband rather than her father. The pair demanded castles and powers in Normandy, and that the Norman lords should swear allegiance to them in King Henry's lifetime. Henry, though, says Orderic Vitalis, 'Had no inclination to allow anyone, while he lived, to have any pre-eminence over himself, or even to be his equal'.

Through the summer of 1135 tensions simmered in southern Normandy, only held in check by the formidable presence of Henry himself, visiting and strengthening his frontier castles. Then, in November of that year, he took a little respite in the form of a hunting expedition to the Forest of Lyons. There he ate a meal of lampreys – a meaty-tasting eel-like fish – one of his favourite dishes, although, reputedly, it did not agree with him and his doctor had warned him against it. Shortly afterwards he fell ill, possibly due to the famous 'surfeit of lampreys', but more likely from straightforward food poisoning, and a few days later, on 1 December 1135, he died.

His body, accompanied by his illegitimate son Robert, was taken to Rouen and embalmed. Then in the New Year, when the weather permitted, it was taken across the Channel to England to be buried before the altar in Reading Abbey, which Henry had founded some years earlier. Before the cortège reached Reading, however, it was met by a new King of England. Stephen of Blois had pre-empted his fellows, slipped across the Channel and with the aid of his brother Henry, Bishop of Winchester, persuaded the Archbishop of Canterbury to crown and anoint him at Westminster Abbey on 22 December 1135.

Shadowed as it was by the anarchy that followed, it is difficult to make a fair assessment of Henry and his reign. 'A good man he was,' says the *Chronicle*, 'And there was much awe of him,' but he has also been described as cruel and avaricious, overrated intellectually, and ruling by fear rather than love. Rule he did, though, for more than thirty-five years, and if his scheming for the succession did not succeed, it was not for the want of trying. He established peace, in England at least, for long enough to put in place the groundwork for a settled system of government and justice. These solid foundations would survive to be built upon by his grandson, the second Henry, giving us institutions that have lasted to the present day.

2

Henry II

'The most renowned among the kings of the earth'
— William of Newburgh

Born at Le Mans on 5 March 1133, the child that became Henry II was very definitely intended to sit upon the throne of England. He was the legitimate male heir his grandfather, King Henry I, had longed for for more than a dozen years, and surely his arrival would persuade the nobles of England and Normandy to stand by the oath they had reluctantly sworn to accept Henry's daughter Matilda as ruler after his death. This birth seemed to secure the throne for Henry's line for the next two generations at least, though the child's christening, in the cathedral at Le Mans, maybe hinted at trouble ahead.

The chronicles tell us the boy's mother Matilda and grandfather Henry were present, but his father, Count Geoffrey of Anjou was not. Geoffrey – only nineteen at the time of his son's birth – was part of the family because Henry had needed a father for his grandchildren and an alliance with Anjou, against the ill-will of the French King Louis VI. His role in the succession was never defined, and the marriage itself never fully accepted by the Norman nobility in England or Normandy. It was, indeed, used as an excuse for depriving Matilda of her promised inheritance. Significantly, the second son, Geoffrey, was born at Rouen in 1134, but by the time of the third son's birth, in 1136, all King Henry's careful plans had been overthrown, and it was clear that his grandson and namesake would have a far rockier road to travel than his doting grandfather had ever anticipated.

At the time of the king's death on 1 December 1135 Matilda and her family were far away in Anjou and she was pregnant with this third son. No doubt her half-brother Robert of Gloucester, who was present at the deathbed, would have got the news to her as quickly as possible, but by the time she received it her cousin Stephen had already embarked for England, there to be crowned king a few days before Christmas. So would begin the eighteen years of struggle for the crown which later ages referred to as The Anarchy.

Over the next few years, the boy Henry would have had very little of his parent's attention. Unable to mount a direct challenge to Stephen in England, the immediate response of Matilda and Geoffrey was to take over those castles on the frontier of Normandy and Anjou which had been promised as Matilda's dowry – hence the birth of her third and last child, William, in the castle at Argentan. It is likely Henry remained with his mother's household at this time, while Count Geoffrey launched a series of savage and unsuccessful raids into Normandy on her behalf. Later, though, Matilda herself, supported by Robert of Gloucester, landed in England to inspire her followers and pursue her claim to the throne more forcefully. Then the boy stayed behind in Anjou.

By the time young Henry first set foot in England in October 1142, his mother's campaign had experienced something of a roller-coaster ride. At the Battle of Lincoln in February 1141, Stephen had been utterly defeated and taken prisoner. Matilda then advanced cautiously towards London, and actually took up residence in the royal palace at Westminster before a combination of rioting Londoners and an army led by Stephen's queen drove her out. Retreating to Winchester, she again had to escape through a besieging army, losing her chief supporter, Robert of Gloucester, on the way. He was taken prisoner and eventually exchanged for King Stephen, leaving both parties, at the end of that eventful year, right back where they started.

Robert had then travelled to Normandy to seek help from Count Geoffrey and had assisted him in consolidating his gains in that duchy, so that within a few years, Geoffrey would be recognised as Duke of Normandy. The Count was reluctant, however, to compromise his position by splitting his forces. Instead, he dispatched the nine-year-old Henry to England in company with Robert of Gloucester, to act as a figurehead for his wife's claim to the throne, and a promise for the future.

It was not exactly a triumphal entry to his future realm. The fortunes of war had once again turned against Matilda, and she was closely besieged in Oxford Castle at the time her son arrived in the country. Before a rescue could be contrived, however, the resourceful lady escaped, by one account letting herself down from a high tower and crossing a frozen river in the depths of winter. 'I have never heard of any woman having such marvellous escapes,' declares a chronicler of the time.

Henry, of course, was not there to fight, and he was immediately established in Bristol Castle, along with one of Robert of Gloucester's sons, receiving an education that would stand him in good stead for the rest of his life. He seems to have been an able pupil. We are told he could read and write Latin and French, and, more surprisingly for the time, could speak English. He also seems to have acquired a life-long love of learning, probably sparked by the tutors he had at the time. One of these, Adelard of Bath, was a foremost traveller and scientist of his day, having brought back from his travels not only Greek but also Arabic texts on philosophy, mathematics and astronomy. He later dedicated a book on the astrolabe to Henry, urging him to be a philosopher king, with an open mind to different cultures and ideas.

After something over a year in Bristol, Henry returned to Normandy, where Geoffrey had now confirmed his position as duke, thereby securing at least a part of his wife's inheritance. That was not the end of the boy's youthful adventures in England, however. In 1147, without the knowledge or approval of either parent, Henry gathered a small band of mercenaries and launched his own expedition to that country.

The raid, however, was reckless in the extreme. The mercenaries had not been paid, only promised a share of supposed rich pickings to come. Nor were they at all successful, attacking two small castles and being driven away from each. Then it appeared Henry had no money to pay them off. Appeals to his mother at Devizes and his uncle Robert at Bristol were both refused, and in the end an outrageous appeal to King Stephen – 'to implore him humbly that, of his goodness, he would make provision for his pressing wants' – produced the money needed to get the boy and his potential nuisances out of the country again.

Two years later Henry was back, not as an invader this time, but as a slightly more mature sixteen-year-old seeking knighthood at the hands of his uncle, King David of Scotland. Slipping quietly through friendly territory in the west of England, he made his way to Carlisle, being received there by the king with 'sumptuous provision and costly munificence', and was knighted on 22 May 1149. The return journey was rather more eventful. Stephen, who by know knew of his presence in the country, sent men to try and intercept him, while the king's son, Eustace, himself set ambushes, which Henry evaded on his way to Bristol. Some fighting followed in the most disputed areas of Wiltshire, but Henry was never in a position to pose a serious challenge and withdrew to Normandy in January 1150.

At this point, Geoffrey of Anjou, who had always seen himself as something of a caretaker duke, handed Normandy over to his seventeen-year-old son, who immediately found himself challenged by his nominal overlord, Louis VII of France. A short but vigorous campaign was led by Louis and his brother-in-law Eustace, the son of King Stephen, and was equally vigorously defended by Henry and Geoffrey. It ended abruptly when the French king fell ill. A brokered truce was followed by a peace treaty, which involved Henry and his father travelling to Paris in order that the new duke might properly pay homage for his duchy. It was during this visit that he would first have laid eyes on Eleanor of Aquitaine. At that time Eleanor was the wife of King Louis, at least nine years older than Henry and the mother of two little daughters. Nevertheless, at least one chronicler declares that, from this time on, Eleanor desired to obtain a divorce in order to marry the young duke, and the attraction may have been mutual.

Henry, though, had his mind set on England. He began immediately to plan an invasion, no doubt urged on by his mother's supporters in that land. Matilda herself had retired to Rouen some time before, though by no means giving up on her claim to the crown, which she now passed on to her son. The invasion was to be twice postponed, however, first owing to the unexpected death of Count Geoffrey in September 1151, and then to the equally unexpected marriage of Henry himself, in May 1152.

Although Louis of France and Eleanor of Aquitaine had been married for 14 years, the marriage had been on the rocks for some time, only continued at the insistence of the pope. Whether it was Louis's desire for a son, or Eleanor's desire to be rid of a husband she regarded as no better than a monk, the end finally came in March 1152, when a church council was persuaded to annul it on the ever-useful grounds of consanguinity. This left the beautiful, clever and desirable Eleanor, who was Duchess of Aquitaine in her own right, one of the wealthiest unmarried women in Western Europe.

Various chronicles declare that, as she travelled south to her own lands, both Theobald of Blois and Henry's own younger brother Geoffrey tried to ambush and abduct her, but without success. As soon as she arrived, however, according to William of Newburgh, she sent for Duke Henry to come and marry her, which he duly did. Newburgh has no doubt that the marriage was pre-arranged by the pair of them and carried out 'not very splendidly ... but with guarded prudence'. At a stroke, Henry obtained not only a wife but control over a territory stretching from the Channel to the Pyrenees. He fully intended to add to that the crown of England.

Before he could do so, however, he had to fight off a concerted effort by all his enemies to deprive him of what he had already obtained. Once again Eustace attacked the north-east of Normandy, while King Louis and the Blois brothers attacked its southern borders. This might have been expected, Henry's sudden increase in wealth and power posing a threat to both the French and English kings. What was more surprising was that they were joined by Henry's own brother Geoffrey, who now attacked him in Anjou.

William of Newburgh states that on his deathbed Count Geoffrey had bequeathed Anjou to Henry only until he could win the throne of England. Thereafter it should go to Geoffrey. No other chronicle of the time endorses this, indeed Robert of Torigny, closer both in time and distance to the event, says the second son was left only four castles. Nevertheless, Geoffrey seems to have been sufficiently aggrieved by Henry's actions, either in assuming Anjou or in marrying Eleanor, to challenge him for their father's county.

It is Torigny again who tells us that nearly everyone now 'thought that Duke Henry would speedily lose the whole of his possessions'. Henry disagreed. Acting with the speed and energy which would become his hallmark, he drove back the southern invaders, while nowhere directly confronting his feudal lord, the French king. Within a short time he was secure enough to tackle his brother in Anjou and Geoffrey quickly submitted, leaving Eustace, still besieging a castle in the north-east, as his sole adversary. It was in England, not Normandy, however, that Henry would challenge Eustace.

By this time, King Stephen had revived his attempt to defeat the supporters of Matilda and was closely besieging a major fortress at Wallingford that had held out against him for the past dozen years. At the end of 1152, the defenders communicated to Henry that he must either send help to them or permit them finally to surrender the fortress to the king. In January 1153, therefore, Henry himself arrived in England, though with a relatively small force, being unwilling to leave Normandy and his other territories weakened.

He didn't go to Wallingford but to Malmesbury, an outpost of Stephen's close to Henry's own strongholds at Bristol and Gloucester. There he prepared to confront the combined forces of Stephen and Eustace, thereby relieving the pressure on Wallingford. Both sides lined up for a major battle – but it never took place. The weather was against it for a start. Rain, sleet and snow poured down, driving in the face of the king's army 'so they could hardly support their armour'. Moreover, behind the scenes circumstances had changed in the past few years. Great magnates who had benefitted from the Anarchy to increase their own power, were now reluctant to risk all in continued warfare. Agreements had been made across the divide to respect each other and give only the minimum support required by their feudal obligations to the chief belligerents.

At Malmesbury it was Stephen who withdrew, apparently doubting the loyalty of some of his followers. Some sort of truce was agreed under which Malmesbury Castle was to be destroyed. Instead, it was handed over to Henry and over the next few months, a series of defections showed the tide was running strongly in favour of the young duke.

In August 1153, Henry set out to relieve Wallingford and here again, it seemed inevitable there would be a final showdown between the warring parties. This time, however, it became clear that the armies would refuse to fight. 'Traitorous nobles interfered,' says one chronicler, and it is clear Stephen and Henry only reluctantly accepted the truce then declared. One of its terms was that the rivals must meet in face-to-face negotiations, and following this, over a period of months, a peace agreement was thrashed out by skilled negotiators, chief of whom were Theobald, Archbishop of Canterbury, and Stephen's own brother, Henry, Bishop of Winchester.

The negotiations were helped by the fact that Eustace took himself off to rampage through East Anglia and died, probably of food poisoning, though deliberate poisoning has not been entirely ruled out. The younger son, William, showed no interest in inheriting the crown, and thus it was that in November 1153 Stephen and Henry met again at Winchester to ratify the terms of the treaty that had been negotiated on their behalf. In the cathedral, before assembled clergy and magnates, Stephen agreed to adopt Henry as his son and heir 'by hereditary right', while Henry, in return, agreed to pay homage to Stephen as his liege lord. 'Thus, through God's mercy,' says a chronicler of the time, 'after a night of misery, peace dawned on the ruined realm of England.'

Henry felt confident enough to return to Normandy in March 1154, while Stephen travelled round an England at last unconditionally acknowledging his kingship. He had little time to revel in his success, however, falling ill at Dover in October of that year and dying a few days later. Once again, Henry showed his confidence, delaying his return to England by more than a month. Then, at Westminster Abbey on 19 December 1154, he was finally consecrated and crowned as Henry II, king of England. He was twenty-one years old.

He may have been young, but for the past half dozen years at least he had been fully involved in the political and military manoeuvrings taking place on both sides of the Channel and was a seasoned campaigner. Although it was his grandfather, the first King Henry, that he idolised and sought to imitate, much credit for his upbringing must also be given to his father, Count Geoffrey. The count, necessarily absent for much of the boy's childhood, had provided the best of tutors to educate him for his future role. Nor was there any apparent rivalry between father and son, such as had plagued the relationship between William the Conqueror and his sons. As early as 1145, Geoffrey was cheerfully anticipating that Henry would 'by the grace of God ... surpass me and all my predecessors in power and dignity'. It was Geoffrey, too, that first bore the name 'Plantagenet', supposedly from his wearing a sprig of broom in his helmet.

It is as well Henry was prepared, for the task ahead of him was a stiff one. Though some have suggested the ruin of England during the Anarchy has been overplayed, it was far from being the prosperous, well-governed land that Henry I had left some nineteen years before. The south-east and south-west regions had got off lightest, being firmly under the control of the rival parties. A wide strip across central-southern England, however, from Gloucester to Oxford in the north, and Bristol to Winchester in the south, had been repeatedly fought over and ravaged. Further north, the earls of Chester and Leicester had fought each other for control of the Midland shires, while Geoffrey de Mandeville had, for a short time, rampaged across East Anglia. Wales had been completely lost, and the northern counties of Northumberland and Cumbria had been ceded to Scotland. Everywhere, royal authority and royal justice, so carefully established by Henry I, had broken down, while over-mighty lords had imposed their own rule over areas under their sway.

It was this situation that the young king now set about repairing, and in many ways he was fortunate. The powerful Earl Ranulf of Chester, for example, had turned his coat several times during the Anarchy but ended up on the winning side, and would have expected a suitable reward had he not died a few days before the coronation, leaving a six-year-old son as his heir. This allowed Henry to take back all the lands the earl had acquired by force during the lawless time, leaving the boy only those held at the time of the death of Henry I.

Similarly, in the west of England Henry was dealing with the heirs of his mother's major supporters, and neither William of Gloucester (son of Robert) nor Roger of Hereford (son of Miles) had shown the enthusiasm for the fight that their fathers had evinced. When Roger died in 1155, Henry had no problem reclaiming royal castles at Gloucester and Hereford and extinguishing the earldom of Hereford. He had, though, to besiege the castles of Hugh de Mortimer at Wigmore, Cleobury and Bridgnorth in order to get back the latter, another royal castle, and similar action was needed in Yorkshire to strip William, Earl of Aumale of all the castles and royal lands he had obtained during the time of anarchy.

Over the next year or so, in full accord with the Winchester treaty, lands and castles were returned to their previous owners, and many castles built without royal permission were destroyed. Then, in 1157, Henry turned his attention to territories that had been lost. The sixteen-year-old Malcolm, King of Scotland, was persuaded to hand back the northern counties of Northumberland and Cumbria, setting the boundary between the two realms once again at the Solway and Tweed, despite the fact that both his grandfather and father had been staunch supporters of Matilda and her son. Henry was dealing with King David's heir, not King David himself, and took full advantage of the fact. In exchange, Malcolm was given the earldom of Huntingdon, which had been his father's until 1141.

In that same year, forces were dispatched into Wales to reclaim territory lost during the Anarchy. In north Wales, Owain Gwynedd had taken control of all the area of the old kingdoms of Gwynedd and Powys, a region extending across the north from Anglesey to the River Dee. After losing some ground, Owain quickly came to negotiate with Henry, accepting him as overlord in return for confirmation of his own position in the area.

In south-west Wales the sons of Gruffydd ap Rhys had consolidated their hold on most of the old kingdom of Deheubarth, comprising Carmarthen, Ceredigion and Dyfed, though they never succeeded in taking Pembroke. The youngest son, Rhys ap Gruffydd, had, however, only come to power at the same time as Henry. Though he managed to defy the English king for a while, eventually he was forced to hand back all that had been taken from the Normans in the area. Henry kept the castles of Pembroke and Carmarthen in his own hands, but Ceredigion was returned to the Clare family, in the person of Earl Roger de Clare.

Of course, King Henry was now effective ruler of a much greater area than any of his predecessors, and all his drive and energy was needed to keep everything under control. As early as 1156 he had been recalled to Normandy, partly as a result of troublemaking by his brother Geoffrey, and partly in order to fulfil a requirement to perform homage to Louis VII of France. This was something the earlier Norman kings had always avoided, but to Henry it seemed expedient at the time, not least in obtaining recognition of his right to rule in all his continental territories. It would, however, severely limit his future actions, since directly opposing a feudal lord in warfare could lead to the loss of all the territories within the sway of that lord.

The meeting with Louis may have been a little tense. The wife who had given him only daughters had already presented her new husband with two sons, though the elder would die that year, at the age of three. The encounter with brother Geoffrey, however, was of a more violent nature, as he was again pressing his demands for Anjou. His castles at Chinon, Loudun, Mirabeau and Montsoreau had to be besieged before he finally came to terms, afterwards retaining only Loudun and receiving an annuity of £1,500 in exchange for the others.

Shortly afterwards, Geoffrey became Count of Nantes. One story declares he was chosen by the citizens after they expelled their previous count, while a more plausible version claims the count was ousted as part of Henry's plans for a takeover of the duchy of Brittany. Certainly, when Geoffrey died a few years later, Nantes was not returned to the twenty-year-old Conan, Duke of Brittany, who was also Earl of Richmond and firmly under Henry's control. In 1166, Henry insisted on the betrothal of Conan's daughter, Constance, aged five, to his own son Geoffrey, aged eight, and thereafter Conan was forced to abdicate in favour of Constance, the takeover then being complete.

It may have been a streak of his father's youthful recklessness, or maybe the completeness of his early successes that now prompted Henry to try and add the county of Toulouse to his 'empire'. He had a claim, of sorts, through his wife, and in fact King Louis had tried to press that claim when he was married to Eleanor. In the meantime, however, Raymond, Count of Toulouse, had married the French king's sister, and when Henry launched his attack he found Louis standing shoulder to shoulder with his brother-in-law. The disadvantage of that oath of homage, so easily taken a few years before, now became apparent and Henry was forced to give up his campaign rather than risk all he had so far achieved by engaging in warfare with his liege lord.

For a twenty-six-year-old, however, he had not done badly. It was also clear that he intended to learn from mistakes made by his predecessors. Henry I had been one of the wealthiest monarchs in Europe, while both Stephen and Matilda had been perennially short of money. The use of foreign mercenaries had been one drain on the finances of both, and Henry lost little time in sending them packing. Another great loss had been the practice, particularly on the part of Stephen, of giving away land and privileges in order to keep his followers sweet. Henry saw no need to do this and decreed at the start of his reign that Stephen's charters, and, indeed, some of his mother's, should be reviewed. Many were declared no longer valid. There was also a general review of land ownership up to the time of his grandfather's death and a great deal of formerly royal land was recovered, all of which went some way towards refilling the royal treasury.

Key to stabilising the royal finances was the re-establishment of the Exchequer as the bureaucracy at the centre of royal administration. This had been closely linked to Bishop Roger of Salisbury and his kin before their fall from power under King Stephen, and Henry was lucky enough to have on hand Nigel, Bishop of Ely, a nephew of Roger of Salisbury, to take over as Treasurer and guide the reconstruction. So successful was this that a continuous set of 'Pipe Rolls' exists from the very first year of the new king's reign. Among the various revenues recorded we now find loans from moneylenders, including Jewish moneylenders.

Jewish communities had been introduced into England by William the Conqueror, and, as the Christian church began to frown on the practice of usury – the taking of interest on a loan – so the Jewish moneylenders came to prominence. Early in his reign, Henry made considerable use of such loans, until, with a change of policy, taxes began to be levied not only on landholding but on the value of a person's moveable goods. This considerably widened the range of those taxable, bringing in citizens living in towns, merchants and, of course, Jewish moneylenders, under a tax that became known as tallage. In fact, after 1162 the ancient geld was quietly discontinued. So many exemptions had been granted by this time that it was not the major fundraiser it had been. Nevertheless, the ending of this longstanding, customary tax would cause problems for later medieval kings.

The increasing use of 'scutage' – money payable as an alternative to providing military service – also helped to fill the royal treasury. Henry claimed he would prefer to risk professional soldiers rather than ordinary English lives in his campaigns, but greater certainty and flexibility were also advantages, especially when estates began to be subdivided, and a 'knight's fee' or obligation for service could be spread over dozens of pockets of landholding. In 1166, he required all his tenants in chief to provide lists of their sub-tenants and what knight service was owed by each. While this helped to confirm the hierarchy, it also enabled him in future years to levy scutage, not only on the knight service owed to him personally, but on the total knight service owed to his magnates. At roughly a pound per knight, this could provide a useful amount, though in fairness, scutage was only levied seven times in the reign.

In fact, William of Newburgh praises the king for his frugality. 'He never imposed any heavy tax on the realm of England, or on his lands overseas,' he says, the only exception being a tax to raise money for the relief of the Holy Land, levied in 1166 and again in 1198, which was in line with that levied in other lands of Western Europe.

Taxes were paid in silver pennies, received and accounted for at the Exchequer, which, over a period of time, moved its base from Winchester to Westminster. The silver content was checked, and in 1156 found to be so debased that in 1158 a new coinage was minted and the number of authorised mints severely reduced. By 1178 the whole procedure had become so standardised that the Treasurer at the time, Richard fitzNigel, son of the previous Treasurer, was able to produce the 'Dialogue of the Exchequer'. This took the form of a question and answer textbook going into minute detail on the origin of the Exchequer, the roles of its various officials and the duties and liabilities of the sheriffs who must account to the Exchequer for the revenues from their areas.

These sheriffs were at the time the backbone of local administration. Appointed by the king, they were responsible for collecting revenues, upholding the royal peace in their areas, the general maintenance of law and order, and putting into practice the orders of the king. During the reign of Henry II their duties and responsibilities would increase, but in real terms their power would diminish as Henry brought more and more of the legal system under central control.

It has been said that Henry had the mind of a lawyer. Walter Map, a courtier who knew the king from the beginning of his reign, describes him as showing keen discernment, and skill in finding unusual ways of solving a problem, while another who knew him, Peter of Blois, says one of his favourite leisure activities was striving with a group of clerics to untangle some knotty matter of law, or government. All agree that the solutions he sought were practical, rather than theoretical, and the aim was to benefit the people as a whole, and in particular those below the top levels of society.

He would have had before him the situation he had inherited, where over-mighty lords in some areas had become petty kings and tyrants. He could not, without provoking another civil war, directly attack the feudal rights they had to hold their own courts for their own people, but he could, and did, make his own courts more attractive, and provide access to them for a great range of people. Very little that he did was entirely new, but he took pre-existing structures and shaped and moulded them, so that, by the end of his reign, it was clear some subtle revolution had occurred in the legal process. Indeed, the year of his death, 1189, is still recognised as the point at which what we now call the Common Law of England was firmly established.

Land was the most valuable commodity in medieval England, and disputes about the ownership or possession of land were the commonest disputes. A person dispossessed by his lord, however, would either have to plead in that lord's own feudal court, or, if sufficiently wealthy, appeal to the king. Henry's innovation was to introduce simplified procedures, known as 'petty assizes', bringing at least the initial inquiry into the jurisdiction of his own courts. The assize (inquiry) of Novel Disseisin, introduced around 1166, allowed any freeman to obtain a writ from the king's chancery claiming he had been dispossessed of his land without a lawful judgement. The assize of Mort d'Ancestor, introduced around 1176, similarly provided for a claim that an heir had not been allowed to inherit. The writ would be addressed to the local sheriff, requiring him to summon twelve men of good repute who could answer the simple questions in the writ. For example, it might ask, 'Was X possessed of this land before he died?' and 'Is Y his heir?' The answer/verdict would be delivered to the royal justices when they visited that area, and, if in Y's favour, the sheriff would be ordered to put him in possession of the land. This quick and relatively cheap procedure became extremely popular. It was not, of course, a trial of who had a *right* to the land. This would be introduced a little later as a Grand Assize, which would provide an alternative to the trial by battle which had previously been the means of settling land disputes. To use the more formal Grand Assize, a writ of right had to be obtained alleging the lord had failed to deal properly with the case, but both assizes involved the use of what we would call 'jurors', though their verdicts were based on their own knowledge of the facts, rather than on evidence presented to them.

These new procedures were revolutionary in that they opened up the king's justice to an increasingly wide range of people. Any freeman could apply for a writ, and a freeman was any landholder who did not provide labour for his lord in exchange for his land. Similarly, the jurors were drawn from the knightly class, involving them more and more in the provision of justice. The manorial courts of the greater lords were not specifically undermined – a lord could still show he was doing justice for his tenants – but the writ of right in particular provided a strong supervisory element by which the king could exert control over his barons.

Of course the king himself had his own court and was constantly pursued around his various lands by streams of petitioners, whom, according to contemporary chroniclers, he treated with commendable patience. The very nature of his 'empire', however, made it imperative that justice should be firmly established even in his absence. To this end, at the start of his reign he appointed co-Justiciars: one, Robert, earl of Leicester, with sufficient weight to ensure commands were obeyed, and the other, Richard de Luci, providing continuity with the previous regime. It was around this time, too, that the Exchequer, based increasingly at Westminster, expanded its judicial role and began providing clerks to be sent around the country as royal justices.

Henry I had sent justices around the country at times, but it was during the reign of his grandson that these visitations or 'eyres' became a regular feature. The country was divided into circuits with bands of justices assigned to each, so that, sitting simultaneously all over the land, from the mid-1170s onward, they could cover the whole country. Hearing cases involving pleas of the crown had previously been the function of the sheriff, but more and more these cases were taken over by the royal justices, leaving the shire and manorial courts only minor matters to deal with.

In a major drive to establish an effective peace-keeping system, the Assize of Clarendon in 1166 formalised the procedure for dealing with the more serious criminals. Twelve men from every hundred, and four from every town, were to form 'juries of presentment'. These were to notify the sheriff of any persons suspected of committing murder, robbery, theft or receiving stolen goods. Sheriffs could enter any jurisdiction in order to arrest such persons and were required to cooperate with other sheriffs around the country to arrest suspects or fugitives from justice. Gaols were to be built to hold suspects, but they would then be tried, not by witness evidence, but by the ordeal of water, binding the accused and lowering him into a pool of water previously blessed by a priest. If he sank, he was innocent. If he floated, he was guilty, on the basis that God had refused to accept his body. The verdict would be reported to the court and punishment imposed, frequently the loss of a foot or hand, or, in more serious cases, hanging. Even if the accused came 'clean' from the ordeal, that is to say, was acquitted of the specific charge, there was a provision for him to be exiled if he was a person of 'evil repute'. The property of those convicted or exiled then belonged to the crown.

This system supplemented rather than replaced the older frankpledge system, and the Assize of Clarendon further empowered the sheriff to check that everyone was in his appropriate tithing group, even when this right to a 'view of frankpledge' had been given away to a local lord. It was a lucrative exercise since fines could be imposed for any irregularity, and this and other powers of the sheriff made corruption very possible. Henry, though, was scrupulous in checking on his officials, and, according to Peter of Blois, 'judging those whom he has made judges of others'. In 1170, on his return to England after a long absence, he carried out an inquiry into the work of the sheriffs, and twenty out of twenty-six of them were sacked and replaced by officials from the Exchequer.

One of those removed but subsequently reappointed was Ranulf de Glanvill, who later went on to become a royal justice and eventually Chief Justiciar, following the retirement of Richard de Luci. It is Glanvill's name that we find on a 'Treatise on the Law and Constitution of England' that appeared around 1189, an attempt to describe both the criminal and civil laws as they stood at that time. This clearly shows the enormous developments that took place in the reign, in royal control over justice, in the use of jury verdicts and in the writs now obtainable from the royal chancery. He describes fifteen of them, and, as he himself remarked, it would be easy to draft writs to deal with many different matters. Soon there would be many more, all of them dealt with in the royal courts, and, initially at least, open to any freeman at the expense of a little time and money. Within a comparatively short period of time, they would increase and multiply to give birth to the entire Common Law system.

With the increased work of the chancery in dealing with all these legal and administrative matters, it was as well that, at the very start of his reign, Henry had appointed a most competent chancellor. His name was Thomas Becket, and he had been recommended by Theobald, the old Archbishop of Canterbury, in whose household he had been employed for some time. Theobald had found him both industrious and loyal, and he probably hoped that, as chancellor, he would be able to protect the church from any challenges that might come from the new king.

Some thirteen years older than Henry, Becket had been born in London and educated at Merton priory, later spending a year studying canon law on the continent. He threw himself into his new job with zest, and soon became not only a trusted servant but an intimate friend of the king. 'Never,' says his contemporary biographer William fitzStephen, 'were two men more of one mind or better friends.' Despite the age difference, he describes them sporting together like boys of the same age when the day's hard work was done, and, no doubt, the competence and efficiency of Becket eased the burden of that work on the shoulders of the king.

It is certainly overstating it to claim, as one biographer does, that the whole government of the realm was entrusted to Thomas while the king engaged in youthful pursuits. Nevertheless, when the marriage of Henry's son to the French king's daughter was mooted, it was Thomas who was sent – in a magnificence that it took pages to describe – to carry out the negotiations on behalf of the king.

A turning point came in April 1161 when Archbishop Theobald died. Over the previous hundred years a growing emphasis on the independence of the church had had the potential to bring it into conflict with royal interests in a number of ways, the Investiture Controversy being only one of many contentious areas. In England, when the archbishop of Canterbury, the leading cleric, had had a good relationship with the king, such conflicts had generally been smoothed over. This had been the case with William the Conqueror and Archbishop Lanfranc, and again with Theobald and Henry. When the relationship was not good, however, as with William Rufus and Archbishop Anselm, the ensuing battles had had serious consequences.

It was no doubt with this in mind that Henry now proposed making Thomas the new Archbishop of Canterbury. In itself it would be a controversial appointment. Thomas was not even a priest, let alone a bishop, and there were existing bishops who were well qualified for promotion. Some people actively opposed the idea, including Henry's mother Matilda, and indeed Thomas himself, who warned the king that in gaining an archbishop he would surely lose a friend. For a year the see remained vacant, but in the end the king had his way. In May 1162, Thomas was unanimously, though reluctantly, elected as Archbishop of Canterbury; his prediction would very soon be proved correct.

Some, even his faithful biographers, describe what happened next as a 'conversion', how the worldly chancellor became the saintly archbishop, but that seems to misunderstand the true character of the man. Even as chancellor he had been pious and temperate, the magnificence attaching, as he saw it, to the office rather than the man. Now he would be more so. What motivated Thomas Becket was not wealth or worldly power, but the personal satisfaction of proving to be the best. As chancellor he had aimed to be the best, most capable chancellor ever. Now, given a new role, he would strive to be the best archbishop. He was almost certainly utterly sincere in both roles, but he knew from the start they would be incompatible, and one of his first actions as archbishop was to resign the chancellorship.

Henry took it as a slap in the face, and further slaps were to follow. Thomas opposed the marriage of Henry's brother William to the recently widowed heiress Isabella of Warenne, he set about reclaiming property that had previously belonged to Canterbury but which was now in the possession of powerful lords, and he was rather free in handing out excommunications, the most severe ecclesiastical punishment, to those who opposed him. The most serious issue between them, however, was to be that of the infamous 'criminous clerks'.

Since the establishment of ecclesiastical courts by William the Conqueror, the custom had grown up that any cleric committing an offence would be tried in those courts, rather than by the sheriff or king's justices. Since holy orders in those days encompassed not only priests and bishops, but also a host of minor orders – almost anyone who could read and write – it has been estimated that this covered roughly one sixth of the population. The only punishments they could incur involved penance, reprimand, demotion or expulsion from their order, considerably lighter than in other courts. As William of Newburgh expressed it, the clergy, who 'ought to shine on earth like stars placed in the firmament of heaven, yet take licence and liberty to do what they please with impunity.' In 1163, it was reported that more than a hundred murders had been committed by clergy in England during Henry's reign.

As part of a wider drive for law and order he determined to do something about this, and the matter was discussed at a council at Westminster in October 1163. There the king proposed that a clerk found guilty of serious crime should be handed over to the secular court for appropriate punishment. Canon law, the church's law, he claimed, permitted this. Archbishop Thomas, however, contended that under church law the clergy were completely independent of secular authority. It was a moot point and Thomas was backed by the other bishops. Henry then pointed out that in earlier times clergy had been handed over for punishment, and the bishops' oath of fealty to him accepted such 'royal customs'. The argument shifted then to what had been accepted by fealty, and Thomas insisted that the phrase that was included with the oath, 'saving our order', meant they did not accept anything contrary to canon law. At this the king stormed out and the meeting ended.

Over the next weeks Thomas was urged to change his mind and accept the royal customs. Even Pope Alexander III suggested flexibility, though he himself, faced by an anti-pope in Rome elected by the Holy Roman Emperor, was desperate not to lose the support of the king of England. Eventually Thomas agreed, and being told that his reconciliation should be public, attended a great council held at Clarendon in January 1164. Here, though, he and all the assembled bishops and nobility were presented with a document that became known as the Constitutions of Clarendon. Even William of Newburgh admits that in this Henry 'perhaps ... exceeded the bonds of moderation', for this document not only contained the claimed custom relating to criminous clerks, but many other claimed 'royal customs'. Among other things clergy were not to leave the country without royal permission, the king's officials and tenants in chief were not to be excommunicated without royal permission and no case could be appealed to the pope without royal permission.

To be fair to the king, with his lawyerly mind he was probably attempting to set down once and for all in black and white what was at the time a very misty grey area, that is, the boundary between what was legitimately church business and what was legitimately royal business. To Thomas, though, and to the assembled clergy, it could have appeared as the thin edge of a potentially very thick wedge. The bishops, therefore, looked to Thomas for leadership. He in turn claimed it was an attack on the independence of the church and refused to agree to it, and the bishops backed him unanimously. For three days immense pressure was brought to bear to make them change their minds. Then abruptly, without apparently any explanation as to why, Thomas did so. He agreed to the document, at least verbally, and the other bishops, following his lead, signed and sealed it. Almost immediately afterwards Thomas repented his decision, but by then it was too late. If this was a battle of wills, Henry had apparently won.

It sounded the death knell, though, for any possible future partnership between king and archbishop. Feeling bitterly betrayed by his friend, Henry determined to replace him. On 6 October of that year Thomas was brought before a royal court at Northampton, ostensibly to answer a charge of failing to appear before a similar court when summoned on a previous occasion. Having dealt with that matter, however, the king then accused the archbishop of a series of misappropriations of money in his earlier role as chancellor. Twice before Thomas had tried to leave the country without royal permission, a flagrant breach of the Constitutions he had earlier accepted. Now, clearly understanding the king's purpose, he fled in earnest, in the dead of night, taking ship to the continent and landing on an open shore near Gravelines. For the next six years he would remain in exile under the protection of Louis VII of France, while numerous attempts were made to bring about a settlement of the issue.

Louis, of course, was quite happy to see his over-mighty vassal, the King of England, put in the wrong. The English bishops, meanwhile, as on many earlier occasions, supported Henry. As Gilbert Foliot, Bishop of London, wrote to Thomas, it was the Archbishop who had caused the problem, first by opposing the document at Clarendon, then changing his mind. They had accepted the Constitutions because he had, and when he had changed his mind once more and then fled, he could not expect them to follow him further. Thomas, however, claimed to be defending the church, and in that the pope had to back him. Alexander, though, was still walking a tightrope between supporting Thomas and alienating Henry, who might then give his approval to antipope Paschal. More than once, threats of excommunication and interdict on one side were met with threats to acknowledge Paschal on the other.

The Constitutions of Clarendon were the initial battleground, but when in January 1169 Henry began to give ground on that, the archbishop's insistence he could not submit to an earthly power without using the phrase 'saving God's honour', became a new point of conflict. In November of that year, however, at a meeting at Montmartre between the kings of England and France, the archbishop, and papal legates, almost everything was settled.

Under threat of a papal interdict on England, Henry made great concessions on the Constitutions, while Thomas was persuaded to abandon his provocative phrase and be reconciled, with a return to England to follow. Now, however, with all trust between them lost, the archbishop wanted some guarantee of his safety once he returned. The pope advised that, if the king gave the traditional kiss of peace, Thomas should take this as a guarantee. When this was suggested to Henry, however, he declared he could not do so because he had previously sworn, in a fit of anger, that he would never do so publicly again. At this, the meeting once more broke up in anger and suspicion.

In January 1170, with Pope Alexander stronger than he had been for some time, new legates were sent to settle the matter once and for all. Before the next meeting, however, Henry had made an uncharacteristic false step. Following continental rather than English custom, he had had his son consecrated and crowned as king of England in his own lifetime, and, with the Archbishop of Canterbury in exile, the ceremony had been performed by the Archbishop of York. The pope had written forbidding this, but Henry claimed the letter had arrived too late. Thus, not only did the pope feel aggrieved and Thomas slighted, but Louis of France was also angry that his daughter Margaret, who was married to the new Young King, as he was known, had not been crowned at the same time. Against this fractious background, in July 1170 the dispute between king and archbishop was finally, formally, settled on the same terms as those accepted the previous November. The kiss of peace was not mentioned, nor was it given, either then or on the two subsequent occasions when king and archbishop met before Thomas set off for England on 1 December.

His return was greeted with great joy, particularly in Canterbury and London according to his biographers, though other reports show the king's agents furiously opposing him still. The homecoming was slightly marred, however, by his immediate action in suspending the Archbishop of York, and excommunicating the Bishops of London and Salisbury, for their part in crowning the Young King. Thomas apparently had Henry's permission to do this, and a letter of papal authority, but the bishops immediately set off to Henry's court in

Normandy to protest. In doing so, says William fitzStephen, they greatly exaggerated the archbishop's actions, even accusing him of treason, and of careering around the country with a force of armed men. 'While Thomas lives,' one is alleged to have said to the king, 'You will have neither peace nor quiet.'

That the king was infuriated is undeniable. William of Newburgh describes him as 'losing the mastery of himself in the heat of his exuberant passion', but the specifically provocative words, 'Will no-one rid me of this turbulent priest?' were never spoken. Contemporary writings refer only to him ranting about courtiers who allowed him to be mocked by a low-born clerk, while a little later Newburgh simply says he 'poured forth the language of indiscretion'.

Four of those present, however, Reginald fitzUrse, Henry de Tracey, Hugh of Morville and Richard Brito, read into that language a command for action. They set off at once for England, and on 29 December confronted the archbishop at Canterbury, first raging at him in his own chamber and stirring up a riot in the town, then, in full armour, following him into the cathedral itself, where his monks had persuaded him to go for safety. The cathedral was full of monks and visitors to the town, for Vespers was being sung, but ignoring the panic caused by their appearance, the four knights dragged Thomas from the very altar steps and attacked him. A visiting monk, Edward Grim, who later wrote a well-researched biography of the archbishop, tried to protect him and was seriously wounded. Thomas himself received four sword blows to the head that severed the top of his skull and left his lifeless body sprawled in a mess of blood and brains beside the altar.

When news of the death was brought to King Henry on 1 January 1171, he was horror-struck. Uttering loud lamentations he withdrew to an inner chamber, and for three days remained alone, refusing all food and comfort. Probably his grief was quite genuine, but it must have been at least a little tinged by the realisation that he would be blamed for this sacrilegious act. As soon as he emerged, he sent a delegation to the pope protesting his innocence of any intention to harm the archbishop. He had, in fact, even sent to recall the four knights as soon as he realised where they were bound. Promising any penance the pope should require of him, Henry must also have known his hopes of establishing limits to church jurisdiction were doomed.

As an object of revulsion throughout Europe and beyond, the king found himself, for the first time, in a position of weakness. It was a time, too, when he particularly needed strength, with many enemies poised to threaten his extensive domains. Louis of France in particular, since the birth of a longed-for son in 1165, had felt a sharpened envy for the mighty 'empire' Henry commanded, most of which was, in theory at least, part of Louis's domain. This led the king to do all in his power to disrupt the quiet possession of those lands. Support for Becket was just one part of this, while active encouragement of rebellions, and raiding along the border areas, kept Henry constantly on the move to counter the continuing display of malice. In Wales, too, and even in Ireland, there was a potential for imminent trouble that would need the king's attention.

In 1169 Henry had attempted to allay the fears of Louis by showing an intention to divide up his domains among his own sons. His eldest, Henry, the Young King, would have England, Normandy, Anjou and overlordship of Brittany. Richard would have his mother's lands of Aquitaine, and Geoffrey would have Brittany, paying homage for it to his brother. Homage was immediately paid to Louis by the 13-year-old Henry and 11-year-old Richard, and, more reluctantly, to the young Henry by 10-year-old Geoffrey, who, in theory, had already been Duke of Brittany for several years through his betrothal to Constance. This division, while appeasing Louis, seemed to leave Henry's youngest son, John, who was still little more than a baby, with no landholding to look forward to. Some have suggested that this was the reason why, in 1171, the king's eyes turned towards Ireland, while others have claimed the Irish expedition was an attempt by Henry to escape the aftermath of Becket's murder and win back favour with the church. In fact, the situation was a little more complicated than that.

As long ago as 1155, according to Robert Torigny, Henry had considered the conquest of Ireland at a council at Westminster, and a papal bull known as *Laudebiliter*, approving such a move, is mentioned by the writer Gerald of Wales as existing at that time.

The pope's motive was to reform the Irish church and bring into line with Rome the practices of a people he referred to as 'ignorant and barbarous'. What Henry's motive might have been we don't know, as he quickly gave up the idea.

By 1171, the situation was different. In 1167 Dermot MacMurrough, King of Leinster, had been driven out by Rory O'Connor, King of Connaught, and came to Henry offering him homage in return for help to regain his kingdom. Henry gave him money and a rather lukewarm letter allowing him to recruit freelance adventurers to his cause. At first, only a few minor, disaffected Norman lords of West Wales supported him, but in 1170 they were joined by Richard de Clare, sometime Earl of Pembroke, and still Lord of Striguil, now known as Chepstow. He made a bargain with Dermot that, in exchange for his help, he would marry Dermot's daughter Aoife, and inherit Leinster after his death. It soon appeared that the Irish had no answer to the Norman forces of archers and disciplined foot-soldiers. Leinster was retaken, and when Dermot died in May 1171, Richard de Clare seemed set to be king.

Unlike Louis of France, Henry was not prepared to have a vassal elevated to kingship without his consent, and he was already preparing an expedition when de Clare visited him offering appeasement. Both Gerald of Wales and a nearly contemporary French song declare that Leinster and the Norse towns of Dublin, Wexford and Waterford were surrendered to the king of the earl's free will, though other sources say Henry threatened confiscation of English and Welsh estates to bring him to submission. Either way, de Clare was to receive Leinster in return as a fief from Henry and, as all his conquests were now imperilled by a concerted counter-attack by the numerous Irish kings, the expedition went ahead as planned.

Arriving in Ireland with a strong force in October 1171, Henry found little need for fighting. Almost at once the majority of the Irish kings and Norman barons submitted to him, together with the archbishops and bishops of the Irish church. Leinster was confirmed to de Clare, and Meath to another Norman, Hugh de Lacy, if he could conquer it, for the kings of Meath and Connaught were not among those submitting. It is clear Henry was intending a further campaign to complete the conquest of the whole island, but in April 1172 he discovered the pope had at last made known his response to Becket's murder, and papal legates were already waiting in Normandy to examine him on oath as to his involvement.

His return was so swift the French king was moved to remark, 'The English king does not go by horse or ship, he flies.' The important thing for Henry, though, was to establish his position in relation to the archbishop's death. Becket was already being talked about as a martyr for the church, his saintliness being confirmed by the discovery that, under his robes, he had worn a hair shirt, 'of the roughest kind and swarming with lice'. The lice are a very Beckettian touch.

In a matter of days, negotiations with the papal legates cleared the way for Henry's reconciliation with the church, and on Sunday 21 May 1172, in a public ceremony in the cathedral at Avranches, he laid his hands upon the book of the Gospels and swore to his innocence of any intention to harm the archbishop, though he admitted his hasty words had been the trigger for the deed. He also swore to carry out whatever acts of penance should be required of him, and the terms of this penance were then pronounced. Henry was to provide 200 knights to serve in the Holy Land for a year. He himself was to take the cross and serve for three years, either in the Holy Land or in Spain (though, in fact, the pope soon released him from this obligation). The estates of the church of Canterbury were to be fully restored, and, though the Constitutions of Clarendon were not specifically mentioned, the king was to abolish the evil customs contrary to the church which he had introduced. The implicit release of the bishops of England from their oaths to the controversial parts of the Constitutions was confirmed a week later in Caen, and the Constitutions themselves were allowed to quietly fade into history, though both the church and king felt a significant compromise had been reached in their favour. There were other personal penances that were also required of Henry, and though these remained secret, we might surmise that the subsequent scourging of the king before the tomb of the, by now, Saint Thomas in July 1174, was one of these.

Having agreed to these terms, Henry was then led out of the cathedral and before its main door was, pronounced absolved from guilt over his part in the archbishop's death. He was then formally re-admitted, both to the cathedral and the church. As for the murderers themselves, after an audience with the pope they were sent to fight for Christendom in the Holy Land for 14 years, after which they were required to remain there in religious retreat until they died.

The bruising contest with Becket and the church left its mark on Henry. In the future he would be less dogmatic and more open to diplomatic compromise. He was a boy no longer, now in his fortieth year, and still a constant traveller about his far-flung lands. If he looked for peace and support from within his family, however, he looked in vain.

It was a problem that would have been very familiar to his great-grandfather, William the Conqueror. Just as William had made his eldest son Duke of Normandy but given him no power, so Henry had crowned his eldest king of England, but with no estates of his own, and no share in government. In both cases the son was seen by his father as an idle wastrel, and in both cases the son found a willing supporter in the king of France.

The crisis came in the spring of 1173. In arranging a marriage for his youngest son, John, Henry promised that John should have the castles at Chinon, Loudun and Mirebeau, the same that had been given by his father to his own younger brother. At once the Young King protested that he had not been consulted and had no intention of allowing such valuable castles to pass to his brother. All his other grievances came pouring out, and when he was overridden by his father, he shortly afterwards fled to Paris, to the court of his father-in-law, Louis VII. When Henry sent placatory messages after him, 'from the king of England', Louis is said to have declared, 'Behold, the king of England is here.' Henry, he said, 'as king is dead ... for he resigned his kingdom to his son, as the world is witness.'

Now it appeared that a plot against Henry had been incubating for some time. Most accused Louis of fomenting rebellion, but Queen Eleanor was also implicated. For some years she had lived separately from her husband with her own court at Poitiers. Her sons, Richard and Geoffrey, and potential daughters-in-law were with her, and it was claimed she had turned them against their father. Richard and Geoffrey now quickly joined their brother in Paris. Nor were they his only supporters, as the extent of the rebellion became apparent. In England a number of disgruntled nobles declared for the Young King, including the earls of Chester, Norfolk and Leicester. William the Lion of Scotland, who was promised the counties of Cumbria and Northumberland, also came out against Henry, but the Welsh rulers, Dafydd ap Owain in Gwynedd and Lord Rhys in Deheubarth, remained loyal. Philip, Count of Flanders, and Theobald, Count of Blois completed the encirclement of Henry by his enemies.

William of Newburgh is scathing about the motives of this grand alliance. Though they declared they were supporting the rights of the Young King, he says, 'Nothing could be more absurd.' In fact, they were motivated by private hatred and the hope of gain. Nevertheless, 'In the month of June, when kings are accustomed to go to war,' a series of attacks were launched against the lands of the English king. From Flanders into north-east Normandy they came, from the south against castles at Pacy and Verneuil, from Brittany against Avranches, and from Scotland against Carlisle and the north of England.

Henry must have felt he was reliving the events of some 20 years before, but once again his cool head and speedy action thwarted his enemies. Though Newburgh speaks of all his vassals wavering, in fact the majority of Normandy, and indeed England, stood firm, and Henry made good use of the wealth of England in hiring mercenaries from Brabant. By the end of the year the Count of Flanders had withdrawn after his brother and heir was fatally wounded, and the Scots had been forced to a truce by the English justiciar, Richard de Luci. Louis had been driven from Verneuil and a lightning march from there to Brittany had resulted in the capture of the earl of Chester. In October the earl of Leicester, who had landed a fleet in East Anglia and joined forces with Hugh Bigod, was also defeated by de Luci and taken prisoner. Most surprising of all, Queen Eleanor was intercepted, dressed as a knight and riding astride, attempting to flee her lands of Aquitaine to join her sons in Paris.

These successes, however, were only the end of Round 1. Round 2 began again the following year when, once again, the Scots king invaded the north, while his brother David joined with rebels still holding Leicester to attack Northampton and Nottingham. The intention was to draw Henry away from Normandy, which would then be attacked by the Young King and his allies, Louis and Philip of Flanders. In fact, Henry made sure all was secure behind him before sailing in stormy weather for England at the beginning of July, taking with him his significant prisoners, including Queen Eleanor. If God was against him, he declared, He could sink his ship, but instead he came safely to land, and made straight for Canterbury where he duly performed his penance at the tomb of St Thomas. As if by way of reward, the very next day William the Lion of Scotland was captured outside Alnwick castle by a small royal force which appeared unexpectedly. Thereafter, according to William of Newburgh, Henry threatened to starve to death the earl of Leicester unless his supporters surrendered their castles, and the English rebellion collapsed.

Meanwhile in Normandy the alliance led by Louis of France was struggling to put the mighty city of Rouen under siege. They had not completely invested it before Henry was back with a strong force of defenders, including some thousand Welshmen provided by Lord Rhys. Within a short time Louis was in full retreat, Richard in Poitou was brought to weeping submission, and a peace treaty resulted in the Young King and his brothers promising full obedience to their father.

The two who came off worst out of all this were William the Lion of Scotland and Queen Eleanor. By the Treaty of Falaise, William was forced to accept Henry as overlord of Scotland, pay homage to him and hand over the key castles of Roxburgh, Berwick and Edinburgh. Queen Eleanor, meanwhile, would spend the next ten years effectively a prisoner of her husband, forced to accept the same comfortable captivity as Robert Curthose had experienced many years before. By contrast, the earls who had backed the Young King would soon recover their freedom and their lands, though not their castles.

As for Henry's sons, they were pardoned at once, restored to their previous positions and given greater financial resources. William of Newburgh comments that Henry 'loved his sons with ... extreme tenderness' and no doubt he still hoped to achieve the family confederacy of states that had been his aim all along. For the next two years, though, the Young King was kept on a fairly tight leash, while Richard seems to have been given a free hand in Aquitaine to bring that unruly province to good order.

For half a dozen years, then, Henry enjoyed relative peace, while the Young King and his master of arms, William Marshal, distinguished themselves on the tournament circuit, but the peace would not last. In 1182 the Young King attempted to take Aquitaine from Richard, who had repeatedly refused him homage for the province. In this he was supported by his brother Geoffrey, and by the new young French king, Philip, who also sent backing for the fight. Philip, son of Louis and brother-in-law of the Young King, was only 16 at the time, but had been well taught by his father that the interests of France were best served by stirring up trouble between the sons of the English king. Even with this backing, however, the Young King was no match for Richard and his father, and he was in full retreat when, in June 1183, he died of dysentery. Henry is said to have been distraught.

Though this ended one problem it created others, and once again Henry tried to shuffle his pack and produce an effective distribution of honours. In 1184, with Richard now assumed to be his heir, the king demanded that Aquitaine should be handed over to John. Richard flatly refused, and when John, with backing from Geoffrey, tried to attack, they had no success. For a time, Geoffrey was put in charge of Normandy, with the implied threat that Normandy, and possibly Anjou as well, could be added to his inheritance at Richard's expense. Nor would Henry publicly acknowledge Richard as his heir to England, while young John, now aged 18, was increasingly recognised as the king's favourite son.

Now, though, John was dispatched to Ireland, a semi-conquered land over which he had been named king as far back as 1177. He spent a large part of 1185 there, mocking the native rulers, upsetting the Norman lords, and generally, perhaps deliberately, showing he was completely unsuitable for the role. In the meantime, Richard was brought to heel by the ploy of removing Queen Eleanor from her long-time seclusion and taking her to Normandy, where it was then demanded that Aquitaine be handed back to her, since she was its rightful duchess. Richard, who was certainly his mother's favourite, was quick to comply. Having achieved this advantage, though, Henry unwisely still refused to acknowledge Richard as his heir, no doubt thinking that uncertainty was the best way to ensure his loyalty.

Once again, it appeared Henry was master, and he was certainly regarded as the elder statesman of Europe, on several occasions mediating between warring parties to find peaceful solutions. With his own sons, however, such solutions were beyond him, for now Geoffrey, with his larger ambitions thwarted, joined his great friend Philip of France in Paris. There they were clearly plotting against Henry when Geoffrey was trampled to death by horses while taking part in a tournament melee. He left two daughters from his marriage to Constance of Brittany, which had finally taken place some five years before, and in addition there was a posthumously born son, whose custody Philip immediately demanded as overlord of Brittany.

Philip now hardened his attitude towards Henry. There were territorial disputes over Toulouse and Berry while the Vexin, dowry of the Young King's widow Margaret, was another sore point. Philip offered it as dowry if Richard married the king's half-sister Alice, to whom he had been betrothed for over 20 years, but Richard showed no inclination to do so. The situation was complicated by a crisis in the Holy Land, where, in 1187, Jerusalem fell to the Muslim leader Saladin. Henry, Philip and Richard all swore to lead a crusade, but continuing disputes delayed their departure.

Henry's tactic of keeping Richard uncertain of his status now rebounded against him. Philip, working to split father and son, suggested to Richard that Henry intended to disinherit him in favour of John. He even suggested John could be given Richard's unwanted bride. At a meeting between the three in November 1188, intended to settle the dispute over Toulouse, Richard demanded from his father that he be formally acknowledged as his heir. When Henry remained silent, Richard knelt and performed homage to Philip for Normandy and Aquitaine, asking him, as overlord, to see that he was not deprived of his rights.

A truce and a series of fruitless meetings in early 1189 did nothing to mend this situation. By then Henry was clearly ill, but he realised Philip was using his son simply in order to force his hand, and refused to give in. There is, though, no evidence he ever intended to disinherit Richard. At a final meeting in May at La Ferté-Bernard in Maine, the same offer was made by Philip as he had made before – Richard to marry, Henry to confirm him as his heir and John to be sent on crusade – and was again rejected. Henry then withdrew to Le Mans to prepare for the inevitable hostilities. Contrary to convention, however, Philip and Richard did not withdraw, immediately attacking and taking the castle where they had met. They followed this up with an attack on Le Mans itself, and, with the town in flames, Henry was forced to flee.

He was pursued with reckless haste by Richard, though what his intentions were we will never know, for Richard in turn was ambushed by Henry's rearguard. The mighty William Marshal was its leader, and, with Richard at his mercy and pleading for his life, he is said to have declared, 'I will not kill you. I will let the devil do that,' and he killed his horse instead.

Henry had first made at speed for Alençon and the safety of Normandy, but abruptly he turned about and rode south again, sending most of his followers away. Maybe some inkling had come to him of what would be confirmed a few weeks later. In any case, he was too old and ill to want to go on fighting. He went home to his favourite castle at Chinon in Anjou. When pursued and called to a meeting by Philip and Richard, he could barely sit on a horse, but he listened and agreed to the terms demanded of him – all the usual, plus a payment of 'compensation' to Philip. He was also told he must give the kiss of peace to Richard, and, as he did so, he is said to have whispered, 'May the Lord spare me long enough to have my vengeance on you.' It was not to be. He was carried back to Chinon in a litter, and there, given a list of those who had deserted him to join Richard, he found the name of John at the top.

Some accounts say he collapsed at once into delirium. Others give a selection of words spoken before unconsciousness and death took him. 'Now let everything go as it will,' is one offering. Another says, 'Cursed be the day I was born, and cursed be the sons I leave behind me.' It is generally agreed that his last words were, 'Shame, shame upon a conquered king.' Henry died on 6 July 1189.

'In his own days he was unpopular with almost all men,' says William of Newburgh. Well, that would be expected for a decisive ruler who relentlessly trimmed back the powers of over-mighty lords. He continues, though, 'Yet it now becomes clear that he was an eminent and valuable prince,' and it is hard to argue with that assessment. Finding England a country in tatters, he left it in excellent order, and by sheer energy and strength of will, held together an 'empire' that would not long survive him. Further, although he spent only around a third of his time in England, his logical mind and practical administrative skill left it with a unique legal system that lasts to the present day and has been exported around the world. Henry may have felt he died in shame, but the English Common Law system stands as a fitting epitaph for a mighty king.

3

Henry III

'Behold the king of simple life and plain, Harry of England…'
– Dante Alighieri

Few kings can ever have begun their reigns in such challenging circumstances as Henry III. Just a little over 27 years had passed since the death of his grandfather, the previous Henry, but the actions of his uncle Richard and father John in the interim had had enormous consequences for the lands that had been the empire of Henry II.

Richard, born in England but growing up with his mother in Aquitaine, had only one aim when he came to the throne, that of fulfilling his crusading vow. To that end England was treated solely as a bank. He arrived in that country in August 1189, was crowned on 3 September, and left again on 11 December, in between squeezing every penny he could from both nobles and church. William the Lion of Scotland was able to buy back Roxburgh and Berwick and free his country from the overlordship of England, while important offices, such as that of justiciar, were freely sold to the highest bidder.

Then, in the course of his crusade Richard managed to make enemies of all his allies, in particular Philip of France and Henry VI, the German emperor. Instead of marrying Philip's sister, to whom he had been betrothed since childhood, he married Berengaria of Navarre, causing Philip, his erstwhile friend, to hurry back to

France, intent on making mischief. Later, returning to England, Richard was blown off-course, shipwrecked, and fell into the hands of Emperor Henry VI, who imprisoned him.

Prince John had not been trusted with any share in government while his brother was away, though he had been amply compensated with a rich heiress wife and the control and revenues of seven English counties. He also felt himself slighted when Richard declared Geoffrey's young son Arthur his heir-apparent. So when he heard of Richard's capture, he at once declared he was dead and travelled to Paris to pay homage to Philip for the English lands in France, at the same time handing over key territory in the Vexin. His endeavours to take England, however, met with little success. It was soon learned that Richard was alive and well, though the ransom demanded for his release would once again drain the country of wealth. When he returned, John immediately threw himself on his brother's mercy and was quickly forgiven.

Reclaiming lands given up to Philip required expensive military operations, however, and once again wealthy England was called upon to pay. No king of England, declared one contemporary chronicler, had ever taken as much from his kingdom. When Richard died from a sniper's wound turned gangrenous in April 1199, the English barons were already chafing from what they saw as unfair and excessive demands. Justice and peace were what they required from a new king. Instead, they got John.

Named as heir by Richard in his last hours, John immediately faced a rival claimant, the twelve-year-old Arthur, earlier recognised as heir-apparent. Philip, still making mischief, initially backed Arthur, until John agreed to perform homage to the French king and pay a feudal 'relief' of 20,000 marks for the right to enter into his inheritance. Such a relief had never been paid by John's predecessors, and immediately converted the rather theoretical overlordship of the French king into something more solid.

Then in 1200 John put aside his previous wife and married Isabella of Angoulême, who was already betrothed to Hugh de Lusignan. Hugh complained to Philip's court, and when John refused to appear at the court to answer the charge, Philip exercised his right as feudal overlord to forfeit his lands and give them instead to Arthur, all bar Normandy, which he intended to keep for himself. In the renewed warfare that followed, John captured not only Arthur but the Lusignans and many other rebellious Poitevin lords. Many prisoners were starved to death, and Arthur himself disappeared at this time, almost certainly killed by John. Says the chronicler Matthew Paris, 'Many people from that time forth were wholly alienated from the king,' and when Philip again invaded Normandy, John did little to defend his lands.

By the time his first son, Henry, was born on 1 October 1207, the Angevin 'empire' was irretrievably lost. Philip –known to the French as Philip Augustus – had taken Normandy, Maine, Anjou, Brittany, Touraine and Poitiers, leaving only part of Poitou, Bordeaux and the duchy of Gascony in English hands. Thereafter, largely confined to England, John seemed to do everything possible to endanger his son's inheritance.

His overriding aim was to raise money, ostensibly to enable him to win back his lands overseas. Taxes were imposed on all manner of laymen from nobles down to the lowest level, as well as on the church. Then a dispute arose over the appointment of a new archbishop of Canterbury. John refused to accept the pope's appointee, the Englishman Stephen Langton, expelled the monks of Canterbury, and seized all their property for himself. In March 1208, England was put under an interdict, whereupon John expelled all the bishops except his own supporter Peter des Roches, Bishop of Winchester, and took their property as well.

In 1209, John himself was excommunicated, and two years later Pope Innocent absolved all his subjects from their fealty to the king. By Easter 1213 a French fleet had been assembled to attack England, again at the urging of the pope. Then, in an abrupt about-face, John declared himself repentant for his sins and handed over his kingdoms of England and Ireland to the pope, receiving them back again as a fief, and doing homage for them. In future, any attack made by Philip of France would be an attack on the pope's lands and the pope's vassal. Though this manoeuvre stopped the invasion, Matthew Paris has a sour opinion of the matter. Thus, he says, 'of a country of the most perfect freedom, he made a slave'.

An attempt to regain the continental lands in 1214 ended in failure, largely due to lack of support from disaffected English barons. Some of these were already demanding John accept the Charter of Liberties of Henry I as a basis for their relationship. Then, in the spring of 1215, an outright rebellion broke out. John was forced to negotiate, and on the open meadows at Runnymede, under the guidance of Archbishop Stephen Langton, a charter was thrashed out.

Later, though not at the time, known as Magna Carta – the Great Charter – it was largely based on that of Henry I though with additional clauses, such as the freedom from arbitrary arrest and punishment. Not only were royal actions to be restricted by this charter, but a council of 25 barons was to enforce it, with seizure of royal goods and castles as the punishment for breach. It was signed by King John on 15 June 1215, probably under duress, though many of the lords named in the preamble were loyal to the king. Almost at once, however, it was clear that neither side intended to abide by it.

John appealed to the pope for help and Innocent quickly proclaimed the charter void. The barons then declared John deposed and offered the throne to Prince Louis, son of Philip of France, who had a very tenuous claim to it through his wife. In the fighting that followed, John was largely successful until, in May 1216, Prince Louis landed with a mighty force backed by the resources of France, whereupon the tide turned. By August both London and Winchester were held for the rebels with around two-thirds of the senior barons supporting Louis, while Alexander of Scotland had taken Carlisle. Then in October the king fell ill at Kings Lynn, possibly of dysentery, though Matthew Paris blames peaches soaked in new wine and cider. Following this, he says, in continuing northwards he 'irrecoverably lost his carriages and much of his baggage' in the Nene estuary, 'swallowed up by a quicksand,' or more likely by a rapidly rising tide. John himself made it as far as Newark, and there he died on the evening of 18 October 1216.

So it was that John's son Henry, less than three weeks after his ninth birthday, became heir to a kingdom riven by civil war, with something like half of it in the possession of a foreign prince.

It could have been the end of the Plantagenet dynasty, but in fact things were not quite as black as they seemed. Among these still supporting John, and named as executors of his will, were William Marshal, foremost warrior of the age, and Ranulf of Chester, England's most powerful earl. Much depended on the choices of these men, and within days it was clear they would throw their weight behind the boy king. Even as his father's body was being carried to Worcester, his nominated place of burial, Henry was travelling from Corfe to Devizes, and thence to Gloucester for his coronation on 28 October, a mere ten days after John's death.

There was so much wrong with that coronation – wrong place, wrong crown and wrong person bestowing it on the young head – but it was the best that could be contrived in the circumstances. Westminster Abbey was in the hands of Prince Louis, the crown of England was lost, and in any case far too large for a nine-year-old king, and the Archbishop of Canterbury was in Rome, explaining to the pope why he had failed to publish the excommunications of those who had rebelled against King John. So Henry, only knighted the day before by William Marshal, was crowned by Peter des Roches, the highest ranked English bishop available, with a simple circlet of gold provided by his mother. He did, however, recite the traditional coronation oath, promising to preserve the peace and protect the church, and give good laws and justice to his people.

Immediately after the coronation, Henry did homage for his new kingdoms of England and Ireland to the papal legate Guala, who had also been named executor in John's will. Pope Innocent had died earlier in the year, but his successor, Honorius III, was equally interested in affairs in England, not least as a source of funds for his projected crusade. Papal support would initially be of great benefit to Henry, though later it became more controversial. At the time, the immediate excommunication of Prince Louis for attacking the pope's land of England, meant no bishop could crown him king, which gained a useful breathing space for the party of the new King Henry III.

We know very little of the earlier childhood of this boy, or indeed the early years of his mother's marriage. She may have been as young as nine when she married John, and there is certainly a considerable gap between the marriage and the birth of the first child, Henry, at Winchester in 1207. The following year she took up residence at Corfe Castle in Dorset. Matthew Paris claims the king accused her of adultery and locked her up there, but that may be merely malicious rumour. A brother for Henry was born in January 1209 and christened Richard, followed by three sisters, Joan, Isabella and Eleanor, born in 1210, 1214 and 1215 respectively.

Of course, Henry himself would have little to do with the government of the country for many years. In the meantime there must be a regent, and William Marshal was urged to take the role. On his deathbed, according to Marshal's biographer, King John himself had begged that Marshal be given custody of his son, 'who will never succeed in holding this land without him'. Initially reluctant, claiming his great age as an excuse – he was then in his seventieth year – Marshal was inclined to defer to Ranulf of Chester as the leading earl, who in turn deferred to Marshal. It was the legate Guala who pointed out that such delicacy might lead to factions and divisions that the king's party could not afford. Marshal was then prevailed upon to take the post, and immediately showed by his energy and shrewd statecraft that age had put no limit on his abilities.

His clear intention was that the regency should be a collegiate matter, and at once a great council was called to meet at Bristol on 11 November 1216. There the momentous decision was taken to reissue the Runnymede charter in the name of the new king. A few changes were made, particularly the removal of the clause concerning the supervising council, and the clauses relating to the king's forests would be revisited in the near future. The charter was signed on behalf of Henry, and sealed not only by William Marshal, 'our guardian and the guardian of our realm', but also by the papal legate, giving the church's support to this new regime.

The ground had now been cut from under the rebels. Their personal hatred and distrust of John had nothing to do with the boy who had replaced him, and the most serious of their grievances had now been firmly dealt with. Furthermore, splits had already appeared between the English barons and their French supporters, with the former complaining about rewards disproportionately being given to the French. The winter truces gave time for thought, and a few barons came over to the royalist side, but Louis still held around half the country and controlled the Channel. The besieged Dover castle still held out for Henry, though, under the Justiciar Hubert de Burgh, while the Weald and the Cinque Ports were wavering. Lincoln Castle, too, was besieged, and it was there that a decisive blow would be struck for the new king.

An attack on Mountsorrel in Leicestershire by the royalist earls of Chester and Derby succeeded in splitting the rebel forces. While Louis pressed the siege of Dover, a large part of his army marched north, first to Mountsorrel, and then to assist in the siege of Lincoln. There, the castle was ably defended by the female hereditary castellan Nicola de la Haye, but the rebels had occupied both the town below and the space on the hill-top between castle and cathedral. Now, in May 1217, Fawkes de Breauté – one of John's leading mercenary commanders – got into the castle with a force of crossbowmen, who then lined the castle walls. While Ranulf of Chester attacked the north gate, and Fawkes' men poured their bolts down from above on the startled besiegers, Marshal and his force, entering the town by another little-known gate, charged the rebel forces and put them to flight. Their leader, the young Count of Perche, was one of the very few killed in a battle that became known as the Tournament of Lincoln, but over half the knights in the rebel army were captured and it was a major turning point in the war.

Louis abandoned his siege at Dover and retreated to London, and as more and more barons and their followers deserted his cause, sent to France for reinforcements. By the time they sailed for England at the end of August 1217, however, the Marshal and his council had organised a fleet of their own, led by Hubert de Burgh. Letting the French, with some 80 ships, pass first, they sailed out of Sandwich, manoeuvred to windward, and launched powdered lime into the eyes of those on board the enemy vessels. The French flagship was quickly taken and the smaller supply ships captured and looted, while the rest of the French fleet escaped back to France.

It was the end for Louis. Under the Treaty of Lambeth he agreed to quit the country and never return in exchange for a payment of 10,000 silver marks. In addition, there was to be a general amnesty for both sides, no new ransom demands and a general restoration of lands, the sorting out of which occupied the royal justices for some time to come. Once again, the charter of liberties was reissued, for the first time referred to as the Magna Carta, to distinguish it from the Forest Charter issued at the same time. By the end of the following year peace had been achieved, not only in England but also with Alexander in Scotland, and in Wales, where Llewelyn the Welsh leader was now styled Prince of Wales.

By the time William Marshal died in May 1219 he could fairly claim he had achieved all he set out to do. The young king was firmly on the throne, the Exchequer was working again, the king's justices were once more making their way around the kingdom, while at Westminster, according to the requirement of Magna Carta, a bench of justices was sitting regularly to hear the Common Pleas. The only danger was that rival factions bidding for control of the king might split apart this fragile peace. Peter des Roches had already claimed the right to take over the regency and been rebuffed, while to give it unfettered to his great enemy Hubert de Burgh might be equally catastrophic. The Marshal avoided the problem by committing his young charge to the care of the new papal legate, Pandulf, who was already well-known from an earlier visit to England. According to his biographer, in his parting words Marshal asked that God should give the young prince the grace to be a good man, but added that if he should go astray as his father had done, he prayed God to make his life short. Henry replied, 'Amen.'

One person given no share in the regency, or indeed in bringing up her own son, was his mother, Isabella of Angoulême. In July 1217 she left England for good, returning to Angoulême where she was at least countess in her own right. No-one appears to have made any objection to her going, and her children were left behind in England, all bar young Joan who, at the age of four, had been betrothed to Hugh de Lusignan, son of the man Isabella herself had been intended to marry. Joan was being brought up in the household of her prospective in-laws, but when she reached the age of ten the marriage was called off and her mother took her place as the bride of Count Hugh. This was a far more suitable match, both parties being in their thirties, but it caused upset at the time. Having no permission to remarry, Isabella's English dower was confiscated, and in retaliation Hugh gave his allegiance to England's enemy, France, and threatened to hold on to his rejected bride, Henry's sister. A compromise was finally achieved. Joan married the king of Scotland, and Hugh and Isabella went on to have nine children over the next nine years, all of whom, of course, were half-brothers and half-sisters to the English king.

Meanwhile in England the regency continued, with power effectively being shared by Pandulf, the Justiciar Hubert de Burgh and Peter des Roches. In May 1220 Henry, now thirteen years old, was given a second coronation, this time at Westminster Abbey, with full ceremonial, the crown being placed on his head by the Archbishop of Canterbury, Stephen Langton. The day before, beginning a lifetime dedication to promoting fine buildings, the king had laid a foundation stone for a new Lady Chapel at the abbey, and he now took as his patron saint Edward the Confessor, its founder and builder.

A priority for those governing the realm was the recovery of royal castles and lands which had been either given away or simply taken during the recent civil war. Many were held by mercenaries, particularly foreign mercenaries, appointed by John, who now felt their positions to be just reward for their services. Persuading these to give up what they held was a delicate job, and in 1223, at the urging of the pope, it was declared that Henry was sufficiently 'of age' to use his own great seal, so that in future, demands were seen to come from the king, rather than simply the council. It is the first time, too, that we hear mutterings against 'foreigners'. Prior to this it had been accepted that lands and positions in England might be held by people from all over the Angevin 'empire', particularly Normandy. Now, though, that empire was largely lost, and men had, in most cases, been forced to give up their lands either in England or overseas and swear allegiance either to the English or French king. As a result, England was becoming ever more English, with the expectation that important positions would be held by native-born Englishmen.

As it happened both Hubert de Burgh and Archbishop Langton fell into this category, each born to minor gentry in the east of England. With the departure of Pandulf and the ending of Peter des Roches's service as tutor to the king, it was these two who steadily saw through this policy of resumption of castles. Among those to go was Fawkes de Breauté, whose brother William, resisting to the end and imprisoning a royal justice, was hanged along with his garrison after a siege at Bedford Castle.

In 1223, the death of Philip of France brought his more belligerent son Louis to the throne. Refusing to renew the long-standing truce between the countries, he immediately invaded Poitou, and offered Bordeaux and Gascony to Hugh de Lusignan, if he could take them. Despite their pacifist inclinations, de Burgh and Langton agreed that this last foothold in France could not be allowed to slip away, and they set about raising and financing an army to defend it.

Since the old land tax, the geld, had been abandoned, it had become much more difficult to raise large sums of money for extraordinary ventures. Feudal aids might only be levied for specific purposes, and scutage (payment in lieu of military service) brought in less and less. Instead, it was decided to levy a tax payable by everyone, lay and church alike, amounting to one fifteenth of the value of all moveable goods. Such a tax had been levied a few times before, notably to pay the ransom of Richard I, but it was a novelty, and a great council was called in order to approve it. In exchange they were given new, and final, versions of Magna Carta and the Forest Charter, this time sealed with the king's own seal. Clearly this levy was given in response to an extraordinary situation, but the approval by the council, and the grant of a charter in exchange, set a precedent that would be picked up and used extensively in future times.

The expedition to Gascony in 1225 was a success. It was led by Henry's sixteen-year-old brother Richard – recently knighted and created earl of Cornwall – together with his uncle William Longespée, Earl of Salisbury, an illegitimate son of Henry II. Louis provided no assistance to Hugh de Lusignan, who was quickly driven out of Gascony. When the French king died suddenly the following year, leaving a twelve-year-old son, Louis IX, Henry began to have hopes of regaining all that his father had lost. Abruptly declaring himself of age in January 1227, the nineteen-year-old started to push for war, despite the reservations of de Burgh.

In 1229 an army was mustered at Portsmouth, only to find there were not enough ships available to ferry them to France. With a fine display of Angevin rage Henry blamed de Burgh, being barely restrained from drawing his sword and attacking him. When the army finally embarked in May 1230, it made for Brittany where the allegiance of the Duke, Peter de Dreux, had already been bought. According to Roger of Wendover, Henry was then urged to attack Normandy, being told it would easily fall to him; de Burgh, however, vetoed this and a similar attack on Anjou as being too dangerous. On the other hand, Matthew Paris declares the king simply 'wasted his days in idleness, and ... squandered an incalculable amount of money'. Either way, the expedition was a failure, and in September the king 'returned ingloriously to England'.

Wendover was correct in at least one respect, as the blame for the failure fell squarely on the shoulders of Hubert de Burgh. For some time the justiciar had been building up enemies. His marriage in 1221 to the sister of the King of Scotland was resented by the barons, and his recommendation that the king arrest his brother in 1227 after a row over a disputed tenancy, made an enemy of the earl of Cornwall. He had, meanwhile, been accumulating valuable honours since the king came of age and could grant his own charters. To the Marcher castles of Grosmont, White Castle and Skenfrith, were added royal castles at Montgomery, Cardigan and Carmarthen, while on the death of Gilbert of Clare, Earl of Hertford and Gloucester, he was given the profitable wardship of his eight-year-old son Richard. The return to England in 1231 of his long-time foe Bishop Peter des Roches, however, spelt the beginning of the end. Peter had been greatly enhancing his prestige on crusade with the Holy Roman Emperor, and soon began whispering in the king's ear of the failures of the over-mighty de Burgh, both in military and in financial matters. In the summer of 1232, de Burgh was abruptly dismissed, stripped of his castles, imprisoned, and charged with a litany of offences, most of which were preposterous. To avoid a trial, he submitted to the king and was imprisoned at Devizes Castle.

Bishop Peter was triumphant, and quickly filled the vacuum left by de Burgh with friends and relatives including Peter de Rivaux, his nephew, or possibly his son, who became treasurer. Many of these new men came from Poitou. The king, says Roger of Wendover, 'put confidence in no-one except the ... bishop of Winchester and his son Peter de Rivaux', on whose advice, 'he dismissed all the native officers of his court ... and appointed foreigners from Poitou in their places'. Many castles were also placed in their charge. This may be a gross exaggeration – Wendover uses the words, 'as is said' – but it clearly reflects the thinking of the time, recorded by this exactly contemporary chronicler.

On the death of Earl Ranulf of Chester, it was left to Richard Marshal, inheritor of the Marshal name and position, to protest on behalf of the native English. Not only was the king filling the place with foreigners, he claimed, but he was arbitrarily taking lands from English tenants to give to Poitevins, in clear breach of Magna Carta. Bishop Peter's response was that the king could have as many foreigners about him as he chose. Indeed, shiploads of foreign mercenaries – described by Wendover as 'poor and covetous after wealth' – were even then arriving to support the king against his own barons.

The consequence was a short, sharp civil war that dragged in both Wales and Ireland. It resulted in the death of Richard Marshal, and losses, both financial and otherwise, for Henry, before the newly appointed Archbishop of Canterbury, Edmund Rich, intervened to mediate a conclusion. By his advice Bishop Peter was dispatched to care for his diocese with a strong warning not to meddle again in state affairs, while the offending Poitevins were sent packing.

By this time, of course, the boy king was a boy no longer, and at twenty-seven years of age should have been well capable of ruling his kingdom. By the same age his grandfather Henry II had seen off all challenges and had a firm grip on his extensive lands. The later Henry, though, was made of different stuff. Perhaps if he had been a little older at the start of his reign, a little more involved in wresting back his kingdom and setting it on a firm footing, he might then have developed the necessary steel and political nous to follow in his grandsire's footprints. Instead he had been well bought up to be an educated, civilised Christian king, and a good man. Well aware of his status, but used to leaning on others for advice, he had a fatal combination of eagerness to please and an inability to foresee consequences. In another, more settled, age he might have been a star. In the unruly, grasping 13th century, however, he was something of a disaster.

At the age of twenty-seven years it was also high time Henry was married, and in fact the next few years were full of weddings. First, in 1235, at the suggestion of Pope Gregory IX, the Holy Roman Emperor Frederick II married Henry's sister Isabella. It was a prestigious match, though at forty he was nearly twice her age, and the dowry demanded of 30,000 marks drained the royal finances.

Then the following January Henry himself married the twelve-year-old Eleanor of Provence. It seemed a perfect match. Eleanor, too, was well educated, and steeped in the culture of poetry and the arts found in Southern France, which Henry found most attractive. They were married on 14 January 1236 at Canterbury, and Eleanor was crowned Queen of England a few days later at Westminster Abbey. Unusually for such a marriage at the time, they became devoted to one another. The result was five children and a settled family life based at Windsor Castle, as a result of which Henry travelled far less than any of his predecessors.

The ceremonial for his marriage, and especially the magnificent feast that followed, was arranged by Henry's current best friend, one Simon de Montfort. This Simon, a younger son of a younger son, was a descendant of Amaury de Montfort who had been a thorn in the flesh of Henry I in his French wars. His paternal grandmother, though, had been Amice de Beaumont, heiress to the estates and earldom of Leicester. These estates had been confiscated by King John on the death of the last earl, and given to Ranulf of Chester, but with few prospects in his native France, Simon de Montfort came to England in 1231 and made a claim to both estates and title. Of an age with the young king, and with a far more forceful personality, he seemed to make an immediate impression, and quickly recovered the Leicester estates. He had to wait a few years for the title of earl, however, and by that time had perhaps presumed too much on the friendship of the king.

In January 1238, in something of a secret ceremony, de Montfort married Eleanor, sister of King Henry and widow of the younger William Marshal. The king apparently was present and approved of the marriage, but the barons were outraged that this upstart Frenchman should aspire to such a match. In particular, Henry's brother Richard threatened rebellion and had to be bought off with 6,000 marks. Worse than this, it appeared that on the death of her first husband Eleanor, then aged only sixteen, had taken a vow of perpetual chastity, and this new marriage was condemned by the archbishop of Canterbury. de Montfort was forced to hurry off to Rome to secure the pope's dispensation and approval.

On his return he was still on good terms with the king. In February 1239 he was made earl of Leicester, and in June of that year was one of the godfathers at the christening of Henry's new son, Edward. In July, however, a violent row blew up between them. It appeared that Simon had obtained a large loan and used the king's name as security without even asking him. In his fury, Henry also accused him of seducing his sister, claiming he only approved the marriage to avoid shaming her. The de Montforts were forced to flee the country, and spent the next few years on the so-called 'Barons' Crusade' in the Holy Land, a rather disorganised affair that achieved little but added prestige to the participants.

Henry, meanwhile, had some problems of his own. Queen Eleanor's grandfather, Thomas, Count of Savoy, had a settled policy of extending the influence of his county throughout Europe, a policy pursued by many of his fourteen children. In 1236, therefore, Eleanor had arrived for her wedding accompanied by many relatives and fellow countrymen. Henry proved most accommodating, and in particular a number of her uncles gained prominence in England.

Thomas's fifth son William, Bishop-elect of Valence, was the family diplomat. He it was who had negotiated the marriage of Eleanor's elder sister Margaret to Louis IX of France in 1234, and he also negotiated Eleanor's own marriage, becoming a favoured councillor of King Henry, though still looking after family interests. He made such a big impression on the king that in 1238 he tried to have him appointed bishop of Winchester in order to keep him in the country. That attempt failed, but another favoured uncle of the queen, Peter of Savoy, became earl of Richmond in 1241, and another, Boniface, followed Edmund of Abingdon as archbishop of Canterbury.

It was partly this influx of more 'foreigners' that caused such a reaction to de Montfort's marriage, while the king's determination to rule with a small sworn council of favoured advisors, many also from overseas, added to the bad feelings. No new justiciar or chancellor was appointed after 1234, and the barons, who by now were thinking of themselves as 'native Englishmen', felt increasingly excluded, as, indeed, did those below the level of magnate who might have hoped to rise through positions at court.

Something of this split between king and barons was revealed in January 1237 when Henry called a great council of magnates and senior clergy, 'to discuss matters affecting the whole kingdom'. If they thought they were being consulted on some major policy, however, they were disappointed. When assembled they were told, 'The king wishes you to know that he is destitute of treasures,' followed by a request for a tax of one-thirtieth of all their moveable goods. This speech, says Matthew Paris, was heard with indignation, and 'a murmur mingled with groans and grief sounded through the hall.' Henry claimed he needed the money to cover the expenses of his sister's and his own marriages, but the magnates responded that they were continually having money extorted from them 'without their deriving any advantage from it'. In the end Henry got his tax, but only after promising not to make further demands on them, and reissuing Magna Carta and the Forest Charter in their final form with further promises to abide by their terms.

Now, after his father had done his best to make his early reign impossible, it was the turn of Henry's mother to add to his problems. Isabella had never been entirely happy at being a mere countess instead of a queen, and her relationship with the Dowager French Queen Blanche, for many years regent for her son Louis, was not good. A crisis was triggered in 1241 when Louis decided his younger brother Alphonse was now of age, and installed him as Count of Poitou. This was a title – an effectively empty title – that had already been given by Henry to his brother Richard, and Isabella was not only angry that her son should be excluded, but furious when she was snubbed by Blanche at the ceremony to install the new count. As a result, says Matthew Paris, she goaded her husband Hugh de Lusignan to rebel against the French king, and Hugh in turn wrote to Henry urging him to come at once and bring as much English money as he could, with the prospect of winning back at least part of his overseas lands.

Henry, with the naivety he was frequently accused of, took him at his word. Accepting the invitation, he immediately summoned a great council of magnates and clergy to ask for another tax to finance the coming campaign. For the first time Matthew Paris uses the word 'parliament' or debate, to describe this assembly, though there was nothing to distinguish it from earlier great councils. When it sat, in February 1242, doubts were expressed about the chances of success against the well-organised, well-resourced French, with whom there was an existing peace treaty, and it flatly refused the king's request.

In fact, by the time Henry had scraped together enough money and embarked, in May 1242, with a relatively meagre force of seven earls and three hundred knights, Louis had already secured Poitou, and was waiting on the north bank of the River Charente at Taillebourg with an army some estimates put at 50,000 men. In spite of this, Henry delivered his formal defiance in June, and when Louis offered to renew the peace treaty he turned him down. Then on 21 July 1242 the heavily outnumbered rebel army, led by Henry and his step-father Hugh de Lusignan, attempted to force the river crossing over the bridge at Taillebourg.

It was a complete fiasco. According to Matthew Paris, Henry's brother Richard, had won the gratitude of the French king during the recent crusade, and it was he who persuaded Louis to hold off his devastating counter-charge long enough for the English king to escape. Henry fled, first to Saintes and then to Bordeaux, while Hugh de Lusignan also deserted his cause, rapidly submitting to Louis and blaming his wife for the whole affair. Isabella, incidentally, who was also accused of attempting to poison the French king, fled to the abbey at Fontevrault where she died in 1246.

Louis, having crushed the rebellion, made no attempt to drive Henry out of Bordeaux, or indeed his last remaining duchy of Gascony. It took until the following March, however, before the English king could bring himself to request a new peace treaty. In the meantime he lived comfortably at Bordeaux, though berated on one occasion by the newly returned Simon de Montfort as being wholly incompetent and deserving to be locked up as a simpleton. Finally, on 1 August the new treaty was signed, and Henry returned to England, as Paris says, 'poor, landless and inglorious'.

It was the end of any hope of rebuilding the Angevin empire, but the ultimate cost was greater than simply the thousands of pounds wasted in France. With no prospects in their own native land, a new influx of Poitevins was received in England, along with those Lusignan half-brothers of Henry and their followers, all expecting that the king would provide for them, which he did. When his brother Richard, newly widowed, married Queen Eleanor's sister Sanchia the same year, a fresh wave of Savoyards was added. The result was far from harmonious. The Savoyards and Lusignans, competing for the same honours, hated each other, while the English – who tended to refer to all of them as Poitevins whatever their origins – despised them all. The split was reflected within the royal family itself, with Queen Eleanor taking the side of her relatives, and Henry generally supporting his.

Despite this constant drain on his resources, the king made no attempt to rein back on his other spending, though his finances were frequently precarious. So much land and so many honours had been given away by now that the requirement that 'the king should live of his own', that is to say on revenues from the royal demesne, could only be met by the most severe austerity. Instead, Henry continued with his extravagant lifestyle and grandiose plans. He had already built a new Great Hall at Winchester Castle, and in 1245 began his most favoured project, the complete rebuilding of Westminster Abbey as a suitable extended shrine to his beloved patron, Edward the Confessor. No expense was to be spared on this, with the latest designs and most skilled masons employed over the following decades to produce the stunning effect required by the king.

The financial shortfall was made up by every means possible. Although not deliberately keeping bishoprics and abbacies vacant, Henry was happy to take their revenues while clerical squabbles postponed elections. The law, and particularly the forest law, was especially profitable, with even minor breaches being punished by heavy fines. Then there were the demands made on Jewish moneylenders, so great as to bankrupt many of them. Regarded as the king's own property, and only precariously tolerated at the time, they were a source of finance that needed no-one's consent. In 1241, for example, Matthew Paris records that they produced 20,000 marks for the king, 'compelled to submit to a most terrible ransom, under the penalty of death or exile'. Pressure on the Jews, of course, meant pressure on those who had also borrowed from them, many of them from the lower levels of gentry, the knights and freemen, so the king's exactions were felt throughout society.

Henry was not the only one demanding money, particularly from the English clergy. The pope, who had been such a great support in the early part of the reign, was now continually drawing money both from the king and the church in all its forms throughout the land. In constant need of finance for crusades in the Holy Land, for combating perceived heresies in southern France, and in resisting the attempts of Emperor Frederick II to reclaim lands in Italy, one pope after another regarded England as a legitimate source of funds.

Not only were subsidies regularly demanded, with papal officers sent to collect them, but vacant benefices were also scooped up by the pope. At one point he directed that the next 300 vacant benefices should be assigned to his nominees. All of these would be Roman clerks who drew revenue from the benefice but never set foot in England. The English church protested repeatedly, not only that it was being drained of money, but also that those actually employed, at a pittance, to care for the souls in these benefices were ignorant and neglectful of their duties. Complaints to the king were ineffectual. Henry was still too much in awe of the pope to refuse his demands. It was only when, in 1250, Robert Grosseteste, Bishop of Lincoln, delivered a stinging rebuke to Pope Innocent IV, that any reduction was made in demands on the English church, which by then was providing in the order of 70,000 marks per year to Rome.

The year 1250 was significant – a jubilee year, completing the twenty-fifth cycle of 50 years since the birth of the Lord Jesus. It saw, however, the defeat and capture of Louis of France – later Saint Louis – while on crusade, and the death of the excommunicated Holy Roman Emperor Frederick II. Louis's ransom took roughly a third of France's annual revenue, but Frederick's death was more significant.

He intended his son Conrad, also excommunicated, to become Emperor in his place and inherit all his kingdoms including Germany and Sicily, the latter covering roughly half of Italy. Pope Innocent, however, was determined he should not have Sicily. He even offered it to Henry's brother Richard, who firmly refused, commenting, 'He might as well have offered me the moon.' Conrad soon took over in Sicily, but his own death a few years later re-opened the whole matter again.

In 1250, Henry decided that he, too, would go on crusade, formally taking the cross, and setting a date for departure in 1256. There were other matters, though, that needed to be settled before he could leave. Gascony had been promised to his eldest son Edward, possibly at the insistence of Queen Eleanor, but the always unruly duchy had reached such a state by 1248 that Simon de Montfort had been sent, apparently with a free hand, to subdue it. The typical Montfort energy and severity of approach quickly lost him the king's support, and a rising tide of complaints led in 1252 to de Montfort himself being brought before the king's court at Westminster to answer for his actions. Henry, we are told, was excitable and angry, Simon calm and reasonable. No firm conclusion was reached, but de Montfort resigned his post in favour of Prince Edward, and Henry undertook his own expedition to Gascony the following year, successfully placating and calming those earlier outraged by his lieutenant. de Montfort himself retired to France where his welcome and prestige were secure.

While in Gascony Henry arranged for the marriage of Prince Edward to Eleanor, the half-sister of the new king Alphonso of Castile, thereby turning a rival into an ally for his southern lands. The wedding took place in October 1254, with Edward, now fifteen years old, being endowed not only with Gascony but with extensive lands in Ireland and Wales, with Chester and with Bristol. Even before this, though, Henry was seeking to arrange an equally bright future for his younger son, the nine-year-old Edmund.

The sudden death of Conrad in May 1254 had once again thrown open the question of Sicily, and now Henry eagerly accepted an offer of the kingdom on behalf of Edmund. The arrangement made with the pope, however, proved to be disastrous. The king was released from his crusading vow in order to concentrate on securing Sicily, and all the money he had raised or could raise was now to be paid to the pope to cover his expenses in this venture, a debt that eventually mounted to some 135,500 marks.

Pope Innocent also suggested a lasting peace with France would help in the struggle against what he saw as the German enemy, and in December 1254 Henry met Louis face to face for the first time. Given their past it could have been a difficult meeting, but with Henry and his brother, and Louis and *his* brother, married to four sisters from Provence, it rapidly turned into a family gathering, and the two kings became firm friends. Louis was by some years the younger of the two, but certainly the wiser, and negotiations were immediately begun for a treaty to end all hostilities between their kingdoms.

At almost the same time Pope Innocent died, his death possibly hastened by news of the defeat of the papal armies at Foggia by Manfred, illegitimate son of Frederick II, who was now acting as regent to Conrad's two-year-old son Conradin. Despite the fact that Manfred was firmly in charge in Sicily, the new pope, Alexander IV, was keen to pursue the same policies as his predecessor. Almost his first action was to demand from Henry payment of the expenses lavished on the Sicilian campaign. Nor did he in any way soften his demands for payment when, in 1256, Richard of Cornwall was elected King of the Germans, having bribed his way to the post, though such an election was clearly to his benefit.

By 1258 it was clear that Edmund was never going to displace Manfred, and equally clear that Henry had no means of paying his enormous debt to the pope, despite threats to excommunicate him should he fail to do so. In April of that year, he summoned a parliament of barons and clerics intending to ask for financial aid, but matters quickly spiralled out of his control.

Quite apart from the king's debts, there were other things on the minds of those he had summoned. Trouble in Wales was one issue, possibly caused by the high-handed actions of Prince Edward. Famine was another, after a failure of the previous harvest. The real flashpoint, however, was Henry's backing for his Lusignan half-brother Aymer, when Aymer's men were responsible for a violent attack on followers of John FitzGeoffrey. FitzGeoffrey was connected to all the great families of the realm, the Clares, Marshals, Bigods, Warennes and Mandevilles, and for them his failure to get justice from the king was the last straw.

On 30 April a group of magnates in full armour, including the earls of Norfolk, Leicester and Gloucester, stormed into Westminster Hall and surrounded the king. Probably fearing immediate deposition, imprisonment or death, Henry was no doubt relieved to find they only demanded reform. A committee of twenty-four was proposed, twelve to be appointed by the king and twelve by the barons, to consider how best this reform should be carried out, though it is perhaps an indication of the king's views that all his Lusignan half-brothers were included among his chosen twelve.

In Oxford, at a parliament summoned for 11 June, the committee began its work. It was a tense time with both sides arriving accompanied by armed followers, but soon the reforms, later known collectively as the Provisions of Oxford, were pouring out. They were nothing short of revolutionary. The appointment of Hugh Bigod, brother of the earl of Norfolk, as justiciar was a revival of an office that had lapsed decades before, but the role was changed beyond recognition. Previously something of a prime ministerial office, now the main task of the justiciar was to deal with complaints and to deliver justice all around the country. These complaints could be made by or about great men or small, and to widen access they were to be presented by panels of four knights for each county. Bribes and presents were forbidden, the only exception being that the justiciar, other judges and their officers could accept suitable food and drink for each day.

Knights were also involved in the reformed position of sheriff. Henceforth, these were to be local men, appointed from the higher ranks of knights of the county. They could hold office for only one year, and initially were to be paid a salary, though this later proved unworkable. Strict anti-corruption rules were laid down. Sheriffs and their officers were to take no presents or rewards, were subject to the jurisdiction of the Justiciar, and had to account for their actions at the end of their year in office.

These measures, by and large, dealt with the many grievances of all levels of society that had grown up during the king's reign. The most revolutionary aspect, though, was an attempt to deal with the king himself, by reviving the idea of a supervisory council that had been quietly dropped from later versions of Magna Carta. This new council, however, was to go much further than its predecessor. Its fifteen members were to be chosen by four members of the committee of twenty-four, two nominated by the king and two by the barons. The fifteen also had to be approved by the twenty-four. Once appointed, the duty of the council was to 'advise' the king on all matters relating to the kingdom. In particular, they were to choose the chief ministers – the chancellor, the treasurer and members of the Exchequer – and control the use of the king's seal, in effect rendering the king powerless to act without their consent.

Furthermore, a parliament was to be summoned at least three times a year, in October, February and June, to deal with 'the common business of the kingdom and of the king'. A commission of twelve, chosen by the community of the barons, would always attend these parliaments, along with the fifteen members of the council, whether summoned by the king or not, though there was nothing to restrict the parliament to this number, and others could be personally summoned. The twenty-four even gave themselves powers to reform the households of the king and queen and to reform the church, and – keeping matters completely in their own hands – inserted their own nominees as castellans of the royal castles.

Oaths were sworn by 'the community of England' at Oxford, that they would stand together, 'each one of us and all of us together', to do right and take nothing to which they were not entitled, and, if anyone reneged on the oath, to treat him as a mortal enemy. The king and his son also swore to abide by the provisions, and, in a proclamation issued on 18 October, Henry declared that everything done and to be done by his councillors was done by his will and should be obeyed by all loyal subjects. Again, it stated that any who failed to obey would be treated as deadly foes. Significantly, this proclamation was issued in three languages, Latin, French and English, the first time the native English language was used in an official document since the time of the Conqueror, nearly two centuries before.

A driving force behind these reforms was Simon de Montfort, Earl of Leicester, probably influenced by his great friend Robert Grosseteste, Bishop of Lincoln. His name comes first after the bishops in the list of councillors of the king, but his insistence that the restrictions on corruption and the provision of justice must apply to the barons and their bailiffs as well as to the king, for the benefit of 'the community of the realm', began to divide those magnates who had previously acted together. It has been pointed out that, as the poorest of the earls, certainly in terms of landholding, he had the least to lose and the most to gain from the new arrangements. As early as the spring of 1259 there were 'words of insult bandied about' between de Montfort and the earl of Gloucester, and soon after Simon departed to France.

In November 1259 Henry himself travelled to France where the Treaty of Paris, a final settlement between the two countries, was signed and sealed on 4 December. Under it the English king formally gave up his claims to Normandy, Maine, Anjou and Poitou, and in exchange was recognised as lord of Bordeaux, Bayonne and Gascony, together with parts of Aquitaine. For these areas, though, he was required to recognise Louis as his overlord and to perform homage, which he did. Christmas was spent at Paris in possibly a more festive atmosphere than he would have found at home, and the friendship between the two kings prospered. The year 1260, though, would see further trials of strength between the king and the English barons.

Early in the new year Henry was brought news that Llewelyn had broken the terms of the truce between them and was attacking the lands of the Marcher lords. He immediately sent to delay the parliament due on 2 February, arguing that the defence of the Marches should have priority. No parliament should be held until he returned, he ordered, but then was delayed in France, first by the marriage of his daughter to John of Brittany, and then by a bad attack of fever. Meanwhile, Simon de Montfort returned to England, challenged Henry's right to delay the parliament, and apparently intended to force the issue by holding a parliament in London in the king's absence. Most worryingly for Henry, he seemed to have drawn Prince Edward into his plans.

Edward had caused anxiety before this. In his teens he had fallen under the influence of his Lusignan uncles, possibly leading to the arrogant behaviour complained of by the Welsh. Now he seemed to be in thrall to Simon de Montfort. He had taken an oath to support de Montfort some months earlier, and now appeared to be backing him in opposition to his own father. The continuator of Matthew Paris's work writes of a 'deadly discord' at the time, between the king and his son, between the king and de Montfort, and between de Montfort and Edward and various other barons.

By the time Henry returned in April, however, he was buoyed by the support (and money) of Louis of France and had not only armed mercenaries but also some of the English barons on his side, notably the earl of Gloucester and Hugh Bigod. In the event, Richard of Cornwall mediated a settlement, Prince Edward was reconciled to his father, protesting he had never been disloyal, and the potential crisis was smoothed over. An attempt to bring de Montfort to trial failed, but the baronial party would never be quite so united again.

When in 1261 a papal bull was received freeing Henry from his oath to abide by the Provisions of Oxford, it must have seemed the king had regained his former position. He justified his repudiation of the Provisions on the ground that he had received nothing that had been promised in exchange – neither backing for the Sicilian venture, nor negotiation with the pope to reduce his debts. Furthermore, he declared, it was the lies of evil-minded men who had sought to turn his people against him, and throughout his long reign he had acted only for the good of the country. Then he cheerfully dismissed the officials appointed by the council – the justiciar, chancellor, sheriffs and castellans – and put his own men in their places.

It was too much, particularly when another bull was received from Pope Alexander ordering excommunication for anyone who tried to deprive the king of his full authority. The disunited magnates became united again, and the outcry from the ranks of the knights and freemen showed how much they had valued the reforms. For some time, as both sides struggled to avert a civil war, there was a ludicrous situation of two sets of officials, two sets of sheriffs, and even two versions of 'parliament' with knights summoned by de Montfort to St Albans, and by Henry to Windsor, on the same day.

When an agreed arbitration failed to resolve the matter, Richard of Cornwall's diplomatic skills were once again called upon, and his finding was in favour of the king. In May 1262, regarding himself as finally free to do so, Henry arranged a two-year truce with Llewelyn, though at the cost of confirming his holding of all the lands he had recently taken. By this time Simon de Montfort had left the country in disgust.

It now seemed to Henry that matters were sufficiently settled in England for him to pay an extended visit to France to deal with matters arising from the treaty and from Gascony. At the same time Richard of Cornwall was spending some months in his neglected kingdom of Germany. With all the major players out of England, however, the situation in that land began to change.

The day after Henry left, his ally Richard de Clare, Earl of Gloucester, died suddenly. At least one chronicler suggested he was poisoned, but in any event his loss weakened not only the king, but also the position of the Marcher lords along the frontier with Wales. His son Gilbert was nearly nineteen, but being still technically underage, was placed in the wardship of Humphrey de Bohun,

Earl of Hereford. Within a short time, he had allied himself with a group of disaffected young Marcher lords, many of them previously members of Prince Edward's household, who, possibly influenced by de Bohun, found common cause in demanding a return to the Provisions of Oxford. When in November Llewelyn launched attacks north and south, complaining of persistent breaches of the truce, little was done to resist him.

To complicate matters, in September both Henry and his son Edmund had fallen seriously ill of an epidemic sweeping through Paris. Though the king was well enough to return to England later in the autumn, he was still clearly convalescent at Christmas, and he sent for Prince Edward to return urgently from Gascony. In his view, Llewelyn was the most serious threat, but the rebellious group demanding the Provisions of Oxford was daily attracting more and more support, including many from the shires whose hopes had been dashed by the papal bulls. In the spring of 1263 they sent for Simon de Montfort to lead them, and at the end of April he came.

From Oxford, late in May, a demand was made that the king once more return to the Provisions of Oxford but he flatly refused to do so. de Montfort's response was to incite his followers to seize the city of Gloucester and Edward's own city of Bristol. Then he turned his attention to the south and east, securing the support of the Cinque Ports on the south coast and of the men of Kent. For the first time the city of London rose against the king, who with Queen Eleanor was residing in the Tower. When the queen attempted to escape to Windsor, safely held by Prince Edward, she was pelted with stones and mud (and probably worse) by the Londoners as her barge passed along the Thames and was forced to turn back and seek shelter at St. Paul's.

On 13 July 1263 Henry gave in and once more accepted the Provisions of Oxford. Prince Edward was forced to hand over Windsor and also Dover Castle, which he had been holding for his father. A new council was installed with de Montfort firmly in charge. A new justiciar and new chancellor were appointed, new castellans and new 'wardens of the peace' in the shires, working alongside the sheriffs. de Montfort, however, no longer had the undivided support of the baronial class.

Heavy-handed actions against those who had opposed him made new enemies, while Prince Edward refused to be reconciled and soon drew away his former friends. The crucial question of who should appoint members of the king's household divided the October parliament, and gradually Henry, still declaring support for the Provisions, won back a measure of control.

At the end of the year it was agreed to submit the whole matter to the arbitration of Louis of France, famed for his saintliness and commitment to justice. Henry made it to France, where for some time his wife and the archbishop of Canterbury had been gathering support. de Montfort did not, having suffered a broken leg in a fall from his horse. It is doubtful his presence would have made any difference, however. Louis may have been a saint-in-the-making, but he was also a king. In January 1264, in the so-called 'Mise of Amiens', he utterly condemned the Provisions of Oxford, and found for Henry on every disputed point. The result was civil war.

With more than half the barons now on the side of the king, de Montfort's most prominent backer was Gilbert de Clare, the new young earl of Gloucester. He had, however, substantial support in the towns and among the knights of the shires, especially in the Midlands. The unifying cry was for control of the oppressive power of king and magnates, and a general hatred of 'foreigners'. Most popular was a call for the cancellation of debts owed to the Jews, which affected almost every landowner in the country. Massacres of Jews had already taken place, led by de Montfort's sons and by Gilbert de Clare.

Initially, the war went well for Henry and Edward, with gains in the Severn valley and at Northampton. When de Montfort moved south to threaten Rochester and links to the continent, however, the king and his son were also drawn south, and on 14 May battle was joined outside the little town of Lewes. de Montfort was carelessly allowed to dominate a ridge, though his army was far outnumbered and described as 'for the most part striplings, novices in arms'. He lined them up in three divisions with a force of Londoners to the left, Gilbert de Clare commanding the centre, and his sons commanding the right wing.

At the outset an impetuous charge by Prince Edward leading the royal cavalry drove the Londoners from the field, but then, with his force comprising roughly a third of the army, he rashly pursued them for some hours, by which time the battle was over. With more even numbers and the advantage of the hill, de Montfort had won a crushing victory, capturing both the king and his wiser brother, Richard of Cornwall. Edward had little option but to surrender.

There was no question of deposing the king, but the views of both sides are succinctly summed up in an almost contemporary work called the Song of the Battle of Lewes. 'The king,' it said, 'Wishes by the removal of his guardians to be free, and wishes not to be subject to his inferiors but to be over them, to command his subjects and not to be commanded.' If he were 'deprived of a king's right, he would cease to be a king.' The opposing view was that the king had been led astray by malicious foreigners, to the destruction of the realm and the degradation of its native people. It was therefore in the name of the community, the 'commonalty', that de Montfort justified his actions:

> ...it concerns the community that wretched men be not made guides of the royal dignity... They who guard the king, that he sin not when tempted, are themselves the servants of the king, to whom let him be truly grateful... Therefore, let the community of the realm take counsel, and let that be decreed which is the opinion of the commonalty, to whom their own laws are most known.

Furthermore, it concludes, it is the 'duty of the magnates' to guide the king, and if he degrades his own men by trusting to foreigners, he cannot complain if they refuse to obey him, 'nay, they would be mad if they were to do so.'

Unfortunately, it seemed that there were very few de Montfort himself could trust at this time. Once again, the king was to have a council imposed on him, but the nine councillors were to be elected by just three men, de Montfort himself, Gilbert Earl of Gloucester and the Bishop of Chichester, and of these three de Montfort was clearly the man in charge. However, even holding all the leading royals, the king, his brother and their heirs, his grip on power was fragile.

A number of barons had escaped from Lewes to France, including Hugh Bigod and the king's Lusignan half-brothers. There, together with Queen Eleanor and with the good will of King Louis, an army was already gathering. The pope, too, was outraged at the turn of events in 'his' kingdom, and excommunicated the leading figures. Furthermore, unrest in the Welsh Marches forced de Montfort to release some of the Marcher lords taken at Lewes, notably Roger Mortimer of Wigmore, with Prince Edward and his cousin Henry of Almain specifically named as hostages for their good behaviour.

Richard of Cornwall was securely held in the Tower of London, but Henry himself, now in his late fifties, was trailed around the country behind de Montfort, who, in practice, could do nothing without the king's authority. The cancellation of debts owed to Jews was a popular move, but as royal castles were taken and distributed among the de Montfort sons, a suspicion grew that the earl was becoming a dictator, merely acquiring wealth and power for his own family.

A parliament in June 1264 had been attended by knights, but by January 1265 de Montfort needed more than that to prop up his tottering regime, and this is the occasion sometimes referred to as the birth of 'Parliament' as we might recognise it. Not only were two knights to be elected to represent each shire, but two burgesses were to be chosen from each of a selection of boroughs, among them London, York and Lincoln. Of the magnates, only twenty-three were summoned, together with a large group of churchmen, who in general favoured the earl, or at least the idea of a settled peace.

The main business of the parliament was settling the future of Prince Edward, who was deprived of Chester and Bristol but promised some other lands in exchange, though only after there had been five years of peace. In March 1265, Henry and his son were forced to swear to uphold this settlement, but it was already being undermined by the defection of Earl Gilbert.

His complaints concerned the continued humiliation of the king and the aggrandisement of the de Montfort family, and his defection drew de Montfort westwards to Gloucester and Hereford, taking Henry and Edward with him. Then, at the end of May, Prince Edward escaped his captivity. Whether Gilbert's complaints were simply a ploy we will never know, but it is fairly clear his brother Thomas was part of an elaborate scheme to free the prince. As one of Edward's guards, Thomas accompanied him on a riding excursion, not that unusual for a noble prisoner who may have given his parole not to escape. One chronicle declares the prince had ridden and tired a series of horses, before suddenly speeding away on the last fresh mount along with Thomas de Clare. First stopping at Mortimer's castle at Wigmore, then moving on to Ludlow, Edward met up with his fellow Marchers, the earls of Gloucester and Warenne, and his uncle William de Valance, and all swore to act against de Montfort.

The Earl of Leicester himself seemed slow to act, and when he called up his son, also Simon, to meet him with an army, the younger Simon was even slower. de Montfort was detained in Wales making an alliance with Llewelyn, and then delayed by royalist forces in re-crossing the Severn into England. It was 3 August before he got as far east as Evesham, expecting to meet there the forces rallied by his son at their stronghold of Kenilworth. Unknown to him, however, there would be no forces. Prince Edward had caught them outside Kenilworth two days before, and though Simon the Younger had escaped into the castle, most of his men had been captured along with their battle standards.

Early in the morning of 4 August these standards were seen approaching Evesham from the north-east, but they were borne by the royalist forces. By the time de Montfort realised what was happening, one division of Edward's army under Roger Mortimer had blocked the bridges at the south of the town, while the other two, one led by Gloucester and one by the prince himself, had moved across Green Hill to the north, sealing the earl into a loop of the River Avon.

The only possible means of escape would be to punch through the forces at the top of the hill, and that is what was attempted, though when he saw the numbers holding the ridge de Montfort knew he had little chance. It is recorded that Edward and his men displayed the cross of St George as their badge, perhaps indicating to the French-born earl that they were the Englishmen on that battlefield. In the event, the day was recorded as the 'murder of Evesham, for battle it was none.' de Montfort and his men were quickly surrounded, and in a storm of rain, thunder and lightning, slaughtered in great numbers. The earl himself was savagely mutilated, his head cut off and sent as a trophy to Mortimer's wife at Wigmore, his limbs and genitals also hacked off. What was left was buried by the monks at Evesham abbey, and when word went round that he had worn a hair shirt under his clothes, his tomb became briefly a place of pilgrimage, until that practice was sharply stamped on by the king and his son.

Henry himself had been carried unwillingly to the midst of the battle wearing borrowed armour, and had only saved his life by crying repeatedly, 'I am Henry, the old king of England. Do not hit me.' Understandably he was in vindictive mood afterwards, or perhaps it was at the urging of his fiercer son that all the lands of even the least of de Montfort's supporters should be taken into the king's hands. Had this policy been persisted with, it might have prolonged the conflict indefinitely, but even so Evesham was not quite the end of the troubled times.

Simon De Montfort's eldest son, Henry, had also been killed at Evesham – Edward himself attended the funeral of a man who had been a childhood friend – but Simon the Younger had secured himself at Kenilworth, where Richard of Cornwall was now being held prisoner. While the rest of the country was submitting to the king, Simon refused to surrender until, early in 1266, he was offered generous terms, albeit requiring at least a temporary exile. Even then the garrison held out, and it took a siege and a compromise to persuade them to hand over the castle at last in December of that year.

The compromise was a settlement known as the Dictum of Kenilworth, negotiated with the aid of a papal legate. This allowed most of the surviving supporters of de Montfort to buy back the lands they had had confiscated, by payment of a fine on a sliding scale, according to their degree of involvement in the rebellion. This could be up to ten times the value of their lands, and prompted a further brief protest rebellion by Gilbert de Clare. Acting on behalf of the 'dispossessed', he occupied London in April 1267 demanding changes to the Dictum. Men without lands, he said, had no means of raising the fines required. In a matter of weeks it was arranged that those returning to the king's peace could have their lands returned and pay the fine later. Shortly after this, the last group of rebels was dislodged from Ely by Prince Edward, and the conflict, later known as the Second Barons' War, came to an end.

The de Montfort lands, of course, were not returned. They were, in fact, given to Henry's younger son Edmund Crouchback – the name referring to his right to bear a crusader cross on his back, rather than to any deformity. Edmund, having finally been deprived of the crown of Sicily in 1263, became successively Earl of Leicester, and later Earl of Lancaster. When the lands of the Earl of Derby were added, he became the wealthiest magnate in the kingdom, holding the nucleus of the later Duchy of Lancaster.

England was now once more a peaceful land. In November 1267 Henry issued the Statute of Marlborough, effectively enshrining in law the controls on sheriffs and other legal matters contained in the earlier Provisions, but without the encumbrance of a compulsory council of advisors. Two years later he was able to attend the translation of the body of his beloved Edward the Confessor to its magnificent new shrine in Westminster Abbey, the place previously occupied by the saint being now designated as the king's own future resting place. By the following year, 1270, matters were sufficiently settled for the princes Edward and Edmund to depart for the Holy Land, intending to join their uncle Louis of France on crusade. Louis had died of dysentery before they arrived, but the princes remained on crusade for several years, despite a call for them to return home in 1271.

In that year Henry had fallen ill and feared he was dying. Although he rallied, he is thought to have been hit hard by three deaths that occurred in little more than twelve months. First, in March 1271, his nephew Henry of Almain was murdered in Tuscany by Simon and Guy de Montfort, in revenge for the death of their father. Then in August of that year, his grandson, the five-year-old Prince John, son of Prince Edward, died. Finally, in April 1272, came the death of his brother Richard, the loyal supporter of his entire reign.

Henry, King of England, breathed his last on 16 November 1272, at the age of sixty-five, and a few days later was laid to rest beside his sainted predecessor in the abbey that remains his lasting memorial. It says much for the peace of the realm that, even when told the news in Sicily on his way home from the crusade, Edward did not hurry back. He was proclaimed king in London by Gilbert de Clare, the first instance of a new reign being deemed to begin immediately on the death of a king and not at the moment of crowning, and it would be more than eighteen months before he set foot in his new kingdom.

Henry, a decent but flawed man, had reigned for more than fifty-six years, through good times and bad. When all is said and done, Powicke's assessment is probably as accurate as any. 'He got through all his troubles,' he says, 'and left England more prosperous, more united, more peaceful, more beautiful than it was when he was a child.'

4

Henry IV

'an honour snatch'd with boist'rous hand'
– Shakespeare

More than 125 years would pass before another Henry came to the throne of England. Henry III, following his devotion to Edward the Confessor, had named his son Edward, and though that Edward had used the names of John, Henry and Alphonso for his first three sons, all had died in childhood and it was another Edward, the child of his later years, who eventually succeeded him. A third Edward followed, avenging the death of his ill-fated father, and there would have been a fourth had his eldest son, Edward the Black Prince, not predeceased him in 1376. Of the three Edwards, the first and third were renowned as fierce and largely successful warriors, but it was the fate of the second that would have more influence on the affairs of Henry Bolingbroke, setting a precedent for events within his own lifetime.

Of course, much had changed in England in the course of that century and a quarter, both in its relations with other states and in its own institutions. The conquest of Wales by Edward I in the 1280s proved to be long-lasting, but his attempts to reduce Scotland to a similar condition were less successful. This latter struggle gave rise to the earliest manifestation of what would later be known as the 'Auld Alliance' between Scotland and France, a relationship that would plague the English again and again down the years.

Indeed, the happy relationship between the royal families of England and France did not long outlive Henry III, and the year 1337 saw the outbreak of the intermittent conflict between the two countries known as the Hundred Years War. Early English successes, including the naval battle of Sluys and the land battles at Crécy and Poitiers, saw an expansion of the French lands subject to the English King Edward III, including Guienne, Gascony, Poitou and Limousin, as well as the useful port of Calais and its environs on the Channel coast. Following the battle of Poitiers in 1356, the French king himself, John the Good, was held prisoner in England pending payment of an enormous ransom of three million gold crowns. This, however, was the high point of English achievement, and by 1380 all that was left to England was its old territory of Gascony and the area around Calais.

It was in part due to these wars and the need to finance them that the institution of parliament had now become securely established. What was experimental in the time of Simon de Montfort became acceptable as necessity in the hundred years after his death, and from the time of Edward I and his Model Parliament in 1295, not only were the nobles and higher clergy summoned, but also two knights from each shire and two freemen or burgesses elected from the boroughs. From 1341 these knights and burgesses sat apart from the nobility, and from 1377 had their own representative, 'the Speaker', forming in embryo the House of Commons of today. By this time, too, these 'commons' had won considerable rights and privileges. Their consent was needed for the levying of taxes and the making of statute law, and, in return for this consent, they had the right to present petitions and grievances, and could even impeach royal ministers.

Much of this increasing power of the common people was down to the emergence of a 'middle class' of merchants and craftsmen in towns, but there had been major changes in the countryside too. In 1348-49 the Black Death had swept through England as through the rest of Europe, carrying off something between a third and a half of the population. Those left had seen an increase in their value, despite efforts like the Statute of Labourers in 1351 to keep them in their place and hold them to the same wage levels as before.

Further outbreaks of plague in 1361, 1369 and 1375 were less devastating, but equally disruptive in a society where previously few had questioned their status.

The man who would eventually become Henry IV was born at Bolingbroke Castle in Lincolnshire on 15 April 1367, during the later years of King Edward III. There was at the time not a suspicion that he would one day wear the crown of England. His father was John of Gaunt – more correctly John of Ghent, his birthplace – who was a son of the king, but John had two older brothers living and thriving, Edward, known as the Black Prince, and Lionel. Edward was everyone's popular hero, sharing in his father's glory in the French wars, and at that time winning a notable victory in Spain. Though he had married relatively late in life, he had already fathered two sons, another Edward born in 1365, and Richard, just four months older than his cousin Henry. Lionel, too, had a child, a daughter named Philippa, and though his wife had died some years earlier, there was likely to be another marriage and further children. No, there was no reason for young Henry Bolingbroke to come anywhere near the throne of England.

Circumstances can change, however, and change was underway almost from the time of Henry's birth. It was in Spain that very year that the Black Prince first fell ill with a sickness that would break his health and eventually lead him to an early grave. The following year, still celebrating his new marriage to Violante Visconti in Italy, Lionel died suddenly, some said poisoned by his new father-in-law. Already John and his son Henry were several steps closer to a throne that it was rumoured John himself coveted, and when, in September 1370, the little prince Edward died at the age of five, they came another step closer.

John would not achieve the popularity of his brother Edward. Some ten years younger, his exploits in the field were less successful, and he had not the charisma of the Black Prince. By 1370, however, he certainly outstripped him in wealth. Edward had married for love, against the wishes of his father, but John had accepted the bride chosen for him by the king, and, at the age of nineteen, had married the wealthy heiress Blanche of Lancaster. On the death of her father Henry de Grosmont in 1361, and her older sister

Maud in 1362, all the wealth, lands and titles of the former had fallen into his hands. Since Henry de Grosmont was a grandson of Edmund Crouchback, these were considerable. At a stroke, John had become Earl of Leicester, Earl of Lancaster and Earl of Derby, while the new title of duke, created by Edward III for his closest family, and originally bestowed on Henry de Grosmont, was bestowed afresh on John of Gaunt, who in 1362 had become Duke of Lancaster.

Young Henry Bolingbroke was less than two years old when his mother died. A few years after that, while replacing his ailing brother in Aquitaine, John of Gaunt married again. His bride was Constance of Castile, daughter of Pedro of Castile, in whose support the Black Prince had lost his health and wealth. With Pedro now dead, murdered by his half-brother who had taken the throne, this marriage gave John at least a claim to a crown, and from that date on he referred to himself as King of Castile. A daughter, Catherine, followed, half-sister to Henry, and then, more significantly, a new family of illegitimate half-brothers and sister. Around 1372 the newly widowed Katherine Swynford was engaged as a governess for the duke's daughters, and quickly became John's mistress. Sons John, Henry and Thomas were born at regular intervals through the 1370s, followed by a daughter, Joan. They were given the surname Beaufort after a castle of Gaunt's where the eldest was born.

By this time King Edward was in his sixties and in severe decline, mentally if not physically. The French war, which had resumed in 1369, was going badly, undermined by bad harvests and sickness, while high taxes made for unrest at home. Gaunt's forays into France convinced him that the war was unwinnable, but his role in negotiating a peace treaty made him unpopular with those who still dreamed of glory on the battlefield. Both he and Edward the Black Prince became more involved in government but were often arguing for different policies. By the time the Black Prince died in 1376, some at least believed John would take the crown after his father, and his general unpopularity led to a petition to the king to formally recognise young Richard as his heir, which he did.

King Edward III died on 21 June 1377. Richard was immediately proclaimed king at the age of ten, and Gaunt took the first opportunity of publicly declaring his loyalty to his nephew and repudiating the rumours that had linked him to the throne. He took no part in the regency council appointed for the new king, but he was clearly a major influence behind the scenes.

In 1380, a poll tax was levied for the third time in three years. This was a tax payable by everyone over the age of fifteen who was not a beggar, and, unlike the previous tax, fell at the same rate on rich and poor alike, the stipulation that the rich should help out the poor in their payment being more of a request than a command. In the event it triggered an uprising known as the Peasants' Revolt. In the south-east thousands marched on London, being admitted to the city by sympathisers. Prisons were opened, houses and documents burned and officials summarily beheaded. For several days the city was out of control, and anyone connected with the Duke of Lancaster, who had supported the tax, was a special target of the mob. Richard had retreated to the Tower, which was besieged by the rebel mass, and from there, together with his cousin Henry Bolingbroke, he watched as the smoke rose from the Savoy Palace, London home of John of Gaunt, utterly destroyed by fire and gunpowder. The duke himself was far away in the north of England, but his son only narrowly escaped with his life when some of the rebels got into the Tower and seized and beheaded a number of those sheltering there, including Simon of Sudbury, the Archbishop of Canterbury.

It was the fourteen-year-old king who ended the revolt, riding out to meet the rebels and, by his quick thinking, averting a likely massacre when their leader, Wat Tyler, was slain. This, Richard's first taste of real personal power, may have gone to his head a little. Certainly, he was soon in conflict with his council over his lavish spending and over-generous gifts to favourites. Two special counsellors were appointed, 'to counsel and govern his person'. One, Richard, earl of Arundel, he disliked from the start, but the other, the lowly born Michael de la Pole, soon became another favourite, particularly when he negotiated the marriage of the king to Anne of Bohemia. This marriage took place in 1382, and the young couple quickly became devoted to each other – a successful marriage in every way but for a lack of children.

Meanwhile John of Gaunt had not been neglectful of the interests of his own son. He had married for wealth and intended that Henry should do the same. Some years before, John's brother Thomas of Woodstock had married Eleanor de Bohun, elder daughter and co-heiress of Humphrey de Bohun, Earl of Hereford. There was a younger daughter, Mary, and this was the wife Gaunt wanted for his son. Either Thomas or Eleanor, or both, however, aimed to reap the entire fortune of Earl Humphrey for themselves, by pressuring Mary to enter a convent. Gaunt acted decisively. Money was paid, Mary was abducted, probably willingly, and Henry Bolingbroke was married to the girl of his father's choice early in 1381.

One account claims Henry and Mary had a first, short-lived child in 1382, when he would have been fifteen and she only thirteen. More certainly the first child to survive was born in September 1386 and christened Henry. Three more surviving sons, Thomas, John and Humphrey, were born over the next few years, and then two daughters, Blanche and Philippa, before Mary died giving birth to the latter in June 1394. By that time Henry Bolingbroke had taken part in events of national importance, the repercussions of which would shape the remainder of his life.

In July 1386, John of Gaunt sailed from Plymouth with some 7,000 men, with the intention of making his claim to be king of Castile into a reality. Henry Bolingbroke, now nineteen years old and recently created Earl of Hereford, was left in charge of the Lancastrian interests at home. The departure of the duke, however, seemed to take the brake off all the conflicts and tensions in England that had been on the increase for years. The king's extravagance, his unpredictability, his lavishing of badly needed funds and lands on his inner circle of favourites, particularly Robert de Vere, Earl of Oxford, all had drawn criticism from both lords and commons. Sometimes it seemed as if Richard's actions were designed specifically to provoke such criticism. In the course of a disastrous campaign in Scotland, he bestowed the titles 'duke of York' and 'duke of Gloucester' on his uncles Edmund, Earl of Cambridge, and Thomas of Woodstock respectively. At the same time, however, he made Michael de la Pole Earl of Suffolk, and Robert de Vere Marquis of Ireland, later to be Duke of Ireland.

Since de la Pole was, at the time, being blamed for the failures in the wars, and de Vere for encouraging the king in idle pursuits and extravagance, neither appointment was well received.

By October 1386, with a serious threat of a French invasion hanging in the air, parliament was in no mood to grant the king's request for new funds without some real changes. A demand was made that de la Pole be removed as chancellor. Richard refused, saying he would not remove the meanest kitchen scullion at their request, and thereupon stormed out. Nor would he return to parliament as they required. Instead, he demanded a delegation from parliament should come to him. The bitterest enemies of de la Pole and de Vere at the time were Thomas of Woodstock, Duke of Gloucester, and his friend Thomas Arundel, Bishop of Ely, brother of Richard's hated counsellor the Earl of Arundel. Instead of the delegation of lords and commons Richard might have expected, these two were sent to the king, ostensibly to speak for parliament as a whole. At first Richard was defiant, but then Knighton's Chronicle records the delegates 'reminded' him of an 'ancient law, and one followed not long ago', whereby if a king followed evil counsellors or his own whims and refused to be guided by the wholesome advice of the lords and commons, these same lords and commons could 'pluck down the king from his royal throne' and substitute 'some very near kinsman' instead. It is easy to believe Gloucester saw himself as the 'very near kinsman', but the clear reference to the fate of Edward II was not missed by the young king, who capitulated at once.

Returning to parliament, he was forced to agree to remove de la Pole from office and the earl was immediately put on trial accused of 'frauds, falsehoods and treasons'. Despite a spirited defence and remarkably shaky evidence, he was convicted, fined and imprisoned 'at the king's pleasure'. Parliament next insisted that a council be formed to hold office for one year, to govern in the king's name and inquire into all matters concerning the king's household and expenses, the conduct of foreign affairs, and all complaints from the time of Edward III onwards. Fourteen were nominated to this council and on paper it looks fairly balanced, including the Duke of York and the archbishops of Canterbury and York. Three leading members, however, were the Duke of Gloucester, the Earl of Arundel and Thomas, Bishop of Ely. Furthermore, it was declared that anyone counselling the king to oppose this council should be treated as a traitor.

Richard's response to this was to spend much of 1387 travelling through the north and the midlands trying to raise support for himself, and spreading the view that, now aged twenty, it was time he was allowed personal rule. He canvassed the views of the leading judges who tended to support his claim that the council was infringing his royal prerogative, and that those promoting it were therefore traitors to the crown. He also recruited a small private army, particularly from Cheshire and north Wales. When he returned to London in the autumn, however, it was to find that Gloucester and the earl of Arundel had taken fright and also recruited considerably more supporters, including the Earl of Warwick. When the Londoners refused to support him, Richard was compelled to accept the formal 'appeal', or accusation of treason, against five of his leading friends, made by Gloucester, Arundel and Warwick, and agree that they should be put on trial before parliament. The date set for this trial, however, was 3 February 1388, nearly three months into the future.

The five accused were Michael de la Pole, Earl of Suffolk, Robert de Vere, Duke of Ireland, Alexander Neville, Archbishop of York, Robert Tresilian, Chief Justice of the King's Bench, and Nicholas Bembre, a former Lord Mayor of London. Of these, all but Bembre had been allowed to disappear before the trial date. Suffolk fled to the continent, and the Archbishop of York to his diocese. Tresilian went into hiding, but de Vere, with Richard's blessing, rode north to raise an army for the king.

It is at this point that Henry Bolingbroke becomes drawn into the story. There had been talk of deposing the king, though this was vetoed by the Earl of Warwick. It may be, however, that this brought the Lancastrian heir into the camp of the 'appellant lords', safeguarding his father's interests against the ambitions of Gloucester. For whatever reason, Bolingbroke, along with Thomas Mowbray, earl of Nottingham, now joined forces with the 'appellants' to oppose de Vere. As the Duke of Ireland led some

4,000 men southward to support his friend and king, he found the crossing of the Thames at Radcot Bridge held against him by forces led by Bolingbroke. With the army of Gloucester closing in behind, the position was hopeless. In the fog of a cold December day de Vere managed to slip away to London and thence to the continent, never to return.

Despite the absence of all but one of the accused, the so-called Merciless Parliament met at Westminster on 3 February 1388. Now five 'appellant lords', including Henry Bolingbroke and Thomas Mowbray, made their appeal of treason, and all the accused were found guilty. All but Archbishop Neville were condemned to death, and Bembre and Tresilian, who had been discovered during the trial, were executed. As a clergyman, Neville was exempt from the death penalty, and soon after he was translated to the see of St Andrews in Scotland and therefore beyond the reach of his accusers.

Now the Merciless Parliament lived up to its name, purging officials and members of the king's household, including his former tutor Sir Simon Burley, who was accused of leading the king astray. Despite pleas from Bolingbroke, Mowbray and even the queen, he was condemned and beheaded. All this was done with the usual excuse, that it was not the king they were attacking but his evil counsellors. Then, having voted the sum of £20,000 to be divided between the Lords Appellant for their good services, the lords and commons renewed their oaths of allegiance to the king.

For nearly a year afterwards Richard submitted to rule by the council, but when in May 1389 he reminded them that he was now twenty-two years old and fully of age, power was quietly handed back to him. The return of John of Gaunt later that year freed Bolingbroke to take himself off for the whole of the following year to support the Teutonic Knights at the siege of Vilnius in Lithuania. This was followed by a further two year's absence from 1392 to 1393, first in Lithuania and then on a prolonged pilgrimage to the Holy Land.

The other Lords Appellant also took steps to distance themselves from former conflicts. Warwick retired to his estates, while Gloucester and Mowbray made their peace with Richard, the latter being appointed captain of Calais. Only the Earl of Arundel still appeared to nurse a resentment against the king. In particular, his actions on the death of Queen Anne in 1394 could have been deliberate provocation. He came late to her funeral and then asked leave to depart early. For answer Richard struck him violently across the face and imprisoned him in the Tower for a number of weeks.

There followed a period of relative calm while the king achieved some success in Ireland and accepted a policy of peace with France, which resulted in a long-term truce signed in 1396. As part of this treaty Richard was to marry Isabella, the seven-year-old daughter of the French king, and both Lancaster and his son, who had spent much of his time away from court, accompanied the king to France. Lancaster's reward for his part in the negotiations, and for his 'paternal and sincere affection', was the king's permission to marry Katherine Swynford in January 1396, his second wife Constance having died a few months before the queen. A little later the legitimation of the Beaufort children was accompanied by the earldom of Somerset for the eldest.

All was not quite as it seemed, however. The French treaty was not universally popular, and the childless king's marriage to a seven-year-old was deemed inappropriate by many. Nor had Richard forgiven and forgotten the treatment of himself and his close friends at the hands of the Lords Appellant some ten years earlier. When rumours began to circulate about concessions made to the French and Richard's future intentions, the chief critics of the policy were seen to be the Duke of Gloucester and the Earl of Arundel, and now the king felt strong enough to take his revenge on his enemies.

In 1397, Gloucester, Arundel and Warwick were invited to a state banquet. Gloucester pleaded ill health, possibly genuine, and Arundel stayed away with no apparent excuse. Warwick, however, attended, and at the end of the evening found himself led away to imprisonment in the Tower. Shortly after this, Arundel's brother Thomas, by this time elevated to the archbishopric of Canterbury, persuaded the earl to surrender himself to the king, Richard having sworn that he meant him no harm. Nonetheless, when he did so he was immediately imprisoned in Carisbrooke Castle on the Isle of Wight, and the archbishop was exiled. The king himself went to arrest his uncle, Gloucester, who, realising what was afoot, immediately fell to his knees and begged for mercy. Richard replied he would have as much mercy as he had shown to Sir Simon Burley, and handed him over to Thomas Mowbray, who carried him off to Calais.

Now the king sweetened his revenge by employing the same dubious procedure as these lords had used against his friends. Eight new 'appellant lords' came forward to appeal Gloucester, Arundel and Warwick of treason. Among them were Lancaster's son John Beaufort and two members of the Holland family, Richard's relations from his mother's first marriage. Proceedings before parliament were conducted by the Duke of Lancaster, and it appeared that the accusations related not to new treasons but to their acts of ten years before, their earlier pardons being revoked by the king. First a defiant Arundel was convicted and sentenced to death. Then Warwick, confessing to everything and throwing himself on the king's mercy, was condemned to exile on the Isle of Man. When it came to Gloucester's turn, however, no prisoner was produced. Gloucester, it was claimed, had died of an apoplectic fit in Calais, but before his death he had dictated a full confession. This was now read out, allowing his guilt to be established and his property forfeited to the Crown. Most likely the confession was forced from him before he was murdered, either by Mowbray himself or on his orders, but at least it spared Lancaster from having to condemn to death his own brother.

With this matter tidily dealt with, as far as Richard was concerned, rewards could be handed out to the participants. Mowbray, who had been heavily involved throughout as gaoler, murderer and even supervisor of the beheading of Arundel, became Duke of Norfolk. The king's half-brother John Holland and nephew Thomas Holland became Duke of Exeter and Surrey respectively, while John Beaufort was made Marquis of Dorset. Henry Bolingbroke had not been involved, but his promotion to Duke of Hereford may have been due to his father's participation, and to Lancaster's lack of protest at the easy disposal of his brother Gloucester. According to a chronicle of the time, the king's lavish scattering of dukedoms led to these new dukes being referred to as 'dukelings'.

This arbitrary 'justice' for crimes apparently pardoned a decade before must have sent a shiver of apprehension through many who had previously offended the king in some way. It certainly led directly to the next major change in the life of Henry Bolingbroke, for in January 1398 the young duke appeared before the parliament held at Shrewsbury and recounted a recent conversation with Thomas Mowbray, the new Duke of Norfolk. In this, he said, Norfolk had warned him that the king meant to destroy them both because of their actions at Radcot Bridge and as Lords Appellant. Their pardons would count for nothing, Norfolk claimed, as had the pardons for Gloucester, Arundel and Warwick. The king could not be trusted, and indeed was plotting a way to take the whole Lancastrian inheritance back into royal hands.

Mowbray of course immediately denied this treasonable conversation. A committee appointed to look into the matter found no evidence either way. It was one man's word against another, and therefore the matter must be settled in the traditional way, trial by battle. A date and place was fixed – 16 September at Coventry – but before the contest could begin Richard intervened. It is highly likely he did not want the claim proved one way or the other. Nor was he especially attached to either party, while he may have recognised the power of each to provoke mischief among their followers.

In the event, he banished Henry for a period of ten years, later reduced to six. The Duke of Norfolk, he claimed, had confessed certain 'points' to him which were likely to have caused great trouble in the land, and therefore he was banished for life. It is perhaps revealing of the king's mind when he further admonished Henry that, during his period of banishment, he should have no communication with either Norfolk or the exiled Archbishop, Thomas Arundel.

No protest is recorded from the Duke of Lancaster against the banishment of his son. Possibly he felt Henry was not entirely innocent in the affair. He had, after all, backed the opposition to the king ten years before. Interestingly, Froissart's version of the dispute has Mowbray telling the king of Henry's treasonable remarks, though it is generally believed he was mistaken. Alternatively, Lancaster may have negotiated the right of Henry to receive revenues from his estates during his exile, and he may have expected a quick pardon. Henry, in fact, settled down fairly comfortably in Paris to await his reprieve.

Various chroniclers record other capricious actions of the king at this time, though the date and authorship of one is controversial, and another clearly prejudiced against Richard. He is said to have demanded large sums of money to confirm pardons for earlier actions and threatened to lead an army to destroy London and seventeen counties that had supported his enemies at the time of the Merciless Parliament, unless they paid vast amounts to buy back his favour. Again, he is said to have required bishops and nobles to sign and seal blank charters which he could later fill in for his own purposes. More eccentrically, it is claimed that, on certain days, he would keep his court standing in silence in his chamber 'from supper until vespers', a period of several hours, with anyone he glanced at being required immediately to kneel.

Be that as it may, the action which provoked the greatest shock and outrage followed the death of John of Gaunt on 3 February 1399. It was widely expected that this would trigger a pardon for Bolingbroke, who would then return and inherit the title and estates of his father. Instead, Richard acted to extend his exile to a life sentence, at the same time cutting off the revenues from his estates and confiscating the bulk of the property that had belonged to the old duke.

It seems impossible to believe that Richard thought Henry Bolingbroke would accept this without a fight, and nor did he. He may well have already been in contact with fellow exiles, Thomas Arundel, and the Earl of Arundel's heir, also Thomas. More than likely he now received offers of support from some in England who felt their own interests threatened by this royal theft. Nevertheless, apparently completely unaware of any potential threat, Richard blithely continued with preparations begun the year before for a campaign in Ireland. The cause of this was a rebellion of Irish chiefs, a problem the king thought he had settled only a few years previously. Worse than that, his Lord Lieutenant in Ireland, Roger Mortimer, Earl of March, had been killed in battle. Mortimer, the son of Richard's cousin Philippa, had been his designated heir, and his death left that role now apparently filled by Roger's seven-year-old son, Edmund.

Richard's uncle, Edmund Duke of York, now in his late fifties, was left in charge in England, while a strong force and the majority of the nobility accompanied the king to Ireland. Two who excused themselves, however, were Henry Percy, Earl of Northumberland, and the newly ennobled Ralph Neville, Earl of Westmoreland. They were needed, they claimed, to guard the Scottish border.

Froissart, writing some five years later and far away in the Low Countries, gives a detailed description of what happened next, but there are so many discrepancies between his account and known facts that much of his detail must be regarded as fanciful. In particular, his description of the breakdown in law and order following the king's departure at the end of May 1399, and the pleas of the populace for Henry Bolingbroke to come and save them, smacks so much of the excuses chronicled for the arrival of that other usurper King Stephen several centuries earlier that it must be discounted. In fact, only a matter of days had passed from the departure of the king before Henry's castle at Kenilworth was preparing to receive him, and only a few weeks before he arrived with a small force at Ravenspur on Humberside.

He was accompanied by Archbishop Thomas and his nephew, and probably no more than three hundred men, and the place of his landing was well chosen. Far enough away from London and the south, and close enough to Lancastrian estates and relatives in the midlands and the Percys and Nevilles in the north, it was ideally placed to test the waters. What support would there be in the country for the return of Henry Bolingbroke?

Within days the Earls of Northumberland and Westmoreland had rallied to his cause, along with Northumberland's son known as Harry Hotspur, and most of the north country. The only issue to be settled was exactly what cause he was pursuing. From his stronghold at Pontefract, Henry moved south to Doncaster and there swore an oath, though what that oath was is a matter of dispute. Most chronicles say he swore he had come only to reclaim his 'rightful inheritance', which might refer to the estates and titles of his father, or equally might indicate that he already saw himself as heir to England itself. There had been prophecies that the crown would be inherited by a Lancastrian, and some commentators have seen the actions of Gaunt and his son throughout as attempts to secure the succession from a still childless King Richard. A contemporary French chronicle declares Henry had already circulated letters to the nobility and to towns throughout the land, claiming Richard intended to ruin them all, and that he had come to save them from that.

Whatever Henry's actual intention, it is clear how his arrival was interpreted by Edmund Duke of York. Immediately sending for Richard to return, he initially attempted and failed to raise a suitable army from London and the surrounding area, then set off westwards with the rest of the council. No doubt he meant to meet up with Richard's returning army, but somewhere along the way his courage failed him. Possibly it was news of the numbers now advancing to meet him with Henry, or maybe hearing that Richard was delayed. In the event, he turned away from Bristol to Berkeley Castle, where soon afterwards he met with Henry and immediately capitulated. Bristol, too, went over to Henry without a fight, and there he executed two members of the king's council.

By now Richard had left Ireland, but he had already made a mistake that would cost him dear. Advised by his cousin, York's son Edward, Duke of Aumale, he split his forces, sending part under the Earl of Salisbury to north Wales, while the rest accompanied him to Pembrokeshire. Whether this advice was honestly given, or whether Aumale, who had been close to the king, had already swapped cousin Richard for cousin Henry, it is hard to say, although soon afterwards Aumale, too, deserted the king.

The chronicles describe Richard looking out from his lodgings to find the greater part of his army already melted away, and once again he followed probably treacherous advice to travel northwards and join up with his forces in north Wales. He travelled the coastal route, while Henry, already giving orders like a king, took his forces up through the Welsh Marches to Shrewsbury. There a delegation from Richard's favoured city, Chester, surrendered it without protest. By the time King Richard reached Conway on 11 August, he found that Salisbury had believed a rumour that he was dead and disbanded his army, while his beloved Chester was in the hands of Bolingbroke.

It must have been clear to the king by now that he had little hope of retaining his kingdom and at best might be able to bargain for his life. The chronicles favouring the Lancastrians suggest he did just that. Visited by Northumberland and Archbishop Arundel, they say, he agreed to abdicate provided his life was spared and he was allowed suitable maintenance. Other versions, particularly the more sympathetic French chronicles, claim that Richard was tricked into leaving Conway by Northumberland, who swore on the Holy Sacrament that all Henry wanted was his rightful inheritance. Agreeing to accompany them to a meeting with Henry, and with guarantees as to his safety, Richard had no sooner left Conway than he was ambushed by Northumberland's men and taken as a prisoner to Flint Castle. Thus, says the Brut chronicle, Richard 'stood all alone, without counsel, comfort or succour of any man. Alas! For pity of this royal king!'

Meeting with his cousin, Henry again claimed he wanted only what should rightfully be his, and asked that his claim be submitted to parliament. However, by the time parliament – summoned in Richard's name – had assembled on 30 September 1399, events had moved on. Henry and Richard had arrived in London together, but on arrival it was Henry that went to the Palace of Westminster while Richard was escorted to the Tower.

There was no precedent for *taking* a crown from an anointed king. The only precedent, and one well known to all parties, was the deposition of Edward II some seventy years before. Then clergy, lords and commons together, in parliament though not necessarily *as* parliament, had unanimously demanded the deposition, articles had been drawn up detailing the unfitness of the king to rule, and he had then been persuaded to resign the throne to his son. Very much the same happened now, though not necessarily in the same order.

Early in September Richard had demanded a hearing before parliament, but this Henry was not prepared to allow. A few days before parliament assembled, a delegation of lords, clergy and lawyers visited the king in the Tower with a document of terms for his abdication. According to the official Lancastrian version, Richard cheerfully accepted this, nominated Henry Bolingbroke as his heir, and to signify this sent him his signet ring. Others tell a different tale, of Richard raging against his imprisonment and later falling into depressed resignation, reciting how many kings, rulers and great men had been 'exiled, slain, destroyed or ruined' in that land. Adam of Usk, who witnessed the situation of the king in the Tower, comments that he 'departed thence much moved at heart'.

There is no doubt that great pressure was put on Richard to 'voluntarily' abdicate, though we cannot know what this was. Edward had resigned to protect and benefit his son, but Richard had no such inducement. However it was obtained, his abdication was read aloud to the assembled lords, commons and clergy when the parliament – which was no longer legally a parliament – assembled on 30 September. Even then there were some, such as the Bishop of Carlisle, who demanded Richard should be brought before them for a fair trial, claiming Henry had 'more erred and offended against King Richard, than has the king against him'. The bishop was swiftly removed, but then, perhaps to silence further opposition, thirty-three articles or charges against the king were presented. These included the murder of Gloucester, the arbitrary 'justice' meted out to Warwick, Arundel and others, and Henry's own exile and disinheritance. After some discussion it was unanimously accepted that Richard should be deposed, 'by all his lords' counsel and by the common consent of the realm', as the Brut puts it. The throne of England was empty.

Now it was that Henry Bolingbroke came forward, and, with his hand on the gold-covered seat, made his bid to fill it. Some thought had gone into this claim. It was by no means clear that he was the rightful heir. That depended on the legality of settlements and dispositions made by earlier kings, a matter that had never been decided. He did not want to claim by conquest, since one conquest can lead to another. Nor did he want election by parliament, a potentially disastrous precedent to set. In the end he claimed the crown 'by the right blood coming from King Henry III, and through that right that God of His grace has sent me, with the help of my kin and my friends to recover it.' It was a strange and garbled way to claim such a prize, but no-one challenged it. Then, says the Brut, 'by all the lords of the realm, with the commons' assent and by one accord', Henry was accepted as king of England.

A splendid coronation followed on 13 October, the feast day of St Edward the Confessor and one year to the day since Henry had gone into exile. It is tempting to wonder if, sitting crowned and anointed on his throne, he felt a glow of satisfaction at a lifetime ambition achieved, or simply a shiver of realisation of the task he had taken on. He had told Archbishop Thomas of his intention to rule with truthfulness and mercy, but already he had tied his hands by promising to 'live of his own' and raise no taxes except in time of war. Even his own 'claim' might be used against him. His kin and his friends certainly expected rewards for their loyalty, while there were many others descended from Henry III, some of whom, the Mortimers for example, might feel they had a better right to rule than the new Henry IV.

He began, though, with mercy. Mercy first to Richard, whose fate was now decided. A special meeting of fifty-eight lords recommended he be held closely guarded in some secret place, and that no-one who had previously served him should be allowed near him. This was approved by the commons and Richard was immediately removed from the Tower, spending time in various castles before ending up in the Lancastrian stronghold at Pontefract.

The young Earl of March and his brother Roger were also shown mercy, held in close custody, but spending part of the time with the new king's own younger children. Similarly, when demands arose to punish those who had supported Richard in his tyrannies, Henry let them argue and accuse each other until it was apparent few could escape such a vendetta. Then, in the name of mercy and forgiveness, he simply removed the titles Richard had bestowed on those involved in his vengeance on Gloucester, Warwick and Arundel, and returned them to their previous status.

At around this time he also indicated the permanence of his takeover by appointing Henry of Monmouth, his eldest son and heir, Prince of Wales, Duke of Aquitaine, Duke of Cornwall and

Earl of Chester, all titles traditionally bestowed on the king's eldest son. Parliament was then asked to confirm the boy, just past his thirteenth birthday, as rightful heir to the kingdom, and duly did so. By Christmas 1399 the new King Henry IV must have felt he had made a very good beginning to his reign.

Not everyone in the country loved the new king, however, as he was soon to find out. On the Feast of the Epiphany, 6 January 1400, Henry planned to hold a grand tournament at Windsor. He and all his family would be present, and it seemed to one group of conspirators that this would be an ideal time to remove the new dynasty and restore the old. Chief among the group were the majority of those lords and relations of Richard so recently stripped of their titles – John Holland, now again Earl of Huntingdon, his nephew Thomas Holland, now Earl of Kent, the Duke of York's son Edward, again Earl of Rutland, and his brother-in-law Thomas Despenser. These, together with the Earl of Salisbury and others, planned to assemble forces between Windsor and London, assassinate the king and his sons and then rouse the country for Richard.

The plan might have worked had they not been betrayed to the king. Edward Earl of Rutland was the likely betrayer, he being the only one to survive the plot. He is believed to have warned his father and, in turn, the king. Henry and his sons rapidly returned to London, raised a force and set out after the conspirators who, again warned by Edward, promptly fled. It then appeared they had sadly misjudged the mood of the country. Thomas Holland and Salisbury got as far as Cirencester where they were beheaded by an angry mob. Despenser reached Cardiff and boarded a ship to take him to the continent. Instead, he was taken to Bristol and also beheaded. John Holland also attempted to flee to the continent but was blown ashore in Essex, where he, too, suffered the same fate. A number of lesser men were rounded up, some of them hanged and some pardoned, among the latter being the man who had saved Henry's life in the Tower of London during the Peasants Revolt some nineteen years earlier.

As a plot it was a disaster, and it sealed the fate of Richard. Within six weeks it was announced he had died, the official story being that he had sunk into depression and starved himself to death. Strangely, the king of France seemed to know Richard was dead by the end of January, abruptly reversing his earlier policy of refusing to confirm the ongoing truce, and then demanding the return of his daughter and her dowry. It seems most likely that, as with the earlier case of Edward II, a method had been found of killing Richard without visible violence. His body was brought to London and displayed to the public in a lead sealed coffin, with only the face showing. Despite this, it seemed few believed the official story. Even the Brut records that Richard was 'enfammed (starved) unto death by his keeper, for he was kept four or five days without meat or drink.' Some people refused to believe it was Richard. In particular, the French chronicler Jean Creton, who knew the king, later travelled all the way to Scotland following a story that Richard had escaped there, but was disappointed to find the man supported by the Scots was an imposter.

From this time on, however, the fortune that had smiled on Henry seemed to desert him. In the summer of 1400, it was thought an expedition to Scotland would confirm the military prowess of the new king. The Scots had internal troubles of their own but had refused to acknowledge Henry, and the constant border raiding was an irritation. Urged on by George Dunbar, the Scottish Earl of March, whose daughter had been jilted by the heir to the throne, Henry assembled a large army. Lack of money, though, meant these forces were supplied by the English magnates with the hope of profit as their incentive. Henry's own expectation of easy glory might be measured by the fact that his two eldest sons went with him. There was to be no glory, however, and no profit. The Scots refused to fight and Henry was outwitted by their skilled negotiators. Arriving in Scotland in mid-August, the army, out of supplies and out of money, was back in Newcastle by the beginning of September.

On the way south, however, a further opportunity for easy glory seemed to beckon. In north Wales one Owen Glendower had escalated a dispute with his English neighbour into a full-scale rebellion. In a few days in mid-September the towns of Ruthin, Denbigh, Flint, Oswestry and Welshpool, among others, were plundered and burned, and Henry immediately diverted his army. Before they could get there, though, local forces had defeated Glendower, who, in traditional Welsh fashion, fled westwards towards the mountains. Although descended from Welsh princes he was an unlikely rebel, a middle-aged, legally trained, landowner, but he attracted other men to his cause and for the next ten years would be a thorn in Henry's side. On this occasion the king led his men in a fruitless expedition along the north Wales coastline as far as Carnarvon, meeting no opposition, but making little profit either. Only John Beaufort, Earl of Somerset, benefitted, being given Glendower's confiscated estates.

By the time parliament assembled in January 1401, Henry's popularity was greatly reduced. Two expensive expeditions had failed in their objectives and already the king was breaking his promise and asking for money. It was to be a recurring theme of his reign. The commons was in a belligerent mood, and before the end of the parliament Henry had been forced to replace his chancellor and treasurer with men experienced under Richard, reform his own household, and inadvertently concede that the commons could have their petitions dealt with before granting the money he needed. In addition, at the urging of Archbishop Thomas, the law De Heretico Comburendo had been passed, allowing the burning of unrepentant heretics, while the general strength of public sentiment led to new laws against Welshmen.

By this time the thirteen-year-old Henry, Prince of Wales, had been established at Chester, theoretically overlord of all the Welsh, although the post of justiciar had been given to Northumberland's son, Hotspur. Both were taken by surprise, however, when Glendower resumed activity on 1 April 1401. On that day, Good Friday, the brothers Rhys and William Tudor overcame the few men left on guard and took over Conway Castle while most of the garrison was hearing Mass. Although the castle was quickly re-taken – the king blaming Hotspur for its loss – this was encouragement enough for the rebellion to spread down through west and south-west Wales. In September, Henry and his son once more led forces right across Wales as far as Aberystwyth and Harlech, in a third expensive and profitless campaign. Once more the Welsh retreated before them and returned as soon as they left.

Matters were not helped by bad harvests in 1400 and 1401, causing the price of corn to double. By now, even with the Lancastrian estates to draw on, Henry was deep in debt, and when in early 1402 both Hotspur and Prince Henry complained of lack of money for their actions against the Welsh, he had none to give. Things were about to get worse.

In April 1402 Glendower captured Lord Grey of Ruthin, the neighbour who had begun all this trouble. A large ransom was demanded but Henry had no mind – and no money – to pay it. At about this time, too, Hotspur resigned his post in Wales and returned to the Scottish border, still complaining about lack of payment. A few weeks later an army led by Edmund Mortimer was defeated to the west of Ludlow, in the heart of Marcher territory. Shockingly, corpses were mutilated and left unburied, but worse than this, Edmund was carried off a prisoner. Not only was he effective head of the Mortimer family and uncle of the little Earl of March, he was also brother-in-law of Hotspur, his sister Elizabeth being married to Northumberland's son.

This time Henry prepared three armies to attack the Welsh. One launched from Chester was led by Prince Henry, one from Hereford by the Earl of Stafford, and one from Shrewsbury led by the king himself. They set off at the end of August and on 7 September were halted, not by Glendower but by torrential rain and fierce winds. The king's own tent blew down and he narrowly escaped death, some accounts say by impalement on his own lance, and others by crushing under the weight of tent and poles. Then, even as the English straggled home, news came of a mighty victory, not against the Welsh but against the Scots.

The Earl of Douglas, having raided and plundered far and wide from Scotland to Newcastle, was leading his men back north when he found himself confronted by the forces of Henry Percy, Earl of Northumberland, his son Harry Hotspur, and George Dunbar. A relentless storm of arrows from the English longbowmen forced the Scots down from the heights of Homildon Hill, and on the plain below the army was routed. Five earls were taken prisoner, including Douglas and the son of the Duke of Albany, effective ruler north of the border. Such a victory should have been a cause for rejoicing, but it led only to further trouble.

Following a little-used precedent, Henry demanded the prisoners be handed over to him. Their highly lucrative ransoms would then ease his financial troubles rather than being paid to the army commanders as was more usual. Reluctantly, Northumberland agreed, but Hotspur flatly refused. He suggested, instead, that the money be used to ransom his brother-in-law, Mortimer, at which, according to the Brut Chronicle, Henry flew into a rage. He called him a traitor and accused him of wanting to aid Henry's enemies. Hotspur observed, 'Would you have a man spend his goods and put himself in peril for you, and then not help him in his need?' Upon which the king 'drew to him his dagger'. 'Not here but in the field (on the battlefield),' Hotspur is said to have retorted, and so it would prove to be – although not just yet. The only immediate consequence of this seems to have been that Mortimer transferred his allegiance from Henry to Glendower, marrying his daughter Catrin late in the year.

In the spring of 1403, Henry, too, married again. His bride was Joan of Navarre, the widow of the Duke of Brittany. It was clearly a love match, made against the opposition of her close family and the royal family of France, and equally unpopular in England. The expense of the marriage and of the new queen's Breton retinue only added to the English disapproval of Henry marrying among England's enemies, while on the French side there was horror that she could marry the man who had replaced and killed the French king's son-in-law.

In exchange for the Scottish prisoners Henry had granted the Percys the estates of the Earl of Douglas, and they had spent the early part of 1403 endeavouring to seize them. Clearly at this time Hotspur was also laying other plans, though how much his father knew of them until the last minute is debatable. As late as the end of June, the earl was still asking Henry for more resources for his Scottish campaign, and, although he at first refused, the king soon changed his mind and set off north with a force to help him. He was therefore at Nottingham rather than in London when, on

13 July, he heard that Hotspur had raised his banner in rebellion against him and produced a litany of grievances.

Among lesser accusations of corruption, illegal taxes and failure to ransom Mortimer, the chief claim was that Henry, referred to throughout as Henry of Lancaster, was no king at all, having broken the oath he swore at Doncaster that he would not seize the throne. Hotspur, therefore, was raising an army in Cheshire to restore Richard, 'if he lives', or otherwise give the crown to his nephew the Earl of March.

There were, in fact, to be three armies, for agreement had been reached with Glendower to bring up his Welshmen, while the Earl of Northumberland was also on his way from the north. The aim was to meet at Shrewsbury where there was an easy prize for the taking, Henry, Prince of Wales, whose governor, Hotspur's uncle Thomas Percy, Earl of Worcester, had slipped away to join his nephew.

If Henry had been in London as they thought, the plan might easily have worked. Instead, he, accompanied by Dunbar, marched swiftly across the Midlands to Shrewsbury, raising men as they went. When Hotspur arrived, with Worcester and the Earl of Douglas, on 20 July, it was to find town and castle already secured against them, and their forces outnumbered. With Glendower and Northumberland yet to arrive, Henry was urged to attack at once, and the very next day the armies lined up against each other across a broad plain to the north-east of the town. Nonetheless, much of the day was spent in negotiating, with Henry attempting to avert the battle and, allegedly, his offers being misrepresented to Hotspur by his uncle, the Earl of Worcester.

It was late afternoon when the fighting began with volley upon volley from the longbowmen on each side. Hotspur, on a slight ridge, may have had some advantage, and certainly serious damage was inflicted on the king's forces, especially when the Earl of Stafford leading the vanguard was ordered to advance. As arrows began to run short, however, the battle turned into a desperate hand-to-hand struggle. Confusion reigned as the forces led by the sixteen-year-old Prince of Wales turned the flank of the rebels and closed in behind. A desperate charge by Hotspur and Douglas cut down the king's standard-bearer, who was wearing the king's surcoat as one of several decoys. The cry went up, 'The king is dead.'

'Harry Hotspur is dead,' roared the king from nearby – and there was no reply. Hotspur was indeed dead, and by nightfall the 'worst battle that ever came to England, and the unkindest', had ended in utter defeat for the rebels. The Earls of Worcester and Douglas were taken prisoner and the former executed, while Hotspur's body, which had been quickly buried, was exhumed, beheaded and quartered, with the pieces sent around the country as an example for others, and the head set on a pole over the gateway to York.

If Henry thought his troubles would be over after this, he was soon disillusioned. Northumberland, who had never reached Shrewsbury, was pursued northwards, protested his innocence and had to be forgiven. His presence was needed in the north to keep the Scots in check. They, in turn, began producing letters apparently written by Richard and sealed with his seal, which only later were shown to be forgeries. Meanwhile Glendower, untouched by the loss of his allies, was now negotiating with the French for their support. In September another foray into Wales by royal forces could do no more than resupply and stiffen the defence of Carmarthen, before withdrawing due to lack of resources.

Lack of money was the recurring theme everywhere. Prince Henry in Wales had no money to fight Glendower. His brother Thomas, who in 1401 had been sent aged twelve to be Lieutenant of Ireland, returned in 1403 with the same complaint, and, soon after, their brother young John, nominally Warden of the East March of Scotland, would report unpaid soldiers, crumbling walls and general hunger from the same cause. All had used up their own resources, jewels and plate in the service of the king, but still parliament accused Henry of wasting money and insisted on economies.

In 1404, with French support, Glendower took Cardiff, Harlech and Aberystwyth, had himself crowned Price of Wales, and held a first Welsh Parliament at Machynlleth. It was 1405, however, that would be Henry's annus horribilis. In February of that year Constance of York, the widow of Thomas Despenser, who had custody of the young Earl of March and his brother, obtained duplicate keys to their rooms and fled with the boys towards Wales. Clearly the intention was to join Glendower and the boys' uncle Edmund Mortimer and set up a claim to the crown. In the event they were overtaken and re-captured near Cheltenham, whereupon Constance implicated her brother Edward, who had become Duke of York on the death of his father in 1402. This same Edward had betrayed the Epiphany plotters in 1401, and it is likely Henry did not believe the accusation. Nevertheless, Edward spent some months in the Tower.

The failure of this escape may have changed Glendower's plans, for immediately after he issued a document known as the 'Tripartite Indenture'. This was an agreement between himself, Mortimer and Northumberland to depose Henry and divide his realm between them. Glendower would have Wales, Northumberland the north of England from the Scots border to Warwickshire, and Mortimer the south. The initial failure to secure the Earl of March was a setback to the Mortimer cause, however, and Glendower's was to suffer similar reverses. Prince Henry himself defeated a Welsh force at Grosmont, and at Usk Glendower's brother was killed and his son taken prisoner. Could the northern arm be more successful?

It was the king's son John who first sent word of Northumberland gathering forces in the north. Thus alerted, Henry dispatched John, just short of his sixteenth birthday, together with Richard Neville, Earl of Westmoreland, to deal with the danger. Neville evaded an attempt by Northumberland to capture him, and quickly divided the earl from forces rallying to join him, before marching south towards York, where Richard Scrope, Archbishop of York, had led some 8,000 men onto Shipton Moor to the north of the city. Scrope was accompanied by Thomas Mowbray, son of the Duke of Norfolk exiled by Richard, and clearly the aim was to join with Northumberland against the king. Instead, on 26 May they were confronted by Neville and Prince John. Outnumbered by Scrope's men, though the majority were York citizens rather than soldiers, Neville resorted to trickery. Inviting Scrope and Mowbray to his tent, ostensibly to negotiate peace terms, he plied them with wine and smooth words. A chronicle relates that while this was going on, a knight was sent to the archbishop's force to tell them agreement had been reached and they could go home, which they did. When this was reported to Neville, at once the rebel leaders were arrested and taken before the king at Pontefract. Both were condemned to death and executed outside the archbishop's own castle at Bishopthorpe near York on 8 June 1405.

The day before this execution, Henry's friend and ally Archbishop Thomas Arundel had arrived in great haste to beg the king not to execute Scrope but to refer him to the pope. To kill an archbishop would be a terrible deed. Think of Thomas Becket and the effect of his murder on Henry II, who had not even intended the death! It was late at night, and, soothing his friend, Henry promised to speak to him again before acting. This time, however, Henry was implacable and Scrope and Mowbray were both dead before Arundel was aware of it the next morning.

That same night King Henry awoke screaming that he was being attacked and his skin was on fire. There was no attack but it was the beginning of an illness, or possibly a succession of illnesses, that would destroy his health and shorten his life. We cannot be sure what it was. Everything from eczema and psoriasis to heart disease, nervous breakdown and even malaria has been suggested. It may have been, at least in part, psychological, one commentator describing the king as 'neurotic'. At the time it was labelled leprosy and the cause widely accepted. A contemporary chronicle records, immediately after Scrope's last words, 'And anon after, as it was said, the king was smitten with leprosy,' before going on to attribute other 'great miracles' to the late archbishop. It was not leprosy, of course. In fact, the symptoms described, including the disfiguring skin rash, fit well with erysipelas, or St Anthony's fire, a bacterial skin condition that can cause fever, bodily weakness and even death.

This first attack lasted a week, before Henry was able to resume his pursuit of Northumberland who had fled northwards. The earl's strongholds of Warkworth and Berwick were taken with the aid of cannon, one of the first uses of such weapons in England. By August Northumberland had crossed the border to Scotland with his grandson, Hotspur's son Henry, but now the king was needed further south to repel a serious threat of invasion.

Glendower had made his pact with the French the year before, but no major campaign had been launched. For some time, in fact, the French had been sabre-rattling, attacking Calais and Gascony, and even, in the person of Louis of Orleans, challenging Henry to a duel. In August 1405, however, a sizeable French force had landed at Milford Haven, joined up with Glendower, and marched across Wales to threaten Worcester. Henry was still gathering men as he arrived in the city, and though seriously outnumbered, immediately confronted the enemy. What followed was an eight-day stand-off as the Welsh hesitated and the king tried to raise reinforcements. In the end, the lack of resources showed on both sides. The Franco-Welsh force backed down, and when later Henry tried to follow it into Wales, once more freak rain storms defeated him. There was a firm belief among the English by this time that Glendower could control the weather.

That was the high spot for Glendower, however. The following year the French withdrew, and a change of tactics on the part of the English gradually forced him into an ever-smaller area of north Wales. In 1406, too, Henry had another piece of luck. The heir to the Scottish throne, David Stewart, Duke of Rothsay, had been imprisoned and murdered by his uncle the Duke of Albany in 1401, leaving his seven-year-old brother as the new heir. Early in 1406 the elderly Scots king, fearing for the boy's safety, tried to send him to France. English pirates attacked his ship, however, and, realising the value of their 'catch', immediately took him to King Henry, who decided he could be equally safe in custody in England. Two weeks later the old Scottish king died, and Scotland entered into a long regency period that weakened and impoverished the whole country.

In April 1406, Henry had another bout of illness, sufficient to prevent him attending parliament for much of its sitting. This 'Long Parliament' sat from March until December with breaks for Easter and the harvest. It has been portrayed as a struggle between an ailing king and a belligerent group of lords and especially commons, though that may be to misread the situation. Certainly, Henry made a series of concessions, trimming his household, cutting his own and his wife's expenses, ruling through his council which must be named and, by implication, approved by parliament, and even having the money voted for the defence of the realm against its enemies audited by the commons. This same parliament, however, formally acknowledged Prince Henry as heir to the throne, and approved his place on the council at the end of the year. An alternative reading, therefore, is that it represented a sick king taking a step back from his former deeply involved personal rule and making some attempt at delegation. The proposed transfer of much of the administration to the king's council in fact originated with the king himself. That he still intended to remain in charge nevertheless is perhaps indicated by his appointment in January 1407 of his great ally, Archbishop Thomas Arundel, as chancellor.

For the next few years Henry seems to have been 'semi-retired'. The firm hand of Arundel did much to sort out the royal finances, which in turn led to improvements in the situation in Wales. The murder of Louis, Duke of Orleans, the chief French aggressor, at the hand of his cousin John of Burgundy in Paris in 1407, also did much to reduce the French threat. Once the commons discovered it could not blame the king for everything, it became more co-operative, particularly in producing much needed finance, while the council, led by Arundel and Prince Henry, adopted a collegiate approach, which for the most part worked smoothly.

Early in 1408 the Earl of Northumberland made a final, almost half-hearted attempt to raise a rebellion against the king. He had been in Wales, in France and in Scotland trying to raise men and money, but his force was small when, in the midst of a harsh winter, he set off southwards towards York. Henry prepared to travel north himself, but before he reached St Albans the rebellion was over. A battle that was little more than a skirmish had taken place in the snow at Bramham Moor near Tadcaster in Yorkshire, and Northumberland was dead. Nonetheless, Henry, whose travelling was severely restricted now, went as far as Pontefract to punish offenders and reward the victors, before returning to London where, possibly as a result of this, he became so severely ill that for some hours he was in a coma.

He remained ill for the rest of the year and was fully expected to die. In December his sons Henry and Thomas were summoned to his bedside, and in January 1409 he made his will. Whether this illness was a continuation of the earlier one is debatable. Some have seen it as a stroke, though there is no evidence of loss of speech or paralysis. Then, slowly through 1409, he began to recover.

The arrangements made in 1406 had been intended to be temporary, but as they entered their third year, divisions began to appear which, maybe with some exaggeration, came to be seen as factions. As one of its first actions the council had confirmed the legitimacy of the Beauforts, but this time with a restriction that neither they nor anyone claiming through them could succeed to the crown. This, largely attributed to Arundel's influence, may have niggled with Prince Henry, who was close to his Beaufort uncles. Two of them, in fact, John Earl of Somerset and his brother Henry, now Bishop of Winchester, sat on the council. Later there would be other issues that divided Prince Henry and Henry Beaufort from the elderly chancellor, particularly relating to the treatment of Lollard sympathisers at Oxford University and relations with France.

In December 1409 Archbishop Arundel resigned as chancellor, possibly under pressure from the prince, but instead of the post going to Bishop Henry as he might have expected, it was given instead to his younger brother Thomas. In spite of this it was now clear that Prince Henry was in charge of the council, which was packed with his own supporters.

For the whole of 1410 and most of the following year it appeared as though King Henry had decided to leave everything to his son – but appearances can be deceptive. Possibly the prince pushed his luck too far. Some have accused the younger Henry of arrogance and attempting to usurp his father's position by stealth, even of suggesting to the king he should abdicate – a dangerous word to use to a man who had achieved his throne by the 'abdication' of Richard.

It was the matter of French policy which proved to be a breaking point. With the French king regularly suffering fits of madness, competition in France to control his powers had created rival factions, principally that of Louis of Orleans and that of his cousin John of Burgundy. The blatant murder of Louis by his cousin in 1407 caused shockwaves through France. His thirteen-year-old heir, Charles, was quickly married to the daughter of Count Bernard of Armagnac, who took up his cause against Burgundy, his supporters now being called Armagnacs. Both Armagnacs and Burgundians appealed to England for assistance, and Prince Henry's choice was to support the Burgundians. Several chronicles record that the prince, approached by the Duke of Burgundy, sent on his own initiative a successful expedition in their support in September 1411, paying for this by temporarily stopping payment of annuities to King Henry's supporters. This was a step too far for his father.

In November 1411 King Henry abruptly resumed personal rule. The prince and his council were thanked and dismissed, Archbishop Thomas Arundel resumed as chancellor and a new council was appointed. Now when the Armagnacs appealed to the king, he sealed a treaty with them in April 1412 and later in the year sent out his own expedition, led by his second son Thomas, in their support. For the first time, the normally united Lancastrian family seems to have been divided. Prince Henry was given no role in government at all, and for a short period appears to have become estranged from his father. He may have been at odds with his brother Thomas, too, while the king favoured his second son with the title Duke of Clarence and backed him in opposition to Bishop Henry in his wish to marry John Beaufort's widow, Margaret Holland.

In his youth King Henry had heard a prophesy that he would die in Jerusalem. He was not yet forty-six years old, but by now he knew his health was gone. Perhaps this is why in November 1412 it is recorded that he ordered the construction of ships to take him to the Holy Land, a voyage he would never make. In February 1413 he was too ill to attend the parliament he had summoned, and a few weeks later collapsed while making an offering at the shrine of Edward the Confessor in Westminster Abbey. He was carried into the abbot's lodging, and, recovering his senses, asked where he was. 'In the Jerusalem Chamber' he was told, and there it was that he died on 20 March, with his son, the new King Henry, by his side.

As a young man Henry Bolingbroke had been an athlete, the popular champion of tournaments in England and overseas, and a lover of books and music. The crown of England robbed him of all of that. It is tempting to wonder how many times he might have looked back with regret to that fateful moment when there was no going back, when he had to take the crown or die in the attempt. Certainly, it brought him far more pain than pleasure. The deaths of Richard and Scrope clearly weighed on his conscience, and in the will he wrote in 1409, he calls himself a 'sinful wretch' who had led a misspent life. Had he been a rightful inheritor of the crown there is no knowing how well this rather serious, well-intentioned man might have ruled. As it was, constantly threatened by rebellions, constantly suspicious, constantly criticised by parliament, the best he could manage was to pass on an undisputed crown to his son.

Like many before and since, he discovered that doing another man's job better than he, was far harder than it looked.

5

Henry V

'England ne'er had a king until his time'

– Shakespeare

Had anyone realised when the future Henry V was born that the baby in the castle at Monmouth was destined to be king of England, they might have made a note of the date and time. We only have Henry's word that it was the morning of 16 September in the year 1386, a date he later gave to a man who proposed to cast his fortune. Even the town of Monmouth celebrates a different date, that of 9 August 1387, though that is unlikely since Henry's younger brother Thomas was born before Christmas that year. At the time, although the baby's father had some importance as the eldest son of the mighty John of Gaunt, there was no hint of the heights to which he would subsequently rise.

The events that finally led to that rise began a matter of weeks after the baby's arrival, and meant that Henry Bolingbroke would be away from his family for much of the early childhood of the boy. There must have been periods in the comfort of his home, however, as evidenced by the arrival of baby Thomas in the autumn of 1387, baby John in June 1389, baby Humphrey in October 1390, baby Blanche in the spring of 1392 and finally baby Philippa in June 1394. A compact family, possibly drawn closer by the death of Bolingbroke's dearly loved wife in her last childbirth.

Involved as he was in matters of state, and later mourning his wife, it seems Bolingbroke never achieved a close, warm rapport with his eldest son. Of course, the children were well looked after and provided with all they needed for their proper upbringing and education. Like his father before him, the young Henry developed a love of books and music and had every opportunity to develop the martial skills deemed essential for a nobleman at the time. It seems, though, that he found the warmth missing from his life only when he entered the household of King Richard.

This may have been as early as 1395, but was certainly from 1398 when he became a hostage for his father's, and indeed grandfather's, good behaviour when Bolingbroke was exiled, coincidently on his son's twelfth birthday. Hostage he may have been, but he was never locked up or threatened. Instead, Richard spent time with the boy, talking to him and encouraging him as his father had never done. He was with the king in Ireland when Bolingbroke raised his rebellion in 1399. Indeed, one chronicler records a possibly invented conversation, where Henry declares his innocence of any involvement in his father's plans, and Richard reassures him that he never suspected him of any such involvement. There seems, in fact, to have been a real affection between the two.

Henry remained in Ireland until summoned by his father in September 1399, by which time Richard was a prisoner in the Tower. It was to Richard, though, that the boy first went, only joining his father when the king insisted. Throughout his father's coronation he carried the Sword of Justice, and his name is found among those committing Richard to perpetual imprisonment, though how much the thirteen-year-old understood of the implications of that sentence is debatable. Since the original proposal specified the former king should be kept securely but comfortably, and well supplied with appropriate meat and drink, he may well have felt he was saving his dear friend's life.

Young Henry of Monmouth was appointed Prince of Wales immediately after his father's coronation, and it was to be no empty title. His original base was at Chester as a newly royal presence in the county that had been the most consistently loyal to Richard, and if this was not challenge enough for a boy in his early teens, by the time he took up his duties at the end of 1400 he also had Owain Glendower to contend with. Of course, the whole weight did not fall on his shoulders. He had a governor or tutor, Hugh le Despenser, and a justiciar to enforce the royal will. This latter was Henry Percy, the Earl of Northumberland's son, known as Hotspur.

Hotspur was some twenty years older than the prince, in the prime of life and one of the most famous soldiers in England. Adam of Usk describes him as 'the flower and glory of the chivalry of Christendom'. They would meet regularly at council meetings, and both took part in the four-week siege needed to recover Conway Castle from the rebels in May 1401. It would not be at all surprising to find an element of hero-worship in the relationship between the young prince and the seasoned warrior, so it must have come as a shock to the boy to find this hero openly rebelling against the king in the summer of 1403. More than that, Hotspur's uncle the Earl of Worcester, who had succeeded Hugh le Despenser as the boy's governor, also joined the rebellion. Henry seemed destined to be forever torn between duty and friendship.

A suggestion has been made that one reason for the king's haste in reaching Shrewsbury before Hotspur at that time, was that by then it was where his son was based, and he was not completely sure which side young Henry would take in the coming struggle. If that was so, the boy must have satisfactorily reassured him, for when the battle lines were drawn, the now sixteen-year-old prince was to be seen leading the forces on the king's left. He had ridden with his father in the campaign in Scotland and made several forays into Wales, but this would be his first full-scale battle. It very nearly became his last.

With both armies fronted by longbowmen, the archery duel that began the contest darkened the sky according to one chronicler. Prince Henry, of course, would have been in full armour with a visored helmet, but at some point he must have raised the visor, possibly to see the state of the battlefield better. At that moment he was struck full in the face by an arrow. By the merest chance it smashed the facial bone below his eye but missed both brain and spinal cord, lodging in the thick bone at the back of the skull.

It was maybe the foolhardiness of youth, or perhaps a sign of things to come, but the boy refused to leave the field. The shaft of the arrow was withdrawn leaving the head embedded in his skull. Then the prince led a charge at the enemy so successful that it smashed right through their lines, and, closing in behind, was able to sandwich Hotspur's forces between his own and those of his father.

When all was over Prince Henry is said to have wept over the body of his former justiciar, but he still had to face an ordeal of his own. He probably owed his life to the skill of John Bradmore, the physician who successfully removed the arrowhead from the boy's skull. And we owe it to Bradmore that we know exactly how it was done, for he left a full account of the procedure. Re-opening and widening the wound a little, tongs designed and made by Bradmore were inserted some six inches deep, through the entry wound and into the metal socket on the arrowhead where the shaft had been removed. The tongs had a central screw which allowed them to be spread to grip the sides of the socket. Then, gently moving this to and fro, the arrowhead could be loosened and removed. Over a period of twenty days the wound was gradually closed up, using probes of decreasing length made of barley flour, honey and flax fibres. Honey had been used in healing for thousands of years, and its antibiotic qualities certainly worked here to prevent sepsis and ensure the prince's complete recovery. Nevertheless, in a time before anaesthetics, the operation and daily changing of probes and dressings must have been excruciating.

A long period of convalescence followed, probably at the Lancastrian castle at Kenilworth, but by the beginning of 1404 the boy was back at his post, now in overall charge of operations against Glendower. It was a frustrating time. With severely limited funds available there seemed little possibility of defeating the growing strength of the Welsh. The loss of Harlech and Aberystwyth and the holding of a Welsh parliament would have been bitter humiliation, and though the prince was active up and down the border, he was paying for these activities with his own money, drawn particularly from his duchy of Cornwall.

An easing of the financial situation at the end of 1404 brought immediate results, and Prince Henry secured a striking victory over some 8,000 Welsh at Grosmont in the spring of the next year. More might have been achieved, maybe even a decisive defeat of the Franco-Welsh alliance in that year, but for the distraction and expense of Scrope's rebellion and King Henry's illness. As it was, the prince passed his twentieth birthday in 1406 with all still to do.

There is clear evidence now of a change of policy in Wales, and parliament's repeated thanks offered to Prince Henry suggest this was down to him. Better finance for campaigns helped, but instead of raiding and withdrawing, consistent pressure now began to force Glendower back into north and west Wales. Castles were taken and strongly garrisoned to dominate the surrounding area, a tactic similar to that of William the Conqueror centuries before. Supply routes were cut, and an effective blockade bottled up Welsh forces in a few strong castles which could then be besieged.

The siege of Aberystwyth in 1407 might have been successful had the prince not, by then, been dividing his time between that and the royal council, now in effect governing England. In his absence the siege was briefly relieved, with all to do again the next year. This time the king's enthusiasm for the new siege weapon, the cannon, had transmitted itself to his son, and while a number were needed in the north to pound Northumberland's castles into submission, several were spared and shipped from Bristol to Aberystwyth and Harlech, to help in the two sieges underway there. They were, perhaps, not quite as effective as Prince Henry had hoped, but he was learning all the time about the different ways sieges could be conducted.

Aberystwyth fell in September 1408, allowing all forces to be concentrated against the last rebel stronghold at Harlech. Surprisingly in view of his earlier guerrilla tactics, Glendower and all his family were trapped inside this castle, including his son-in-law Edmund Mortimer. In March 1409 Harlech fell, not to the pounding of cannon but to starvation. Glendower somehow managed to slip away, but Mortimer had starved to death, and the rest of his family, all but one son, were captured. The Welsh rebellion was effectively over, and much of the credit for that must be given to the tactics and persistence of Prince Henry, who himself grew from boy to man during these turbulent years.

Freed from the demands of this rebellion, the prince was able to devote more time to his council duties at Westminster. It was at this time that he became close to his uncle, Bishop Henry Beaufort, and possibly cooler towards Archbishop Arundel. No doubt he was full of confidence after his success in Wales, and maybe over-keen to be equally successful in England at the expense of the older generation. There were clashes with Arundel, especially with regard to a religious sect known as the Lollards.

These were the followers of John Wycliffe, the notable Oxford scholar who, in the 1370s, had first begun to denounce the church, and in particular the pope and bishops, for its worldly wealth and secular power. This was especially evident at the time, when the pope, exiled from Rome, lived in an immense palace at Avignon, largely paid for by the sale of 'indulgences,' promises to sinners of less time in purgatory and a shortcut to heaven after their deaths. The church, said Wycliffe, should be poor as Christ had been poor, and all grace came from the Bible, which should be available for people to read in their own language. Nor were priests and sacraments essential, and most heretical of all, the bread and wine used in the Mass remained bread and wine after consecration, and were only symbols of Christ's body and blood.

Wycliffe, of course, was condemned by pope and bishops, but had been protected until his death in 1384 by Oxford University and especially by John of Gaunt. His words had been taken and perhaps distorted by the leaders of the Peasants' Revolt, suggesting the church should be stripped of its wealth, and, if the state failed to do this, the state itself should be reformed. Despite, or maybe because of this, his followers increased and were given the name Lollard. Archbishop Arundel became their implacable foe, and his hand was behind the notorious statute De Heretico Comburendo, intended specifically to allow the burning of unrepentant Lollards, though such burnings were infrequent.

When in 1407 Arundel tried to stamp out Lollardy at Oxford, forbidding the translation of the Bible into English and banning Wycliffe's writings and any unauthorised preaching, Prince Henry took the part of the university. He also tried to intervene in the burning of the Lollard John Bradby in 1410, though there he was unsuccessful. It is impossible to know his motive for this. Perhaps it had to do with his grandfather's protection of Wycliffe, or maybe an unusual squeamishness about burning a man alive for his beliefs. He did at the time have a good friend and former companion in Wales, Sir John Oldcastle, who was an unashamed Lollard, and there were Lollard knights in parliament. Certainly his attitude contributed to the division now apparent between prince and archbishop.

Much has been made of the prince's youthful misbehaviour, particularly by Shakespeare who represented it over two plays. The actual evidence for it, however, is vanishingly slight. Until the spring of 1409 Henry was fully occupied in Wales, being repeatedly thanked by parliament for his efforts. Thereafter he is heavily involved with the royal council, particularly in the years from 1410 when he was clearly its leader. The only evidence of any misbehaviour would be King Henry's abrupt return to power and dismissal of his son at the end of 1411, and the prince's stout defence of himself in 1412.

As regards the first, the king may well have felt Prince Henry was exceeding his authority in his policy towards France, especially in dealing directly with John of Burgundy and sending an expedition for his support without his father's approval. The word 'abdication' may also have stung him into action, as, too, the discourteous treatment of his friend Archbishop Arundel, and the threat to the marriage of his younger son.

As regards actual bad behaviour by the prince, the contemporary chronicles are contradictory. While the Brut has a long passage about how 'he fell and inclined greatly to riot,' and 'drew to wild company', Adam of Usk praises him as 'a youth upright and filled with virtues and wisdom'. The detailed stories of consorting with bad company and prostitutes, in fact appear long after the prince's death. The accusations against which he defended himself in 1412 refer to disloyalty and attempting to usurp the throne. They were made, claimed the prince, by those 'sons of iniquity' and 'malicious sowers of discord' who were trying to discredit him with his father.

A further attempt to accuse him of misappropriating funds was refuted by the production of his meticulous accounts.

If there was a rift with his father it lasted a matter of weeks in the summer of 1412, with one, probably fanciful, account describing the prince falling on his knees before his father and offering him a dagger with which to end the young man's life if he had any suspicions of his loyalty. Of course the dagger was thrown away and Prince Henry was embraced as 'My dear and heartily beloved son'.

Nor is there any truth in the story enthusiastically adopted by Shakespeare, of the prince trying on the crown at the bedside of his dying father. This was an invention of the French chronicler Monstrelet in the 1440s, when Burgundian sympathies encouraged him to disparage the English king. In more reliable chronicles, the only thing Henry took from his father's bedside was his blessing and encouragement for the future, and one story describes him as spending that night in prayer with a monk or anchorite of Westminster Abbey for company. If he emerged the next day as a changed man, as some have claimed, it is likely to have been due to a sober realisation of his new responsibilities, and a firm determination to rule in accordance with his own vision of a strong and just kingship.

He began – as indeed his father had done – with mercy. Even before his coronation on 9 April 1413 he had released young Edmund Mortimer and his brother Roger from a captivity that had lasted for most of their lives. The earlier heir apparent of Richard II clearly held no threats for Henry, and Edmund was quickly restored to his estates. In similar vein, Edward, son of the old Duke of York, was restored to the dukedom that had been stripped from him, and his brother Richard became Earl of Cambridge. The only notable prisoner excluded from this general mercy was James of Scotland, as yet far too valuable a bargaining tool to be set free.

The coronation itself took place in a ferocious snowstorm that blanketed much of the country. No omens of doom were drawn from this, however, the mood of the country being remarkably positive. Henry was a young man of twenty-six, already a proven and successful leader in war and experienced in government, with a priceless gift his father had never really achieved – popularity.

This is not to say, however, that everyone was satisfied with the new regime. Within weeks posters appeared in London, though to no effect, inciting rebellion in the name of Richard II, claimed to be still alive. It may have been more than just piety and affection, then, that prompted Henry's reburial of Richard's body alongside that of his beloved wife in Westminster Abbey, before the year was out.

By that time, too, there had been another, more serious threat to the new king, from none other than his old friend Sir John Oldcastle. Despite the actions of Archbishop Arundel, the Lollards had been gaining support around the country. This is not so surprising if we consider that in 1413 there were no fewer than three popes competing to be recognised as head of the Christian church. Persecuting the small fry was achieving nothing. In fact, Capgrave's chronicle claims that bills were being posted on church doors, declaring 100,000 Lollards were preparing to rise up and destroy all those that would not accept their ideas. Be that as it may, Arundel decided the time had come to make an example of some prominent figure.

Sir John Oldcastle, by his marriage, had become Lord Cobham, and as such attended parliaments. In addition, he was a member of the king's household. He was, says Capgrave, 'A strong man in battle, but a great heretic'. It took some time to persuade the new king that his friend should be brought to account for his views. In fact, we are told the king only agreed 'after much labour' to persuade Oldcastle to amend his ideas. In September 1413, however, he was brought before Arundel and an array of bishops and proved totally intractable.

Denying the basic tenets of the church regarding communion and confession, he read from a Lollard tract, and when questioned about the church leaders, declared that the pope 'is the head of Anti-Christ ... archbishops and bishops is the body of Anti-Christ' and 'monks, canons and friars is the venomous tail of Anti-Christ.' He was, of course, condemned as a heretic and sentenced to death. Forty days of grace were allowed in which he might recant and save his life, but before that time was up he had escaped from the Tower of London and begun plotting to overthrow the king, whom he no doubt blamed for his persecution.

As on a previous occasion, the action was to take place around Christmastime, and as before, the plot was betrayed to the king. Oldcastle directed his sympathisers, many of them from different parts of the country, to gather at St Giles Fields, near Charing Cross, on the evening of Tuesday 9 January 1414. He believed that thousands more would pour out of London to support him, but Henry took the precaution of locking and guarding the gates, and quietly stationed his own forces at the gathering place. As the different groups of rebels arrived in the dark, most of them not knowing each other, they were quickly arrested and taken off to prison. Then a show of force by the king soon after midnight put the rest to flight. It has been estimated there were no more than a few hundred of them. Some were killed, some captured, and others, Oldcastle among them, managed to escape. He remained free for a further four years, until he was discovered, apparently living on his own manor in Herefordshire, and executed as a traitor and heretic.

What the uprising intended to achieve, particularly as regards the king, has remained vague. Inquiries across the country, however, revealed a well organised network of many thousands of sympathisers, and the laws for their suppression were now tightened. Lollardy went underground, and, with only occasional outbursts, remained there for the next century, though it is tempting to believe that some at least of the reformers who appeared at the time of Henry VIII may have been descendants of these early 'proto-protestants'.

The Lollards, of course, were not the only ones to be disturbed by the rivalry between three popes. The situation had arisen when, in 1377, Pope Gregory XI had returned from Avignon to Rome and soon after had died. His successor had been so notorious in his conduct that a group of cardinals had quickly returned to Avignon and elected a rival. Various opportunities to resolve the situation had been missed when first one, then the other, and, indeed, some replacements, had died. Both reigning popes were declared deposed by the Council of Pisa in 1409, which, consisting of church leaders and theologians from across Christendom, carried a certain weight.

Neither pope, however, accepted this, nor the election of a 'unity candidate', Alexander V, by the council. Thus, when Henry V came to the throne, Pope Benedict XIII reigned at Avignon, Pope Gregory XII in Rome, and Alexander's successor, Pope John XXIII in Florence.

Over the years different countries had backed different popes, with politics largely determining their choice. Thus England had backed the Roman pope, initially because the Avignon pope was a Frenchman supported, of course, by France. After Pisa many countries, including England and France, switched their allegiance to the pope elected there, but the Spanish kingdoms and Scotland still supported Benedict. In 1413, Sigismund, King of Hungary, King of the Germans and future Holy Roman Emperor, was determined the matter should be settled once and for all. In his eastern kingdom he had been fighting off an invasion of Ottoman Turks and wanted Christendom united to support him in this struggle. Pressure was put on Pope John to call a council to meet on neutral territory at Lake Constance in Germany to resolve the issue, and countries were invited to send representatives.

England at the time might have been seen as one of the smaller, less influential countries of Western Europe, particularly since Henry IV had had little time to spare for foreign adventures. Henry, nonetheless, sent a number of bishops, along with his good friend Richard, Earl of Warwick. When the council assembled in November 1414, Sigismund was determined it must not be deadlocked by the large delegations of French and Italians opposing each other and dominating proceedings. It was therefore decided that four 'nations' would be recognised as having voting rights, these being Germany, Italy, France and England. The English delegation would thus have considerable influence over the council, and the council, in turn, would have a lasting impact on the 'Englishness' of England itself.

However important at the time, and Henry certainly gave it due weight, religious matters would not be the dominant feature of the reign of Henry V. Reports brought back by the English expeditions of 1411 and 1412 of the current weakness and divisions within France may even then have raised ambitions in the king to resurrect the claims of his ancestors to that country. The Hundred Years War had been dormant for some time, but it was about to be revived with a vengeance.

The origins of that war lay in the distant past. Indeed, it could be claimed that it sprang from the moment in March 1314 when the last Grand Master of the Knights Templar was burnt to death as a heretic outside Notre Dame cathedral in Paris. In his last words, so the story goes, he cursed the French king Philippe IV who had caused his death, and all his heirs to the thirteenth generation. Eight months later Philippe died in a hunting accident, and two years after that his son, Louis X, died aged twenty-seven after a strenuous game of tennis, leaving a posthumously born son, John I, who reigned a mere five days before dying. For the first time in generations there was no direct male heir. John's four-year-old sister was passed over, and the crown was given to Louis's brother, Philippe V, who lasted six years before dying aged thirty without a son. It then passed to another brother, Charles IV, who reigned another six years and again left only daughters.

The only remaining descendants of Philippe IV were now the daughters of the last two kings: the daughter of Louis X – and Edward III of England, whose mother, Isabella of France, was the second child of Philippe IV. Neither Louis's daughter, now Queen of Navarre, nor the King of England was acceptable to the French, who gave the crown instead to Philippe's nephew, Philippe VI, claiming descent through the female line was barred by the ancient Salic Law. At the time Edward III was sixteen years old, barely a year on the throne after the murder of his father by his mother and her lover, and in no position to protest. Some ten years later, however, when Philippe threatened to confiscate Gascony, Edward could and did lay a claim to the French crown, and it was this claim, through his great-grandfather Edward, that Henry V now intended to pursue.

The early English successes in the war, including the capture of the French King John II, had resulted in the Treaty of Brétigny, which aimed to consolidate an English territory in the south-west of France, together with the area around Calais, while fixing the ransom for the captive king. Other clauses provided for England to have sovereignty in those areas in exchange for renouncing any claim to the French crown, but these were omitted when the treaty was ratified. Accordingly, Henry saw no reason why he should not claim France itself, and judging by the way he set about raising money at once, he seems to have begun planning for this from the earliest days of this reign. This did not, however, prevent him seeing what he could first achieve by diplomacy.

John of Burgundy, known as the Fearless, had seen his power waning since Henry's expedition in 1411. His daughter was married to the Dauphin Louis, but Louis, now in his mid-teens, loathed his father-in-law and fully supported the return to power of the Armagnacs during a short period when his poor mad father had a brief interval of sanity. It was to the Armagnac court of Charles VI, then, that Henry first sent his claim to the throne of France, though typically he was equally open to negotiations with John of Burgundy. Both Charles and John had marriageable daughters, and Henry would have agreed to marry either if it advanced his ambitions.

Negotiations with the French dragged on, and it was in 1414 that John Streeche, a canon at Kenilworth, records the possibly fictitious story of the Dauphin sending a 'treasure' of tennis balls to the king, suggesting they were more suitable to his youth than warfare. If he did, he had clearly not heard of Henry's exploits at Shrewsbury or in the Welsh wars. At one point the king was apparently prepared to settle for the old Angevin empire and the unpaid balance of the former French king's ransom, but the French were offering considerably less. All this time, though, Henry was preparing men and materials for a major campaign in France. Money was raised by all the usual methods, but also by large loans, particularly from individuals such as Bishop Henry Beaufort, now chancellor of England, and one Richard Whittington – yes, that Dick Whittington – Lord Mayor of London.

By the spring of 1415 Henry's intentions were fairly obvious, and though the French continued to send ambassadors up to the last minute, these may have been more concerned with assessing the extent of his preparations, rather than his willingness to compromise. Men were already mustered around Southampton, and the area was crammed with supplies and equipment, so the king met the French at Winchester instead, and rapidly dismissed them.

The campaign was due to launch at the end of July, but at the last moment Edmund Mortimer, newly restored as Earl of March, came to the king and revealed a plot to depose him and put Mortimer on the throne instead. The ringleaders were Richard, Earl of Cambridge, and Henry, Lord Scrope, nephew of the executed archbishop, but the plot also apparently involved the Scots and Welsh rebels. It seems Mortimer was only told at the last minute and went straight to the king, having no wish to risk life or liberty after spending so many years as a prisoner. There was a necessary delay while the plotters were rounded up, tried and executed, so it was not until 11 August that Henry's invasion fleet set sail for France, leaving his brother John, now Duke of Bedford, in charge in England.

Even with some knowledge of English intentions, the French were slow to organise a defence. Charles VI was still incapable, so the Dauphin Louis, now eighteen years old, was at least nominally given overall charge. It was only on 28 July that the Constable of France, Charles d'Albret, a career soldier, was made commander in chief, with another seasoned warrior, Marshal Boucicaut, as captain-general. Although towns and castles had been warned to look to their defences earlier, if Henry had sailed when he intended, he may have found even less resistance than was apparent when he landed unopposed on the coast near Harfleur on the evening of 13 August.

Harfleur was a fortified town with a good harbour, on the northern side of the mouth of the River Seine. It was a good place to establish a foothold, and d'Albret had guessed nearly right when trying to out-think his rival. His forces, some 1,500 men, were on the south side of the river, with Marshal Boucicaut and another force guarding the first suitable crossing point, around 25 miles away. There were defences built on the shore by Harfleur, but Henry found them unmanned and was able to land his whole army, with supplies and equipment, without difficulty. The intention was to take Harfleur quickly, garrison it strongly, and then move on to other targets, the same tactics Henry had used in Wales. In the time it took to move into position, however, reinforcements were rushed into the town, together with a new commander, Raoul de Gaucort, and its defences strengthened.

In point of fact, Henry had underestimated the difficulty of taking the town, while the besieged felt that every day they held out was a day gained for those slowly, slowly, gathering an army further south. Every kind of siege weapon was used, from catapults to cannon, and by 3 September Henry was still confident Harfleur would fall within the next week. It did not. Surrounded by marshy ground that defied mining under the walls – though Welsh miners had been brought for just such an assault – the small river that ran through the town and supplied its fresh water had also been blocked off. In the hot summer weather these were ideal conditions for breeding sickness, and it very soon began.

It was almost certainly dysentery – though the chroniclers put it down to many different causes – and it attacked besieged and besiegers alike. Henry had begun with a fighting force of some 8,000 men, but the sickness ran through it like wildfire. Nor was it any respecter of persons. The Bishop of Norwich died on 10 September, and the Earl of Suffolk soon after. Inside the town conditions were equally bad or worse, and despite spirited efforts and defiance from de Gaucort and his men, when Henry launched an all-out attack on the south-west of Harfleur on 18 September, a number of burgesses approached his brother Thomas, Duke of Clarence, on the western side, with offers of surrender. A truce was agreed with de Gaucort, to run until the following Sunday. If by then no French army had appeared to relieve the town, it would be handed over to Henry.

There was no French army, or at least none yet ready to take the field. On the Sunday afternoon de Gaucort appeared before the king with a noose round his neck, and surrendered himself, his men and the town into the hands of the English. The following day, barefoot like a penitent, Henry walked through the town his siege engines had smashed to pieces, and gave thanks to God in the church of St Michael for this first victory.

And what was he to do now? It was far too late in the year to continue with his original plan, and besides, he had lost somewhere between a quarter and a third of his army to sickness. There had been little profit so far, just a few potential ransoms, and looting of Harfleur had been forbidden since it was to become a second Calais, re-peopled by the English. To return home now would look like failure. Instead, he decided he would march through 'his' land of Normandy to Calais.

There was strong opposition in the council meeting held on 5 October, but the king insisted. Harfleur would be strongly garrisoned under the command of his uncle, Thomas Beaufort, Earl of Dorset, the sick would be sent home, and important prisoners such as Raoul de Gaucort would be set free on their own parole to surrender themselves at Calais on 11 November. The remainder of the men, some nine hundred men-at-arms and five thousand archers, would accompany the king, trusting to God and the justice of their cause to see them safely to their destination.

An act of reckless bravado, or a calculated risk? Henry clearly thought the latter, but he may have been misled by the almost total lack of organised opposition he had witnessed so far. In fact the fall of Harfleur had finally spurred the French into action, and men would soon be gathering at Rouen from all parts of the realm. Nor did they need to guess at Henry's intentions, the rendezvous with de Gaucort for Calais giving the game away.

On 8 October Henry and his army set off from Harfleur. They were travelling light, all unnecessary gear left behind, and carrying only the rations needed for the anticipated eight days march to Calais. There would be no looting, no destruction of property. The king was visiting 'his people' and wanted their goodwill, not their hatred. For the first few days all went as expected, but the first check came when they reached the Somme on 11 October.

Henry had anticipated using the ancient crossing place at Blanche Taque, as had Edward III before him. Instead he was warned just in time that the ford had been spiked, and d'Albret and Boucicaut were waiting on the far side with an advance guard of the French army some six thousand strong. There was nothing for it but to turn south along the river bank and hope for an unguarded crossing further along.

It quickly became apparent that this would not be easy to find. Furthermore, Henry learned from a prisoner taken in a skirmish that almost the entire nobility of France had now turned out, and an immense army was even then assembling across the river near Peronne. The more cautious counsels of d'Albret and Boucicaut had been overruled and the intention was to bring the English to battle.

It was 18 October before Henry found a crossing place on the Somme, and a whole day after that before the army was safely on the other side. By then they were already three days past their estimated arrival time at Calais, and their rations were exhausted. Worse still, a party of French cavalry had been driven off by the English advance guard at the crossing, so the French now knew exactly where they were. Sure enough, the very next morning heralds arrived from the French army declaring that they would be happy to meet the English in battle at any time and place they cared to choose. Henry's reply, very courteously framed according to the chivalric code of the times, was that there was no need to fix a time or place. He was on his way to Calais and the French might find him on the road or in the open fields, on any day they wished.

Clearly expecting a battle at any time, the English took a day's rest and prepared themselves, but when nothing happened, they pressed on, travelling north now, and living off whatever they could find, even nuts and berries from the bushes. Then, on 24 October, cresting a hill on the far side of the River Ternoise, they found themselves confronted by the French army, 'an incomparable multitude ... filling a broad field like an innumerable swarm of locusts'. A little manoeuvring brought the two armies face to face across that large open field, the common field of the neighbouring three hamlets, but it was too late in the day for a battle, and eventually, as darkness fell, they were stood down for the night. It was a night of heavy rain.

That place, beside the hamlet of Agincourt, had been chosen by the French according to the rules of war to give no advantage to either side. The existence of flanking woodlands, however, probably favoured the English. Two separate French battle plans had been drawn up, both intending to use elite cavalry

Above: 1. **Mont St Michel.** Henry – later Henry I – was besieged here by his two older brothers, depriving him of his first title, Count of the Cotentin.

Right: 2. **Domfront Castle.** The inhabitants of Domfront invited Henry to take over the town and castle. From there he extended his power over western Normandy. The castle was later his favourite when he became Henry I and was also favoured by his grandson Henry II.

Below right: 3. **The Rufus Stone.** This marks the place in the New Forest where King William Rufus, the brother of Henry I, was killed by an arrow while hunting.

Left: 4. **The rocky coast at Barfleur, Normandy.** Here the son of Henry I drowned in November 1120, leaving him without a legitimate male heir.

Below left: 5. **The site of Woodstock Palace.** Woodstock was the favourite residence in England of Henry I. Later it was occupied by Henry II, whose mistress 'The Fair Rosamond' reputedly lived there. The palace was destroyed in the seventeenth century, with many of its stones used in building the adjacent Blenheim Palace.

Below: 6. **Carlisle Castle.** Here Henry Plantagenet was knighted by King David of Scotland in 1149.

22. **Harlech Castle.** In 1409 Glendower, his family and his major supporters were starved into submission when under siege at Harlech Castle. Glendower himself escaped and died a free man some years later, but his revolt was effectively over.

23. **Falaise Castle.** Falaise was besieged by both Henry I and Henry V, but only the latter was able to force a surrender.

24. **Site of 1st Battle of St Albans, 1455.** This was the first battle in the so-called Wars of the Roses. The sons of those killed here were especially keen to avenge them in later battles.

25. **Site of the Battle of Wakefield, 1460.** Here an army mustered by Queen Margaret defeated and killed Richard, Duke of York.

ON THIS SITE STOOD THE TUDOR PALACE OF GREENWICH

BIRTHPLACE
OF
KING HENRY VIII
IN 1491
AND HIS DAUGHTERS
QUEEN MARY I IN 1516
AND
QUEEN ELIZABETH I
IN 1533

BUILT BY KING HENRY VIII

35. **Greenwich Palace.** This memorial marks the birthplace of Henry VIII at Greenwich.

36. **Site of the Battle of Flodden Field, 1513.** Here an invading Scottish army was heavily defeated. The Scottish King James was killed, along with thirteen earls and three bishops. The English army was led by Thomas Howard, Earl of Surrey, while Henry VIII was in France.

37. **Hampton Court.** Built by Cardinal Wolsey, Hampton Court was given to Henry VIII by Wolsey when he fell out of favour. It became Henry's favourite residence.

38. **Tower of London.** Many of the former friends, and indeed wives, of Henry VIII ended their lives at the Tower of London. Anne Boleyn refused to enter through the Traitors' Gate.

to ride down the fearsome English archers, but in the event they could not be attacked from the side, only head on. The second battle plan envisaged fewer men, and in fact not all the French commanders named in the first actually turned up. John the Fearless, in particular, stayed away, and locked up his son to prevent him participating either. Even so, the French army outnumbered the English by at least three to one and possibly more, and so confident were they of victory that when the armies formed up the next morning, almost everyone of rank crammed into the vanguard. They all wanted to kill or capture the king and take high-ranking prisoners for ransom.

The English lined up in three groups, or battles, side by side with archers between. They filled the entire width of the field, and the archers were sheltered behind sharpened stakes driven into the ground at an angle. And then they waited – and waited – and waited – maybe as much as three or four hours. Conventional wisdom said the side that attacked first lost, so the French took their time and relaxed a little. Eventually, Henry took matters into his own hands. At great risk, and keeping their formation, his army advanced down the sodden ploughed field until the enemy were within the range of an English longbow. Then five thousand arrows darkened the sky and battle had commenced.

We have an eye-witness account from an English chaplain sitting with the baggage train behind the battle lines. From him we learn that the French cavalry were slow to respond, that in trying to charge down the muddy field they were cut down in huge numbers by the arrow storm into which they rode, and that their wounded, terrified horses, charging back down the field, caused chaos among the advancing foot soldiers. Even the numbers involved in the French army proved a disadvantage. Those in front, hemmed in by the woodlands, had hardly room to wield a sword, and if they stumbled or fell they were trampled on by those pushing forward from behind. Many were simply suffocated. 'Living fell on the dead,' says the chaplain, 'and others, falling on the living, were killed in turn.' There was little chance of anyone taking prisoners for ransom, and even those that were taken by the English were killed by order of the king, when the stricken enemy seemed to be regrouping and a raid on the baggage train was mistaken for an attack in the rear.

By the time the battle was over and the English king formally awarded the victory by a French herald, the cream of the nobility of France had been lost. Three royal dukes, at least eight counts and an archbishop were among the dead, along with d'Albret and the bearer of the sacred French banner, the Oriflamme. The English chaplain suggests French losses of some 1,600 nobles and knights, together with four or five thousand others, but no-one really knows. There were, in addition, over a thousand French prisoners, most of them pulled alive from the heaps of bodies. Among them were the young Charles, Duke of Anjou, not yet 21 years old, Jean, Duke of Bourbon, and Marshal Boucicaut. English losses were estimated at a few hundred, including Edward, Duke of York, Michael de la Pole, who had been Earl of Suffolk for a matter of weeks since his father died at Harfleur, and Davy Gam, the Welshman immortalised by Shakespeare.

It was an overwhelming victory, but by no means the end of the war. Even as Henry was parading in triumph through the streets of London at the end of November, he was planning his return to France. John, Duke of Bedford, had shrewdly called a parliament in the immediate aftermath of the battle, securing generous funding for the next stage, and some of this was spent on commissioning ships with which to dominate the Channel. Their worth was proved when France managed to blockade Harfleur in the early months of 1416, only to be swept away by an English fleet commanded by Bedford in August that year.

By that time Henry had intended to be back in France, but his plans had to be put on hold by the visit of a most important person, King Sigismund of Hungary. Sigismund's project to reform the church was not going as well has he had hoped. True, two popes had resigned, John XXIII and Gregory XII, but Benedict was stubbornly refusing to do so, and the only real action of the Council of Constance so far had been to burn as a heretic Jan Hus, a Czech follower of Wycliffe, whose safe conduct Sigismund had guaranteed.

In an attempt to promote a unity of purpose Sigismund, now Holy Roman Emperor-elect, had begun a tour of the different countries of the West. So far, he had persuaded the Spanish to abandon Benedict and had visited France, which he had found in turmoil. In May 1416 he arrived in England, hoping among other things to broker a peace with France in order to bring both countries into harmony with his own agenda of church reform.

He was given every possible honour. Henry even moved out of the palace at Westminster, making it over to Sigismund for the duration of his stay, and he spent his considerable powers of persuasion in convincing him of the justice of his claim to France. The result was the Treaty of Canterbury, signed on 15 August. In it Sigismund acknowledged Henry's right, not only to be king of France, but also to use any means necessary to achieve that goal, and promised to give active support if and when called on to do so.

In turn Henry promised to support Sigismund at the Council of Constance, and it soon became clear that the English and Germans were acting as partners there. This provoked an attack on the English delegation by the French, on the grounds that England was too small and unimportant to be entitled to a vote. Why, said the French, they didn't even have their own language. This was a reference to the fact that almost all official documents in England were still written in either French or Latin, and that negotiations between the French and English had all been carried out in the latter language. When this was reported to Henry he decided that all his correspondence would in future be written in English, and that that language should be vigorously promoted by his chancery. Within a few generations a standard form of 'the King's English' had been developed and widely adopted, reinforcing once again the relatively new concept of 'Englishness'.

In September both king and emperor-elect crossed to Calais for a series of meetings with French envoys, and later with John the Fearless. If Sigismund regarded himself as mediator in an attempt to produce a widespread peace, this had little impact on the French, who saw him as solely on the side of the English. The old arguments were put and rejected out of hand, only a short-term truce being agreed. With John the Fearless, though, a little progress was made. An agreement of sorts was concluded whereby John would support Henry's claim to France, but only secretly, and he would not pay homage to him until he had secured a substantial amount of the territory he claimed. Since John had only attended the meeting on condition Humphrey of Gloucester was exchanged as a hostage for his safe return, and as both he and Henry have been referred to as the 'champion double-crossers of the age', it is not at all clear what weight could be given to this agreement. Nonetheless, as far as Henry was concerned, his six months of diplomacy had achieved its main aim, in that his next campaign in France would not be derailed by challenges from either Burgundy or the lands of the Holy Roman Empire.

By the time that campaign was launched at the end of July 1417, there had been substantial changes in France. The Dauphin Louis, who as heir to the throne had been kept away from the Agincourt struggle by the Duke of Berry, had died suddenly in December 1415, his place as heir being taken by his seventeen-year-old brother John. John was married to the niece of John the Fearless, Jacqueline of Hainault, and was fully sympathetic to the Burgundian cause. The Armagnacs, though, still ruled in Paris, where Count Bernard of Armagnac was confirmed as Constable of France in place of d'Albret. The situation changed again when Dauphin John died in April 1417. The new Dauphin was fourteen-year-old Charles, the eleventh child of Charles VI and the last surviving son. For the past three years he had been betrothed to Marie of Anjou, daughter of Louis of Anjou and his wife Yolande of Aragon, and had been living in their household. This put him firmly in the Armagnac camp, and when Louis died within a month of the previous Dauphin, Charles remained in the fiercely protective care of Yolande.

This shift in the balance of power immediately stirred John the Fearless to begin raising forces to launch an attack on Paris. By the time Henry arrived in France, then, whether by their agreement or otherwise, he was proving a useful diversion and once again Henry was able to land unopposed some twenty miles from Caen. It is not clear if these two had agreed to stay out of each other's way, but certainly while John was operating to the east of the Seine, Henry set about attacking targets to the west.

Caen itself was the first to feel the weight of his artillery. It was strongly walled about and had artillery of its own but was too slow in carrying out a plan to raze the suburbs outside the walls and blow up the abbeys of St Etienne in the west and La Trinité in the east, whose towers commanded a view into the town. Instead, the abbeys were seized by Thomas, Duke of Clarence, commanding an advance party, and became the headquarters of the king and Clarence himself. Besieged on 8 August, the town was taken on 4 September and the castle surrendered a few weeks later when no hope of relief was in sight.

At the same time, Bayeux to the west and Lisieux to the east capitulated, and a few weeks later Henry held all the major strongholds in central and southern Normandy, from Alençon to Verneuil – all bar the mighty fortress of Falaise, perched high on its rocky crag. By now it was winter, and most campaigns would be ended and armies disbanded. Henry, though, would not relax his grip on Normandy. Falaise was his target, and with his men given some protection in log cabins, a siege was maintained through December and January, until the castle and garrison were forced to surrender. Then, while Henry retired to Caen for the season of Lent, forces under the Earls of March and Warwick and the Duke of Clarence mopped up all resistance south to Domfront, west to the borders of Brittany, and eastwards to the Seine, on the other side of which the men of John the Fearless were well established.

John, too, had had a boost to his fortunes. Early in 1417 the French Queen, Isabeau of Bavaria, had been denounced to her temporarily sane husband as having carried on an affair with a courtier. She was sent to a rather severe exile in Tours, and endured it until November of that year when, overcoming her dislike of the Burgundians, she appealed to John for help. Immediately he sent eight hundred horsemen to rescue her, and from then on she abandoned Armagnac and threw in her lot with the Burgundian faction. In May 1418 Burgundian sympathisers in Paris were incited to rise up in revolt. The besieging Burgundian army was let in, and they and the Paris mob ransacked the city while anyone with Armagnac sympathies was massacred. The king was handed over to John the Fearless, who now held both king and queen, but the Dauphin Charles was got away by an Armagnac captain, Tanneguy de Chatel.

Strongly suspecting his 'ally' might now turn against him, Henry made a decisive move to enhance his own position. First establishing a base on the Seine at Pont de l'Arche, thus deterring aid from the south, the king turned his attention northwards to Rouen, the ancient capital of Normandy itself.

The attack was not unexpected although Rouen had gone over to Burgundy by now and had been reinforced with Burgundian troops. Unlike at Caen, they had completed the razing of a wide area around the town walls, so that when the siege began on 29 July 1418, Henry was not able to get his artillery close enough to be effective without coming under fire from the French artillery and archers within. Instead, he ordered the digging of a great ditch around the place, topped with a palisade, and prepared to starve them out.

At first the besieged were in good spirits, expecting that at any time John the Fearless would appear with an army to relieve them. He did not. By the end of October they were appealing both to the French king and to John for help. Food was running out, they warned, and if no assistance was forthcoming they might have to give their allegiance to Henry, in which case both king and duke would find them bitter enemies. In mid-November John the Fearless set out with an army, got as far as Pontoise, just north of Paris, stopped for some half-hearted negotiations and moved away to Beauvais. It was known he was also negotiating with the Dauphin for an alliance against the English, and clearly he was not prepared to risk a major battle on his own.

Meanwhile, within the strong walls of Rouen, starvation set in. We again have an eye-witness in the English camp, one John Page, who wrote a long poem, 'The Siege of Rouen', about his experiences there. Before Christmas, he says, with all food gone, 'They ate dogs, they ate cats. They ate mice, horse and rats.' Then, 'within a little space, the poor people of that place, at every gate they were put out, many a hundred in a rout.' Old men, women and children found themselves marooned in the ditch. The city would not take them back and Henry would not let them leave. The only concession made was on Christmas Day when the king sent food and drink to them. When challenged over the many deaths, Henry's only response was, 'I did not put them there.'

Then early in January 1419, as John Page put it, 'hunger breaketh the stone wall.' Negotiations were opened with the king though there was little to negotiate, surrender or starvation being the only options. On 19 January town and castle were formally surrendered, and then the king showed surprising mercy to the living skeletons within. There was no ransacking, no mass hangings. The garrison were allowed to leave, though without their arms, and any citizen who swore allegiance to King Henry could stay, and even keep his property on payment of a fine. Many of them did.

Secure now, at least in northern and western France, it was time for more talks. John the Fearless was almost certainly double-crossing him, but he controlled the king and queen and, when overtures from the Dauphin proved fruitless, a meeting was arranged at Meulan in May, where Henry could meet for the first time not only King Charles and Queen Isabeau, but also their daughter Catherine, now seventeen years old and a most important bargaining piece. The French king failed to attend, once again struck down by his recurring malady. Henry, though, was favourably impressed with the beauty and charm of Catherine – not that this affected his hard-headed bargaining, which, in any case, was carried on by representatives of each side while the royals enjoyed a more social engagement. All the lands promised in the Brétigny treaty, plus his recent conquests, all in full sovereignty, plus Catherine, plus a dowry of 800,000 crowns – these were the current demands, and it is possible Henry bid so high because he knew there was little reality in the apparent good will on the other side.

In fact, John the Fearless could hardly wait to get rid of the English before he was making a peace treaty with the Dauphin. Under this, old enmities would be forgiven and forgotten, even the old labels of Armagnac and Burgundian would be discarded, and the two would work together to expel the English from France.

Henry's response was immediate. Within a month he had dislodged the Burgundians from Pontoise and moved his army down to threaten Paris. John rapidly retreated to Troyes, along with the king and queen and their valuable daughter. Both he and the Dauphin were gathering forces, but before they made any move to oppose Henry another meeting was needed to finalise their reunion.

It was to be face to face this time, though the venue and security arrangements show the clear lack of trust that still existed between them. On 10 September they were to meet on a bridge over the Seine at Montereau. Both ends of the bridge were sealed off, and only the two leading characters with a few of their most trusted supporters were to be allowed onto it. In the event all went as planned until, meeting the son of his king, John the Fearless knelt before him. Then, as he started to rise, he was struck down and killed by Tanneguy de Chatel, supporting the Dauphin.

To this day it is unclear whether de Chatel or the Dauphin Charles, or both of them together, had plotted to bring this about. It has even been suggested it was a mistaken interpretation of John's actions when he put his hand on his sword. With his reputation for double-dealing, it would be unsurprising that he was not given the benefit of the doubt. What is absolutely certain is that, at the time, the full blame for this shocking act fell on the shoulders of the Dauphin. Quickly hustled away by de Chatel, he was now an outcast, and any small hope he might have had of opposing Henry had disappeared, at least for the time being.

The English king, of course, was overjoyed by the news. With his major opponent removed from the contest it was now game, set and match to him, and he quickly set about making his demands known. On 26 September his envoys met the king's council in Paris. All previous proposals were now dismissed. Henry would marry Catherine without a dowry, but instead he would be recognised as the heir to the French king, though the two countries would be administered separately, keeping their own laws, customs and institutions.

It took some time and much careful persuasion, but Henry got his way in the end. First John's son, Philippe of Burgundy, agreed to support him, there being no realistic alternative if he wanted revenge on the Dauphin for his father's death. Then on 24 December a truce was agreed between England and France.

Finally, Queen Isabeau, on behalf of the king, was persuaded to accept Henry as son-in-law and heir, some accounts claiming she had already disowned her own son, the Dauphin. It was May 1420 before the text of a comprehensive treaty was agreed, and on 21 May the Treaty of Troyes was finally signed in the cathedral at Troyes, with Isabeau once again signing on behalf of Charles VI.

Eleven days later Henry married Catherine, no doubt to the relief of his English subjects as well as those of the French, who were sick of the everlasting war. He had shown a fine carelessness as to the carrying on of his dynasty throughout all the dangers of the past few years, as neither he nor any of his brothers had been wed. Now it was hoped an heir for England and for France might soon be produced.

The treaty and the wedding of course did not end the hostilities. By order of King Charles all the French nobles were required to consent in writing to what had been done at Troyes, but the Dauphin was still free, and pockets of Dauphinist support were found all over the country, even in the area close to Paris. Only two days after his wedding, in accordance with the terms of the treaty, Henry returned to the fray, besieging and quickly taking the towns of Sens and Montereau. Another, Melun, proved a harder task, holding out from the beginning of July until the middle of November. The king himself was involved in the fierce fighting, and when the surrender finally came his terms were harsher than usual, especially for a group of Scottish prisoners who had answered the Dauphin's appeal for support. All were hanged.

On 1 December 1420 Henry at last made his triumphal entry into Paris. In his train were not only the king of France, for whom he would now act as regent, but also an impressive selection of the English nobility, among them two of his brothers, his uncle Thomas Beaufort, Duke of Exeter, and the Earls of Warwick, Huntingdon and Salisbury. Christmas was spent in Paris, with the English party holding court in the palace of the Louvre while the French king and queen were relegated to the Hotel St Pol. Then, early in the New Year, Henry and his new queen finally returned to England.

On 23 February Catherine was crowned Queen of England. According to tradition, Henry attended neither the ceremony nor the lavish banquet that followed, being more concerned, in any case, with reviewing the administration of the realm over the more than three years of his absence. Nor did Catherine accompany him on the first part of his tour of the realm, starting at Bristol and working up through the Welsh Marches he knew so well, and then on through the Midlands. They did spend Easter together before moving on northwards to York and Beverley, and it was there the king was told of a major setback in France.

Though the Dauphin had been forced to retreat to Maine, still he was not without friends. At the end of January 1421 he issued his Manifesto Against the Treaty of Troyes, denouncing those who had given away the crown of France 'to strangers ... who are ancient enemies', and calling on 'all those who hate tyranny, and uphold virtue and freedom' to join him in resisting that treasonable action. Among those who answered his call was a contingent of Scots under John Stewart, Earl of Buchan, and by Easter an army of some four to five thousand had been assembled.

At the same time, Henry's brother Thomas, Duke of Clarence, who had been left as his lieutenant in France, was leading his own forces into that area in an attempt to subdue it. It happened to be Easter Saturday when he heard that the Dauphin's army was close by at Vieil-Baugé, south of Le Mans. Clearly seeing this as a golden opportunity to dispose of the Dauphin's challenge, he insisted on giving battle at once, against the advice of his experienced commanders, and despite the fact that most of his army, particularly the archers, had dispersed foraging for food. With something like 1,500 men he engaged a Franco-Scottish force at a river crossing, but when they gave way, found himself facing the full army of the Dauphin in battle array, complete with archers. In the one-sided struggle that followed, Clarence was killed, and the Earls of Huntingdon and Somerset taken prisoner. Worst of all the Dauphin had proved that the English army in France was not invincible.

When Henry heard the news, he took it calmly and continued with his tour, which was, in any case, a mixture of review, triumphal progress and recruiting drive. He would always have known there was unfinished business in France, though the death of his brother and heir-apparent meant he would probably have to return sooner than he had intended.

Once more, men and money were needed, and again the latter was raised largely by loans. The biggest of these came from Bishop Henry of Winchester, buying his way back into royal favour after being under something of a cloud. He had no doubt had Henry's permission to resign as chancellor in 1417, ostensibly to make a pilgrimage to the Holy Land. It was probably also by Henry's direction that his pilgrimage took him to Constance, where the church council was deadlocked over whether church reform should take precedence over electing a new pope, Benedict having been at last deposed. Bishop Henry's influence rapidly undid the deadlock and was also felt in the election of Pope Martin V, who was so grateful that he attempted to make the bishop a cardinal. This was not at all to the king's liking since it brought with it a conflict with his own very capable Archbishop of Canterbury, Henry Chichele. Bishop Henry was told in no uncertain terms to reject the honour, and for a while there was a cooler relationship between the two.

Bishop Henry's loan was only one of many, and for the first time Adam of Usk records the people groaning and cursing under the burden of perpetual money-raising for this ongoing war. With a startling degree of foresight – as he concludes his chronicle of the times in 1421 – he declares, 'Mighty men and the treasure of the realm will be most miserably foredone about this business.'

Arriving back in France in June 1421 the king found matters had rapidly moved on. The Dauphin had now secured a treaty with Brittany and had advanced so far as to be besieging Chartres, while other Dauphinist pockets nearer to Paris were also causing problems. The siege of Chartres was quickly relieved, but the hope of bringing the Dauphin to a decisive battle was not realised. He was pursued to Orleans and beyond, but nowhere would he make a stand against the English army.

Instead, Henry determined to destroy the Dauphinist towns near Paris, and in particular the strongly held town and castle at Meaux, on a horseshoe bend of the Seine some thirty miles away. The siege there began on 6 October and would last until the following May. Once again it was a hard winter siege, maintained through unusually wet weather, and once again hunger and sickness assailed both sides. Dysentery and rheumatic fever were rife, and it has been estimated that one in six of the men of the English army died during this period.

A bright spot came in December when it was reported Queen Catherine had had a baby son, christened Henry, on the sixth day of that month. It was also around this time, however, that concerns were first raised about the king's health. When the siege ended on 10 May he returned to Paris and was joined there by his wife. For a while he seemed to be returning to fitness, but the disease, which was probably amoebic dysentery, would not let go so easily. By July the king was clearly a sick man. When Philippe of Burgundy appealed for English help in repelling a Dauphinist attack at Cosne, Henry attempted to join him. In the event, however, he had to send his forces on ahead under the command of his brother John of Bedford.

Instead the king was carried to the castle of Vincennes near Paris. Over the next few weeks he weakened rapidly, and towards the end of August he drew up his last will. Then, on 31 August, Henry V, King of England and Regent and Heir of France, passed away, 'perfectly and devoutly … in the tenth year of his reign'.

Had he lived another two months he would have been King of France. Indeed, Charles VI died even as Henry's coffin was being carried towards England. As it was, his shrewd administration and attention to detail had left that realm secure, but the unfinished nature of his business in France would have been a challenge to a strong, experienced military leader, let alone the eight-month-old baby who was now his heir.

Henry VI

'… a mild and pious king'
— Whethamsted's Register

Although the youngest person ever to become king of England when his father died in 1422, Henry's position was nevertheless a strong one. He was the undisputed heir of a father of immense prestige, there were precedents for dealing with a long minority, and best of all he had two completely loyal uncles who could be deployed to look after his interests both at home and overseas.

On his deathbed Henry V had made his dispositions quite clear, and in doing so showed a shrewd grasp of the problems ahead and the natures of those tasked with dealing with them. The experienced and ever-reliable John of Bedford had to be regent in France once Philippe of Burgundy made clear he didn't want the job. Furthermore, Henry urged him to continue the struggle against the Dauphin, though his reservations show in the instruction that, should he ever come to make a treaty with him, he should under no circumstances agree to give up Normandy.

With John fully occupied in France, the younger brother, Humphrey, Duke of Gloucester, no doubt expected to be regent in England. He was already the king's lieutenant while Henry was away. Clearly, though, there was not the same confidence in him and he was given only the rather vague title of Guardian and Protector of the young king, subject to the overall authority of John when he was in England. Nor was he given charge of the household and education of the young Henry, although himself something of a scholar. That job went to Thomas Beaufort, Duke of Exeter, with Richard de Beauchamp, Earl of Warwick, later brought in as tutor.

Had the brothers worked harmoniously together, things might have gone as smoothly as the former king hoped. Instead, there were splits from the start, with Humphrey of Gloucester pushing for a regency role, and John of Bedford, backed up by his uncle, the wealthy and powerful Bishop Henry Beaufort, determined England should be ruled by a royal council. It was Bedford who had his way, though with a sop to Humphrey that he should be chief councillor, albeit without a power of veto. Once again, there was no role for the new king's mother, the widowed Queen Catherine, and it was out of the question that she should return to France. Instead she remained with her son for his first seven years, and in that time formed a series of inadvisable attachments that would have long-term consequences.

Only from the time of Edward I had it been accepted that an heir became king automatically on the death of his predecessor. Prior to that, it was the crowning and anointing that made a king – hence the speed with which Henry I organised his own coronation. Clearly crowning and anointing a baby would be impossible, but the child was proclaimed King Henry VI of England from 1 September 1422, and King of France from 22 October. The following autumn the toddler king attended his first parliament and received the fealty of his English nobles. It would be some time, however, before he first set foot in France, and by then the situation in his other kingdom would have changed considerably.

Even before that first parliament a series of marriages had first supported and then undermined the Anglo-French alliance against the Dauphin. In March 1423, in accordance with the terms of the Treaty of Troyes, John of Bedford married Anne of Burgundy, sister of Philippe. On his deathbed Henry V had stressed the importance of this Burgundian alliance and that nothing should be done to upset it, and John was ready enough to comply. Although it was clearly a political marriage, John and Anne were apparently very happy, though childless, through nine years of marriage.

It seems almost deliberately provocative, then, that at around the same time, Humphrey of Gloucester undermined his brother's wishes by marrying Jacqueline of Hainault. Not only did the marriage cause a scandal – her divorce from her previous husband being granted by the no-longer recognised Pope Benedict – but Jacqueline was in open dispute with Philippe of Burgundy over lands in the Low Countries that she felt she should have inherited. She had come to England looking for help from Henry V, and now received it from his brother. In defiance of the royal council and his brother Bedford, Humphrey raised an army and took it to Mons, the capital of Hainault, preparing to give open battle to England's most important ally. It didn't come to that. Nor did a proposed duel between Humphrey and Philippe ever take place, being forbidden by both Bedford and the pope, so each had an excuse to back down. Nevertheless, considerable strain was placed on the alliance, and that it held is largely credited to the supreme diplomatic skills of Anne of Burgundy.

In France at this time the English seemed to be consolidating their position. A Triple Alliance negotiated by Bedford with Burgundy and Brittany, meant that almost all of northern and eastern France acknowledged Henry as king. The Dauphin had retreated almost to the Loire, and it was to prevent his cause being further stiffened by Scottish forces that the long-time prisoner King James of Scotland was finally released. He had grown up in England, been well treated by Henry V, and before returning to Scotland married Joan Beaufort, sister of the Duke of Somerset and niece of Bishop Henry. Before returning to Scotland, James was required to swear that no more aid would be given to the Dauphin. This, of course, did not affect those forces already there, and there was a large Scottish contingent in the army that faced the English at the Battle of Verneuil in August 1424.

Verneuil has been called Bedford's Agincourt. Once again an English army was heavily outnumbered, some 2,000 Burgundian men having been sent away beforehand as of uncertain loyalty. The French not only had around 6,000 Scots to reinforce them, but also 2,000 heavily armoured Lombard cavalry. The French chronicler Jean de Waurin, who had been at Agincourt, declares 'the assembly at Verneuil was certainly the most formidable of all.' The English fought on foot, and an initial cavalry charge might have proved decisive had the advantage been pursued. Instead, Bedford rallied his men and overcame the French, before helping the Earl of Salisbury overwhelm the Scots who refused to flee the field. It was a decisive defeat for both French and Scots; the latter lost both their leaders, the Earls of Douglas and Buchan, and all but a handful of men. The Dauphin retreated south of the Loire to Bourges, and for some time was contemptuously referred to by the English as the 'king of Bourges'.

In England, though, matters were far less settled. The return of Gloucester in April 1425 – with his army but without his wife – led to an escalation in his feud with Bishop Henry. It didn't help that Gloucester was popular with the Londoners and the bishop was not. In October of that year an armed stand-off on London Bridge led to the hasty recall of John of Bedford from France to try and calm the situation.

A parliament was called to meet in neutral Leicester in February 1426. It became known as the Parliament of Bats, since, being forbidden to bear arms, the supporters of the rival factions carried cudgels instead. For several weeks Gloucester's complaints about the bishop were investigated before a reconciliation of sorts was secured. In spite of this, Bishop Henry immediately resigned the chancellorship, which was given to the Archbishop of York. At Leicester, too, on 19 May, the four-year-old King Henry was knighted by his uncle John of Bedford. Afterwards, we are told, he knighted with his own hand some two or three dozen young men, including his close relative Richard, ten years older than the little king and already Duke of York.

Back in France, Bedford's slow and steady approach seemed to be achieving results. By the spring of 1428 it looked to be only a matter of time before the Dauphin could be finally defeated and Henry's rule acknowledged over all the land. In July of that year, however, the Earl of Salisbury returned with fresh men from England and, perhaps influenced by Gloucester, pushed for a more vigorous campaign. Bedford intended to consolidate by attacking Angers but was persuaded that Orléans would be the key to a speedier result, being closer to Bourges.

The siege of Orléans began on 12 October 1428 and initially went well for the attackers. As at Rouen a decade earlier, a wide swathe around the city walls had been razed to keep the English artillery at bay. The tower at Les Tourelles had been left, however, to guard the bridge over the Loire. When this tower and the defences around it were taken by the English in the first two weeks, the bridge was broken down and the French retreated within the walls. Salisbury intended to bring up his guns and pound the city into submission, but on 24 October he was severely injured by French cannon fire and died a week later.

A new commander, William de la Pole, Earl of Suffolk, brought new tactics. Instead of blasting the walls down, Suffolk would blockade the place and starve them out. It would take time, though, and time was a gift to the enemy. Nor did he have the manpower to invest the city fully. He could only build outlying forts on the main routes into the place to the east, north and especially to the west, where lay Blois, and beyond it Chinon, the new retreat of the Dauphin. It was not perfect, but with his own force blocking the bridge, it would probably have succeeded eventually, if it had not been for a young woman smuggled into the city on 28 April 1429.

Joan of Arc, the maid from Domremy, had arrived at the Dauphin's court at Chinon on 6 March. By 22 March she had convinced him of the truth – or at least the usefulness – of the voices of the saints that she heard in her head, telling her God wanted her to lead the timorous Charles to his coronation at Reims. Taken into his service and provided with armour, she proved so inspirational to the citizens and defenders of Orléans that within a few short days of her arrival the English had been forced to raise the siege.

Further victories followed, at Jargeau on 11 June, where Suffolk was taken prisoner, at Beaugency on 16 June, and, most crushingly, at Patay on 18 June, where the famous English longbowmen were almost wiped out. Then, on 17 July 1429, the Dauphin was crowned and anointed at the Cathedral of Notre Dame in Reims. No longer an outcast and a fugitive, he was now King Charles VII of France, while the English claimant to his kingdom was merely an uncrowned child.

There had to be a response and there was. Bedford had wanted Henry crowned in April of that year, as soon as the situation on the ground began to shift against them. The council, though, was reluctant. He was, after all, only seven years old. Now, however, it became imperative that he was at least crowned king of England, if not of France as well. On 6 November, therefore, at Westminster Abbey, in a cut-down set of coronation robes but enduring the whole long ceremony, young Henry VI was formally anointed with holy oil, and the crown was at least held above his head, it being far too large and heavy for a child to support.

The following year he travelled to Calais at the end of April, accompanied by an army of 8,000 men, nobility young and old, and the now Cardinal Henry Beaufort. Ostensibly, he was on his way to Reims for his French coronation, but the surge of support for the new King Charles meant that all the area between Calais, Paris and Reims had now to be considered as hostile, town after town having declared for their new French sovereign.

Philippe of Burgundy, who had retreated from Paris when that city came under attack the previous year, advocated a direct assault on Reims. He had to be persuaded to adopt Bedford's more cautious plan of tackling the main places to the north of that city first. Early in May Compiègne was duly put under siege, and once again La Pucelle, the Maid, as the French called Joan of Arc, appeared to inspire the defenders. This was one campaign too many for her, however. A sortie by the besieged ended in disaster when, hotly pursued by Burgundians, they tried to re-enter the town. In panic the gates were closed before the last few were inside, and among them was Joan, now pulled from her horse and taken prisoner.

To the French she was a divinely inspired saviour; to the English a witch and a sorceress. It should have been a turning point and in a sense it was. In December 1430 Philippe of Burgundy sold her to the English, partly to recoup his losses in lands now heavily attacked by Charles. She was taken to Rouen, where Henry was residing, and in January 1431 an inquisition began into her beliefs and actions. Though conducted by French clergy, it was powered by English malice, and Henry's version, contained in a letter described by Waurin, that she was 'very lovingly and gently admonished', is probably far from the truth. In the end she was convicted of heresy on a technicality – the wearing of men's clothes while in prison – and on 30 May 1431 was burnt at the stake in the marketplace in Rouen.

While this was going on the war was continuing with increasing vigour. The idea of crowning Henry in Reims was quickly abandoned. It would have to be Paris instead, but at least the English had the right regalia, which had been missing from Charles's coronation at Reims. It took until October 1431 to make even Paris safe enough for the young king to approach, and he finally entered the city to great scenes of celebration on 2 December. There was a pause then, waiting for Philippe to join them, but he never came. Finally, on 16 December 1431, ten days after his tenth birthday, Henry VI of England was crowned king of France in Notre Dame Cathedral, Paris.

It should have been a triumph, but clearly it was not. The French were annoyed that Cardinal Beaufort used the English rather than the French coronation rite and were disgusted at the scanty and disorganised banquet that followed. Worse was the news that three days before the coronation Philippe of Burgundy had signed a truce with Charles. Worst of all was the departure of the young king from Paris a mere ten days after his coronation, and from the kingdom little more than a month after that. He would never set foot in France again.

There would be a few more good days for the English in France, but the tide was rapidly turning against them. When Bedford's wife Anne died of the plague on 13 November 1432 the alliance with Burgundy was weakened further. Nor was it helped by the duke's swift remarriage the following April. Possibly he had thought to please Philippe by marrying Jacquetta of Luxembourg, the daughter of his vassal the count of St. Pol. Instead, Philippe was outraged that his sister had been replaced in so short a time and that he had not been consulted beforehand. Already he was inclining towards a rapprochement with his French kin, and with the new Pope Eugenius pushing for peace, it seemed only a matter of time before negotiations began.

Early in 1435, Philippe informed his English allies that he would be meeting representatives of Charles at Arras on 1 July, and he invited them to join this peace conference. Eventually representatives of a dozen different kings, dukes and cities met, along with ambassadors of the pope. Cardinal Beaufort was the last of the English delegation to arrive, and it wasn't until the end of August that the talks began. Rather than negotiate, however, the English and French simply submitted a series of demands and counter-demands, until on 6 September the English walked away. Eight days later in Rouen, John of Bedford died, exhausted after a lifetime of often unappreciated service to his country that had begun when he was barely into his teens. A week after that Philippe of Burgundy signed the Treaty of Arras, bringing to an end the hostilities between France and Burgundy.

It is said when he heard of the treaty the fourteen-year-old Henry wept, but that was not the end of his troubles. Before the end of the year Meulan, Dieppe and Harfleur had been lost, and the Earl of Arundel, commanding the English forces, had been killed. Something had to be done to stem this tide of calamity.

At first it was declared that Henry would lead an army to France in person. Money poured in from around the country in the form of loans and gifts. Then it was decided the risk would be too great for an untried king with no heir of his own. Instead, the two 'heirs' closest to the king would be sent, Richard, Duke of York, to become Lieutenant-General and Governor of France in place of Bedford, and Gloucester, the heir apparent, in the role he had always craved as commander of an army to win France once and for all.

By June 1436, Paris had been lost and Calais was under siege, but an advance party to Calais led by Richard of York and Edmund Beaufort had enough success that the mere sight of Gloucester's fleet arriving in August was enough to end the siege. No battles were fought by Gloucester, and no glory won. Worse still, while he was away Cardinal Beaufort and the Earl of Suffolk became ever closer to the young king.

Henry was growing up. After his dual coronations he had already shown signs of independence, challenging his 'master' Warwick, and looking for some real power. He might have been given it had he shown any of his father's shrewd decisiveness. Instead, at the age of fourteen he was described as a quiet, serious-minded boy, 'more religious than a man of religion' and much given to book reading. His father had been described as looking like a bishop and acting like a warrior. Henry, by contrast, tall and strong even then, looked like a warrior but acted like a bishop, and an unusually pious bishop at that, awkward, even prudish, where women were concerned. Great care had been taken over his education, possibly too much care, for either nature or nurture had left him as impressionable as wax. The council had earlier reminded Henry that he lacked the discernment that came with maturity – he would always lack it – but in 1437 it was decided the time had come when he must rule for himself. One month short of his sixteenth birthday a crown-wearing ceremony marked the formal handing over of power from the council to the king.

Earlier that year his mother had died. Queen Catherine had not been part of his household for some time, having secretly married one of her own household servants, Owen Tudor, after an earlier dalliance with Edmund Beaufort. There had been no permission for this illegal marriage, but Tudor seems to have enjoyed the protection of the king, and they had a number of children, two of whom, Edmund aged around seven and Jasper a year younger, were still in the care of the queen when she died. Whatever protection Tudor had ended at that point and he found himself imprisoned, though he would later be pardoned and given a post at court. In the meantime, Henry arranged for his two half-brothers to be taken in and cared for by Katherine de la Pole, sister of the Earl of Suffolk and abbess of Barking Abbey.

By 1440 the situation in France and England was such that either there must be one last great push to complete the conquest, or there must be negotiations to bring about a lasting peace. Henry and his closest counsellors, Cardinal Beaufort, the Archbishop of York, and especially the Earl of Suffolk, all favoured peace, while Gloucester vociferously favoured war. When Henry proposed, as a goodwill gesture, to release Charles, Duke of Orléans, who had been a prisoner for 25 years since Agincourt, Gloucester exploded with fury, claiming it went against the strict instructions of Henry V. He accused Beaufort of manipulating the king for his own enrichment and excluding close relatives such as himself and the Duke of York, who should be the king's natural advisors.

Nevertheless, the release went ahead. Under the terms agreed Charles was to persuade the French king to negotiate a peace treaty, and to pay a ransom of £40,000. Failing this he was honour bound to return to custody. In the event, very little of the ransom was paid, and Charles's influence, and indeed efforts, to achieve peace were minimal. Nor did he return to custody, so Gloucester probably felt himself vindicated.

However, Charles VII of France had also suffered some reverses by this time, notably a rebellion known as the Praguerie, which was joined by his sixteen-year-old son Louis. (The odd name derives from a similar rising that had recently taken place in Prague.) Over the next few years tentative steps were made towards setting up a peace conference, with much consideration given to finding a suitable wife for Henry as part of the process. He was by now of full age and eminently marriageable, but his heir apparent remained his fifty-year-old uncle Gloucester, who himself had no legitimate heir.

Gloucester's marriage to Jacqueline of Hainault had been annulled soon after he had abandoned her in 1424, and very soon after that he had married one of her household, Eleanor Cobham, who may already have been the mother of his illegitimate son Arthur. No legitimate children had followed, but the couple clearly regarded themselves as heirs to the crown. Then in July 1441 Eleanor was arrested and accused of treason and witchcraft. She had commissioned a horoscope of the king which predicted his imminent death and had allegedly obtained a wax figure of the king from Margery Jourdemayne, known as the Witch of Eye, supposedly to use to bring about this death. She was convicted in October 1441, forced as penance to walk barefoot through the streets of London, and then imprisoned for life, her marriage to

Gloucester being annulled. Gloucester himself was not implicated, but his prestige suffered, the first of a number of blows to come.

Soon after this, as if in a final attempt to bring the king of France to battle, an expedition was planned, financed by Cardinal Beaufort, and led, not by the ageing Gloucester but by the Cardinal's nephew, John Beaufort, now made Duke of Somerset. It was specified that Somerset would be independent of Richard of York, the king's lieutenant in France, thus upsetting York, and his only success, when he finally left England in July 1443, was to seize a fortified town in Brittany, in turn upsetting England's ally, the new Duke of Brittany. By early 1444 he was back in England with nothing to show and a great deal of money wasted. Soon after, he retired to his estate at Wimborne and died. Cardinal Beaufort also retired from politics at this time, perhaps to avoid the outcry over this failure, or maybe to distance himself from the negotiations now begun with France.

In March 1444 the Earl of Suffolk set out for a conference at Tours with the twin aims of securing a peace treaty and a wife for his king. Unfortunately, Henry's eagerness for the second undermined his chances of success in the first. The English position had been weakened sufficiently for a daughter of Charles VII to be out of the question. A connection to the French throne, but not too close a connection, was the best to be hoped for now, and preferably someone of marriageable age to produce children. The fourteen-year-old Margaret of Anjou seemed to fit the bill exactly. Henry had made clear that he was not prepared to sacrifice himself either for peace or for dynasty, but when Margaret arrived in Tours on 4 May she impressed the English party with her looks, breeding and education. The deal was quickly done, and less than three weeks later she was formally betrothed to Henry, with Suffolk standing proxy for the king.

The expectation in England was that the new queen would bring with her peace with France, the prospect of an heir in a short time, and, hopefully, a large dowry. In fact, they got none of that. A truce of two years was the best Suffolk could achieve, with the promise of more talks in London the following year. Margaret's dowry was tiny, and it was nearly a year before she arrived in England to make her marriage vows to the king in person, at Titchfield Abbey in April 1445. Though she was given an enthusiastic welcome to London for her coronation on 29 May, the public would soon cool towards her as years passed with no sign of a pregnancy.

When peace negotiations re-opened in London a series of blunders gave all the advantages to the French. Henry's personal display of friendliness, intended to cut through stiff formality and show his sincere wish for peace, was instead interpreted as weakness. Indeed, reports were growing of the king's naivety, some said simple-mindedness, which seemed to be confirmed by his next gesture of goodwill, the offer to give up Maine. This may have been discussed earlier as a bargaining chip, to be offered in exchange for a solid commitment to long-term peace. But Henry seemed to offer it as a gift, to return it to his wife's family, and having committed himself, the king would not draw back.

How far Suffolk knew or approved of this gift is hard to tell, but he was a prime mover of the peace party and thus bound to support the king's efforts. The other lords specifically distanced themselves from the idea, and strong opposition might be expected from both heirs to the throne, Humphrey of Gloucester and Richard of York. Maine should have been handed over in April 1446, but this was delayed until 1448. In the meantime, allegations of mismanagement were made against York and he was removed from his post in France. Soon afterwards he was appointed Lieutenant of Ireland, supposedly for a period of ten years, thus removing him from the scene entirely.

Different tactics were used against Gloucester. When in February 1447 parliament assembled – at Bury St Edmonds in Suffolk's territory, rather than Gloucester-friendly London – the duke was diverted to his lodgings nearby. There he was immediately put under house arrest and accused of treason. Five days later, before he was given a chance to defend himself, he was found dead. It may have been a stroke or a heart attack, but poison is also a possibility. Those whose sympathies lay with the duke at once denounced Suffolk for bringing about his death, suspicions no doubt confirmed when a few months later the order was given to hand over Maine to the French.

Even now there were delays, and it wasn't until Charles VII took an army to the gates of Le Mans in March 1448 that the duchy was finally given up. In exchange a single year was added to the ongoing truce, now due to expire on 1 April 1450. How the different parties were using this truce is, however, highly instructive of the aims and abilities of each.

In France, with the majority of the country now behind him, Charles was building up his army. Using a system very like the old Saxon fyrd, where every community provided a man for royal service, by 1449 he had at his disposal a reputed force of some 60,000 men, on call at short notice. In England, by contrast, Henry seemed to believe that everything was now settled and did nothing. Edmund Beaufort, now Duke of Somerset, replaced Richard of York in France but only arrived in Normandy in May 1448, more than two years after York had left. He found it a shambles, with defences crumbling and unpaid garrisons deserting or turning to banditry. When belatedly in February 1449 he appealed for money to repair the damage, he was told there was none, or at least what little existed was needed in the north of England.

The country was weary of a war that had been rumbling on for well over thirty years, and with no new victories to cheer would not stomach new taxation. Nor could the king raise money from his own estates or from loans. As recklessly generous as Henry III before him, he had given away so many lands, offices, wardships and other sources of profit, and raised so many loans, that the royal finances were reckoned to be hundreds of thousands of pounds in debt. Every year expenditure exceeded income, with money lavished on Henry's pet projects, Eton College and King's College, Cambridge, and on the upkeep of the royal households. Unlike the meticulous Henry I with his set allowances for each household member, or his own father Henry V with a mind like an accountant, Henry had no idea even how many there were among his household, let alone how much each consumed, and petty thieving and free-loading went on almost unnoticed and certainly unchecked.

The same carelessness was brought to affairs of state. Henry could deal intelligently with things that interested him, but most of the time that didn't include the day-to-day governing of his realm. He would on occasion give an estate or office to one person, forgetting he had already given it to another, often, thereby, adding fuel to ongoing disputes between great families or quarrelsome nobles. And it can only have been carelessness and a monumental misjudgement of circumstances led to the next fateful blunder in the delicate relationship with France.

On 24 March 1449 a mercenary captain in the pay of the English attacked and took the town of Fougères in Brittany, England's long-standing ally. In part the raid was for plunder, but the captain certainly believed it was sanctioned by the king, and expected English support to hold the town. The Duke of Brittany, Francis I, had already shown sympathy with the French cause, locking up his younger brother Gilles, a friend of the English king. If the raid was intended to obtain the release of Gilles and to remind Francis where his loyalties should lie, it spectacularly backfired. Francis complained to Charles, who in turn demanded redress from the Duke of Somerset. A good relationship between Somerset and the French king might have smoothed over the affair. Instead, Charles's opinion of him as either arrogant or ignorant was reinforced by Somerset's reply, both to Charles and to Francis. He had not authorised the raid, declared the duke, but he was glad it had taken place, and he would not meddle in the affair to restore the town or provide compensation for loss. Charles declared the long-standing truce had been broken by the English, and the war began again in earnest, this time with Brittany firmly on the side of the French.

Through summer and autumn of 1449, a three-pronged attack on English Normandy took town after town, fortress after fortress, many of them with little or no show of resistance. In truth the Normans had had enough of their English rulers, and with clear foresight of how this would end, returned thankfully to allegiance with their French countrymen. Through all this Somerset remained at Rouen, seemingly paralysed like a rabbit in headlights, and Henry and his advisors discussed what to do – and did nothing. There was no suggestion the king himself should rally his forces and lead them in the field. The ongoing lack of an heir might be one reason, but surely another has to be a consensus that Henry as a warrior would prove as feeble and incompetent as Henry as a ruler.

By early October the French armies were at the gates of Rouen. Within, only John Talbot, Earl of Shrewsbury, seemed prepared to put up a fight, and when on 29 October Somerset formally surrendered, Shrewsbury was forced to remain as hostage until other Norman garrisons had been given up. On 10 November, King Charles of France rode into Rouen, with the English queen's father René beside him, and the English reign in Normandy was at an end.

The humiliation in England was unbearable. Someone would have to pay for all the lives and money cast away so carelessly, and since attacking the king was treason, it was his close advisors who came in for the largest share of the blame. In particular, Suffolk, William Aiscough, Bishop of Salisbury, and Adam Moleyns, Bishop of Chichester, were the men singled out. All three were also accused of being complicit in the death of the popular Duke of Gloucester.

Moleyns was the first to suffer, killed by a mob in Portsmouth in early January 1450. Before he died, he claimed Suffolk was to blame for everything, and on 22 January the duke was forced to try and clear his name before parliament. Even the honourable war record and long service of himself and his family were not enough to save him. The commons insisted Suffolk be arrested and confined in the Tower. Later he was charged not only with corruption and the disastrous policies which had lost Normandy and given away Maine, but also with having designs on the throne itself.

The matter never came to trial, possibly because, apart from the treason charge, any defence would surely have implicated many other lords and probably have shown the disastrous policies were the king's. Instead, on 17 March, Henry announced that Suffolk had thrown himself on the king's mercy, and neither convicting nor acquitting him, he had decided he should be exiled for five years. The lords had it recorded that this decision had nothing to do with their advice, and the reaction of the commons and the public at large was such that a few weeks later Henry prorogued parliament for a month, requiring it to meet again on 29 April in the calmer surroundings of Leicester.

Getting Suffolk out of London proved difficult, but he must have felt himself safe, as no doubt Henry intended, when he sailed from Ipswich on 30 April. Instead, his ship was intercepted by another, and the duke was forced on board and given a brief trial for treason. The guilty verdict was a foregone conclusion, as was the beheading that followed, and on 2 May the duke's body was dumped on the beach below the white cliffs of Dover, with his head skewered on a pole nearby.

Nor was Suffolk's violent end the last of the bloodletting for that year. In March, far too late and far too little, a force of around 2,500 men at last set off for Normandy. No great lord went with them, and though Somerset added somewhat to their numbers, he himself remained at Caen. On 15 April this small army of defiance was outnumbered and all but wiped out at the battle of Formigny, and Somerset, not daring to return to England, retreated to Calais, the only English plot left in northern France, while King Charles mopped up the rest of the garrisons at his leisure.

Spurred on by this further disaster, the mutterings of discontent in England now became a roar, and in Kent the common people found someone willing to lead them to London to put their case to the king. History knows him as Jack Cade, but he went by a number of other names including John Amend-all and, significantly, John Mortimer. The Brut Chronicle says he was an Irishman and claimed to be a cousin of the Duke of York, while others claim he was a Kentishman and a doctor. Whoever he was, beginning in May 1450 he progressed through Kent to London, gathering many thousands of common people as he went. By the time they reached Blackheath on 11 June, the king and his advisors were taking notice, not only because of the numbers and the fact that most were armed with knives and billhooks, but especially because of the Mortimer name.

For half a century there had been an uneasy and unspoken suggestion that the Mortimers, descended from the second son of Edward III, might have a superior claim to the crown than the Lancastrians, descended from the third son. The Mortimer name had been involved in every plot and rebellion in that time. Even the ill-fated Lollard rising of 1431 had been led by a man calling himself Jack Sharp of Wigmoreland, Wigmore being the major castle of the Mortimers in the Welsh marches. The current head of the Mortimer clan was Richard, Duke of York, and the thought that he may be behind this movement of men was more than enough to persuade the current regime to take it seriously.

Cade told the king's representatives on 17 June that they were not rebels but petitioners, come to lay before the king a list of the 'mischiefs and misgovernances of the realm' and to ask him to put them right. Chief among these was the fact that the king was surrounded by 'insatiable, covetous and malicious' men, who 'daily inform him that good is evil and evil is good.' By lying to Henry that the common people wanted York as king, they made him 'hate and destroy his friends and cherish his false traitors'. They had corrupted the law so no-one could obtain a just remedy, and they took for themselves everything that should come to the king, so that 'his law is lost, his goods are lost, the common people are destroyed, the sea is lost, France is lost, the king himself cannot pay for his meat and drink, and he owes more than any king of England should owe.' The remedy for this, so Cade claimed, was to take back all the grants made to those corrupt advisors, to clear them all out and replace them with men of the 'true blood of the realm', such as the Dukes of York, Exeter, Buckingham and Norfolk, and his true earls and barons.

Henry's response to this was to put on armour – the only time he did so – and lead a force to Blackheath. By the time he got there, however, the men were gone, having retreated to Sevenoaks. Then matters degenerated. A small force sent after them was ambushed and killed, and the retainers of the lords who had been left to guard Blackheath, instead allied themselves to Cade's manifesto. Even the Londoners showed sympathy to the cries for reform. By public demand the treasurer Lord Say was put in the Tower, and when Henry tried to release him, he was refused.

Now if ever was the time for decisive action, but Henry's decisive action was to retreat hurriedly to Kenilworth. 'For the king nor the lords,' says the Brut Chronicle, 'Dared not trust their own household men.' London – and, incidentally, the queen at Greenwich – was abandoned to its fate, and as soon as it was known the king had left, Cade and all his men were let in. Lord Say was one of many given a trial of sorts and beheaded in Cheapside. The Bishop of Salisbury, however, another high on their list of traitors, escaped towards his own diocese. It did him no good, for he was dragged from his own parish church at Edington and killed by his parishioners.

Excited by their initial success, it was not long before Cade lost control over the men he had brought with him. London was enthusiastically pillaged and quickly turned against the rebels. A bloody battle to expel the intruders was fought across London Bridge through the night of 5 July, and when a general pardon was offered them the next day, the remnant rapidly dispersed. Cade himself was at first included in the pardon but soon a reward was announced for his capture. Cornered in a garden in Sussex, he suffered a mortal wound and was dead before his body was brought to London and ritually beheaded. Only then did the king feel it was safe for him to return to his capital.

Another returning at this time, creeping home from Calais, was Edmund Beaufort, Duke of Somerset. Surprisingly he was given a warm welcome by king and queen, his loyal service remembered and his failures quickly forgotten. He rapidly gained the confidence of the royal couple, taking the place of those counsellors Henry had lost in the past few months, and Oman's comment that Henry 'was always unfortunate in the choice of his friends', seems something of an understatement.

No such place was available for Richard of York, returning unbidden from Ireland a few weeks later. He had come, he said, to protest his loyalty to the king, especially as his name had been appropriated by rebels in his absence, but the welcome he received was decidedly chilly. Henry had never taken to the duke. He had never had a place on the king's council, and his loyal and successful service had always been at a distance, in France and in Ireland. His closeness to the throne may have been one reason – Gloucester, too, had never achieved intimacy with his nephew – and his arrogance and love of magnificence may also have irked the king, while his free use of the Plantagenet name might have seemed a deliberate challenge. A more specific reason on this occasion was probably his obvious disapproval of Somerset and his rapid espousal of the cause of reform, a cause popular throughout the country.

There was still unrest everywhere, and York's repeated interventions to restore order, often pre-empting some action of Henry's, did nothing to endear him to the king. Nor did a demand from a parliament packed with York's supporters that he be recognised as Henry's heir. Then, in February 1452, it seemed to York he had enough popular support to force the removal of Somerset. Marching from his castle at Ludlow towards London, he expected to be joined by men from every city, but he had badly miscalculated. The other lords rallied to the king, London would not admit him, and when confronted by the king's army at Dartford in Kent he was forced into a humiliating climbdown, taken back to London, and made to swear an oath of loyalty to the king at St Paul's Cathedral.

Perhaps as a signal to York, in January 1453 the king knighted his two Tudor half-brothers, making the elder, Edmund, Earl of Richmond, and the younger, Jasper, Earl of Pembroke. As a further sign of approval, Edmund was betrothed to Somerset's niece, the nine-year-old Margaret Beaufort. Henry's blood relations were thus brought firmly within the royal, Lancastrian, fold. When soon after this it was confirmed that Queen Margaret was pregnant for the first time, Henry seemed to be firmly in control; but events in France would soon lead to a new crisis.

In 1451 Gascony had come under attack from Charles and the major centres of Bordeaux and Bayonne had been lost. The Earl of Shrewsbury, John Talbot, now in his mid-sixties but still a force to be reckoned with, was dispatched in the autumn of 1452 to lead the resistance. Bordeaux and most of Gascony was quickly recovered, and when reinforcements arrived in the following spring, led by his own son, it seemed only a matter of time before the duchy was once again secure. Instead, at the battle of Castillon in July 1453, precipitate action by Talbot, and the novel use of French artillery led to the deaths of both the earl and his son, and some 4,000 English troops. In a matter of weeks, the French had overrun the duchy and Gascony was lost to England forever.

It was the beginning of August before the news was brought to Henry at his hunting lodge at Clarendon. We don't know his immediate reaction. All that is recorded is that in the middle of the night, the king had a sudden 'frenzy' and lost his wits. It was assumed to be the same madness as had afflicted his grandfather, Charles VI of France, but Henry's illness bore little resemblance to that. Charles's madness was active and violent. Henry simply became catatonic. He couldn't walk or talk, made no reaction when spoken to, seemingly neither knew who he was nor recognised anyone else. This was not a brief interlude. It would last for well over a year, and no attempt to rouse him had the slightest effect.

On 13 October his son was born, but hopes that this might stir the king were soon dashed. In turn the Duke of Buckingham and the queen presented the child to Henry, asking for his blessing, but he did no more than glance at him once and then drop his eyes again. In the absence of any other instruction, the boy was christened Edward.

For a long time the seriousness of the king's illness was kept secret, but without his protection Somerset's position was severely undermined. At a great council in November York's ally the Duke of Norfolk demanded he be arrested and tried for his failures in France, and as a result he was imprisoned in the Tower, though no further move was made to bring him to trial.

By the end of the year the truth of the king's situation had to be acknowledged. A parliament was due in February, and if, as usual, it was full of York's supporters, it would be bound to call for him to be made Regent. Queen Margaret, perhaps under the influence of Suffolk and Somerset, had never liked or trusted the duke, and her belief that he wanted the crown for himself had probably been confirmed at Dartford. In January 1454, therefore, she proposed that she herself be given the regency, to rule in the king's name and make all appointments the king would normally make. It may have seemed an obvious move to her, both her mother and, more especially, her grandmother Yolande of Aragon, had carried out such a role very successfully. Parliament disagreed, and on 27 March, after a visit to the king, Richard Plantagenet, Duke of York, was named Chief Councillor and Protector of the Realm, the same title and powers as Humphrey of Gloucester had assumed thirty years before.

It is probably overstating the matter to say, as the later Yorkist-based chronicles do, that York's rule restored peace to the kingdom. There were ongoing feuds among the nobility in the north, in the west country and in Wales, which now began to show a Yorkist/Royalist split. On the whole, though, there was no display of vindictiveness, although key posts – chancellor, archbishop of Canterbury, and captain of Calais – went to York's supporters. He had not, however, managed to force through an act of resumption – taking back lands granted by the king – when, most unexpectedly, in December 1454, Henry 'woke up'.

It has been said that, if Henry's collapse was a tragedy, his recovery was a disaster. York's Protectorate was ended, and his allies removed from the chancellorship and from Calais, and within weeks Somerset was released from the Tower and declared a true and faithful servant of the king. The young Prince Edward, who had been created Prince of Wales with York's approval, was now recognised and blessed by his father, who declared his birth 'a miracle'.

Henry had come round full of peace and goodwill toward everyone. Not so Queen Margaret and the Duke of Somerset, who were more than ever determined to destroy the power of the Duke of York and his supporters, the Earls of Salisbury and Warwick, who had retired to their estates. A great council was called for 25 May at Leicester, to provide 'for the safety of the king's person against his enemies'. Correctly interpreting this as a direct challenge, York and his allies came south with a considerable force, not to Leicester but to St Albans, where they intercepted the king on his way north.

With the king, among others, were the Dukes of Somerset and Buckingham, the Earls of Northumberland, Pembroke and Stafford, and Lord Clifford, and it was immediately obvious that a confrontation was intended. Barricades were hastily erected across the town's streets but for several hours on the morning of 22 May, York tried to persuade the king to hand over Somerset, 'or they would have him by strength and violence.' The response was that any violence would be an act of treason. Henry clearly believed that, as at Dartford, York would back down. His men were thus not even in their full armour when the Yorkists attacked. Warwick's men smashed their way into the town through houses and gardens, the barricades were torn down, and within half an hour York was in possession not only of St Albans but of the terror-stricken king, who had been wounded in the neck by an arrow.

This first battle at St Albans in May 1455 is regarded as the first strike in the so-called Wars of the Roses, sowing seeds for much of the rest of the conflict, which turned into a struggle first to control the king, and then to replace him. Among the dead was Somerset, killed, as had been prophesied to him, beneath a castle, though it was, in fact, the inn sign of the Castle tavern. Also killed were Henry Percy, Earl of Northumberland, and Lord Clifford, while Somerset's son Henry, and Buckingham and his son, the Earl of Stafford, were wounded and taken prisoner.

There is a tendency, at this stage, to see King Henry as a sick old man. He was, however, only thirty-three years old, and while he may have been enfeebled by his illness, there had never been any suggestion that he should put on armour himself and defend his throne. Now he meekly surrendered to York, and when York, Salisbury and Warwick knelt to him and declared they had meant him no harm while removing the traitor Somerset, he is said to have forgiven them. A few days later at St Paul's in London during a traditional crown-wearing ceremony, it was York himself who placed the crown on the king's head.

It is likely that the shock of St Albans brought on at least a mild recurrence of Henry's illness. When parliament assembled on 9 July the king opened it and later declared York, Warwick and Salisbury to be his faithful men. By mid-November, however, a new parliament was opened by York, with Henry absent for 'reasonable causes'. Again, the commons was packed with York's supporters, and within days they were pushing for him to be named Protector once more. Despite resistance from the lords, the appointment was made, granted by the king to prevent him being 'troubled with numerous matters of business', while suffering 'infirmity'. From 19 November 1455 York resumed his protectorate, with enhanced powers and removable only by the king and lords acting together.

Once more, with the enthusiastic support of the commons, he attempted the reform of royal finances and the resumption of royal grants, but now it was the lords, with much more to lose, who opposed and defeated him. In February 1456 they demanded Henry return to parliament, and when he was brought there, York was once again stripped of his powers.

Now, with no lord high enough or close enough to the king, it was the twenty-six-year-old Queen Margaret who became the force behind the throne. After St Albans she had been allowed custody of both husband and son, and with both to protect, in her eyes at least, she became more than ever hostile to the Yorkist faction. Among the queen's most vociferous supporters were the sons of those nobles killed at St Albans, in particular Henry Beaufort the new duke of Somerset. The Yorkists, meanwhile were dispatched, wherever possible, to far flung corners. York was sent north to deal with the raiding of James II of Scotland, who was suggesting a renewed Franco-Scottish alliance against England. Warwick was ill-advisedly retained as Captain of Calais, which kept him away, but gave him a power base all his own.

A great council was called to meet at Coventry in October 1456, with the expectation that the Yorkist leaders would be brought to book for their actions in taking arms against the king. In the event, however, Henry could not be prevailed upon to condemn them. If they swore an oath of loyalty, he declared, he would accept them back into his grace, though at Buckingham's insistence he did promise this would be their last chance.

Even after this, however, hostility crackled in the air, accompanied by sporadic outbreaks of violence. In August 1457 an unprovoked attack on Sandwich by a French raiding party brought a change of attitude. There seemed a real possibility of a French invasion, and Henry, with unusual energy, demanded that his feuding lords must be reconciled. A great council at Westminster began in October 1457 and continued through the winter. York and his fellows lodged within the city of London and the Lancastrian royalists without, and each side had brought enough armed retainers for a small war. Respect for the king, however, kept the peace, and in March 1458 a reconciliation of sorts was achieved. Compensation would be paid by the Yorkists to the widows and heirs of those nobles killed at St Albans, and, as a gesture of peace, a 'Love Day' procession to St Paul's Cathedral on 25 March paired Somerset with Salisbury, the Duke of Exeter with his bitter enemy Warwick, and York with Queen Margaret, while the saintly king walked alone.

If there was peace that day, however, it did not last for long; indeed, the pairing of enemies in the procession only seemed to emphasise that there were two factions in the land and that the hapless king was the prize for whoever could gain the upper hand. No doubt both could make out a solid case for their position. Richard of York was, by wealth and status, the greatest magnate in the land. Should anything happen to the little prince, which was very possible, he was still the next heir to the throne. Yet his position had never been formally acknowledged, and all could be swept away in an instant should a vindictive woman gain enough influence in the king's council to condemn him for treason. Margaret, on the other hand, saw only an overmighty lord trying to gain control of her husband and possibly deprive her son of his crown. Both views have been expressed by historians over the centuries, with the former more prevalent in the 19th century, and the latter gaining ground since.

However threatened he felt, York realised that to appear an aggressor would lose him the sympathy of his fellows. Margaret, on the other hand, needed some new excuse to move against him as Henry had forgiven his earlier actions, and it became a war of rumours. Margaret was accused of assisting, or at least encouraging, the French raid on Sandwich. Worse, it was claimed that the young prince was a changeling, not her child at all, or alternatively not the child of the king. Coming after eight childless years of marriage, that last was easily believed by those inclined to the Yorkist cause.

On the other side there were constant rumours of York stirring trouble around the country preparatory to an armed rebellion. Again, there were plenty of disturbances to fuel these stories, especially in Wales where the king's half-brother Edmund Tudor had been held captive in Carmarthen Castle, dying of a fever in November 1456. During all this time the court was more often in the Midlands than in London, at Kenilworth, Leicester or Coventry, in the heart of Lancastrian territory. No parliament had been called since York's last parliament of 1455. The (Yorkist) English Chronicle declared, 'The queen ... ruled the realm as she liked... England was out of all good governance.'

The spark that ignited the fire of war came when a great council was summoned to Coventry in June 1459. The presence of the three Yorkist lords was demanded in order that they should answer for their actions. Since armed men had already been gathered at Leicester, and the queen had been busy recruiting an army in the name of her son, the Yorkists stayed away, and this act of disobedience immediately branded them traitors.

Now the Yorkist forces began to move, Salisbury down from the north, York from his stronghold at Ludlow, and Warwick, with some 300 men of the Calais garrison, landing in Kent. Like movements on a chessboard, the queen immediately mobilised men to block the threat to the king, and the first to see action was the elderly Lord Audley, intercepting Salisbury on 23 September 1459 at Blore Heath in Staffordshire. Salisbury was heavily outnumbered, but using tactics learnt in the French wars, drew his enemies forward, downhill and across a brook, by feigned retreat, until they could be decimated by flanking archers. Audley was killed along with some 2,000 of his men, and the decisive victory went to the Yorkists.

Less than three weeks later it seemed there would be a battle to settle the struggle once and for all. At Ludford Bridge, below the steep hill topped by Ludlow town and castle, all three Yorkist lords had drawn up their forces. Facing them was the king's army, with banners flying to proclaim Henry himself was in their midst. The Yorkist artillery, fed a rumour that Henry was dead, fired a volley on the evening of 12 October, before the sight of the king himself silenced them. The discovery that he was alive and that their act was therefore treasonable, caused a mass defection of the Calais men. Further defections followed, and when the sun rose the next morning the Yorkist leaders were gone. York and his younger son, Edmund, Earl of Rutland, fled to Ireland, while Warwick, Salisbury and York's eldest, Edward,

Earl of March, reached Calais via the Devon coast. Behind them Ludlow was sacked, and York's wife, the duchess Cecily, had to kneel to the king and beg forgiveness.

At a parliament held at Coventry in November 1459 York and his allies were attainted for treason, meaning all their lands and goods would be confiscated by the king, a welcome boost for the royal finances. All attempts to get at York in Ireland and the others in Calais failed, however, and it was clear it would only be a matter of time before they regrouped and returned.

On 6 June 1460, Salisbury, Warwick and Edward of March landed with 20,000 men at Sandwich in Kent, and with them was a papal legate. For the past two years Pope Pius II had been trying to raise a crusade against the Ottoman Turks, who had taken Constantinople in 1453. The legate was supposed to be negotiating peace between the rival English factions so that they could join such a crusade, and therefore they were greeted by the archbishop of Canterbury, and, despite orders from the king (or more likely the queen), admitted at once to London. He had, however, been persuaded to believe the Yorkist version of events, and would give his whole-hearted support to their efforts, even excommunicating leading Lancastrian earls.

On 5 July Warwick and March led their army northwards to confront the king, once more residing in the Midlands. The Duke of York was to come from Ireland with another force, but it was decided to bring the king's army to battle immediately, before it could be reinforced. A field to the south-east of Northampton was the chosen site, and though Henry was present, it was left to the Duke of Buckingham to deploy the royal forces. On a bend in the River Nene they were drawn up, protected behind by the river and in front by a rampart, ditch and stakes. Buckingham also intended to use cannon, but in the event pouring rain made them useless. Now it was Henry's turn to suffer defections, probably due to the presence of the legate with the Yorkists. The Earl of Wiltshire left before the battle, and there was to be an even more serious defection during the conflict. Before then attempts had been made to get to the king to negotiate, all of them rebuffed by Buckingham. 'If the earl of Warwick comes to the king's presence he will die,' he declared. To which Warwick replied, 'I will speak with the king at 2 o'clock or I will die.'

At 2 o'clock, then, on the afternoon of 16 July 1460, the battle of Northampton began with the Yorkist forces advancing across a sodden field. It is likely Warwick knew what would happen next, for he had already given instructions not to kill the common soldiers but only to target their leaders. As the Earl of March approached the royal forces commanded by Lord Grey of Ruthin, Grey ordered his men to lay down their arms. The Yorkists poured over the rampart, attacking Buckingham's men from the side and rear, and in half an hour it was all over. Lancastrian losses were relatively small – probably as many drowned in the Nene while fleeing as were killed on the field – but among them were the Earl of Shrewsbury and, almost at the door of Henry's tent, his well-loved commander the Duke of Buckingham.

For Henry it was St Albans all over again. He left the field a prisoner of Warwick, passing the bodies of his faithful men as he went. Returned to London, he was lodged at Westminster Palace while all awaited the arrival of the Duke of York. The king's only consolation might have been that his wife and son had escaped all attempts to capture them, but while Margaret and the seven-year-old prince Edward fled westward to Harlech, Richard of York was travelling in some state in the other direction.

His journey led him to Westminster where a parliament had opened on 7 October, and when he arrived on the morning of 10 October he strode up to the empty throne and laid his hand upon it in a gesture reminiscent of Henry IV some sixty years before. There was, however, no great acclamation. Henry may have been useless as a king, but he was loved, and neither lords nor commons would agree to depose him. A contemporary chronicle declares that York's manner was deemed presumptuous and that people 'began to murmur against him and say he had acted in a rash manner'.

He was forced to justify his claim to the throne, which he did, claiming it as of right by a descent senior to that of the Lancastrians. Though he had not urged this right before, he said, 'Yet it does not rot, nor shall it perish.' Finally, on 25 October, by agreement with the ever-compliant Henry, Richard of York was recognised, not as the king but as the heir to the king, after his death or whenever he should lay down his crown.

While York had control of the king and authority to lead armies on his behalf, however, there were many yet free in the country who would not accept his position without a fight. Queen Margaret and her son had reached Scotland and were negotiating a deal with the newly widowed Queen Mary, now heading the regency council of her eight-year-old son. Jasper Tudor in Wales was joined by an army led by the Earl of Wiltshire, while in the north the Dukes of Somerset and Exeter were gathering forces in the queen's name from among the Percys and other northern lords.

York knew he would have to fight soon to preserve what he had won, but battles were rarely fought in mid-winter so he expected no action until at least the New Year. In the meantime, Edward of March was sent to the Welsh Marches, Warwick remained in London, and York, Salisbury and York's son the Earl of Rutland went north to the Yorkist castle at Sandal to prepare to meet a northern challenge.

It came far quicker that they anticipated. On 30 December, engaged on what was probably a foraging expedition in the direction of Wakefield, they were attacked, cut off and overwhelmingly defeated by a Lancastrian army led by the Dukes of Somerset and Exeter, and Lords Clifford and Roos. York was killed on the field of battle, and Rutland pursued and killed by Lord Clifford because 'your father killed my father.' Salisbury was taken prisoner but killed by a mob at Pontefract the next day. With the heads of all three displayed on spikes over Micklegate at York, and Queen Margaret coming to an agreement with the Scots a few days later, the contest for the crown was once again thrown wide open.

On 20 January 1461 the queen and Prince Edward met with her victorious commanders at York and set off southwards with a northern army including Scots and Borderers. Meanwhile Jasper Tudor, his father Owen and the Earl of Wiltshire aimed to join them with an army gathered in Wales. At Mortimer's Cross near Hereford, however, they met with York's son Edward on

2 February and a bloody battle was fought lasting all day. This time, the Yorkists triumphed, and while Jasper and the Earl of Wiltshire escaped, Owen Tudor was beheaded in the market place at Hereford.

This was now a young man's war. Warwick at thirty-three was the oldest of the leading commanders. The queen herself was only thirty, and Edward of March only eighteen, while the majority of leaders on both sides were the children of those killed earlier in the conflict.

As Queen Margaret and her army journeyed south, they ravaged the land all about, not only foraging but plundering, raping and destroying. That at least is the story put about by Warwick, building on rumours and filling the hearts of the Londoners with terror at the thought of these wild northmen approaching. On 12 February, the helpless King Henry was once more drawn unwillingly into the fight, taken north as far as St Albans with Warwick and his army to act as a figurehead in the coming battle against his own wife and son. To the north of the town Warwick set up his army in defensive formation across the road he believed the queen's army would take, Gregory's Chronicle listing an array of formidable weapons to be deployed. Henry himself was placed in a tent under a tree at the extreme edge of the battlefield, with two men to guard him who swore they would keep him from harm.

On this occasion, however, Warwick's tactics misfired. The queen's army approached by a different route, got into the town behind him and overwhelmed what had been his rearguard before the rest of the army could be reorganised. With artillery and other weapons all in the wrong place, chaos ensued. The Yorkists were routed and Warwick was lucky to escape, to rendezvous later with Edward of March in the Cotswolds.

A joyous reunion took place between the queen, her son and King Henry, found apparently singing to himself in his tent after the battle. For their loyal protection of his majesty his two guards were rewarded by having their heads cut off, nominally at the behest of the young prince, though more probably at the command of the queen, an indication of the ruthlessness now becoming prevalent in this civil war.

A triumphant return to London seemed in prospect, but Warwick's stories had done their job in that capital city. London refused to admit them. This first check became a hesitation, and then an abrupt withdrawal. It was not possible to stay long in one place in this winter-time with an army to feed. Already deserters were heading back north, and soon king, queen, prince and army were joining them.

It was an unlooked-for opportunity for the Yorkist faction, and quickly taken. On 2 March Warwick and Edward returned to London with a bold demand. Henry, by joining with the queen's army, had broken his agreement with the Duke of York. Edward was the heir under that agreement, therefore Edward now claimed the crown Henry had symbolically abandoned. On 4 March London agreed with him. By acclamation of the people he was declared to be Edward IV, king of England, and without waiting for a coronation, immediately set off northwards for a showdown to turn the title into reality.

It happened just over three weeks later, at Towton near York. At dawn on Palm Sunday, 29 March 1461, the armies of Edward IV and Henry VI began what has been described as the largest, bloodiest battle on English soil. Fought in a snowstorm with no quarter given on either side, by the end of the day as many as 28,000 may have died, and Henry, Margaret and young Prince Edward were in full flight, first to Newcastle and Berwick, and then to Scotland. If, as believed in earlier times, God gave his judgement in the outcome of battles, this time he had come down decisively on the side of Edward IV.

It was not the end, of course. Despite a lavish coronation for the new king on 28 June 1461, there were far too many Lancastrians – including the entire royal family – still loose in the country for the struggle to be finished. Over the next few years they were slowly driven out, first from Wales and then from Northumbria. By the end of 1463 Henry was living at Bamburgh Castle on the Northumberland coast, while Queen Margaret and Prince Edward, having toured France and even Burgundy begging for support, were living in a castle owned by her father at Kouer on the borders of Lorraine.

The following year matters became even worse for Henry. On 15 May, in a do-or-die attempt to defeat the Yorkist forces at the battle of Hexham, his faithful commanders the Duke of Somerset and Lord Roos were both captured and beheaded, and Henry himself went on the run. For over a year he managed to evade capture, moving from one small Lancastrian 'safe house' to another, until finally recognised and betrayed in July 1465. He was taken to London, imprisoned in the Tower, but treated with 'all possible humanity'. Supplied with all his needs and left in peace, he was probably considerably happier and more comfortable there than he had been for some time.

All was not well, however, in the Yorkist camp. On 1 May 1464 King Edward had secretly married Elizabeth Woodville, the widow of Sir John Grey who had been killed at St Albans three years earlier. Although she was the daughter of Jacquetta of Luxembourg, it was not the sort of marriage a new king should be making. He did it, says Ingulph's Chronicle, 'prompted by the ardour of youth ... relying on his own choice, without consulting the nobles of England', who took it amiss. It marked the beginning of a split with Warwick, which widened when, 'being too greatly influenced by the urgent suggestions of the queen', honours began to be showered on the extensive Woodville family, at the expense of Warwick's own expectations for his two daughters. The final straw came when Edward signed a treaty with the new Duke Charles of Burgundy, at the same time as Warwick had almost completed negotiations for a treaty with Burgundy's enemy, Louis of France.

In July 1469, Warwick married his daughter Isabel to Edward's younger brother, George, Duke of Clarence, defeated the king's army at the battle of Edgecote and imprisoned him. A brief reconciliation followed, but by the end of August the following year Warwick had travelled to France, sworn homage and fealty to Queen Margaret, and made an alliance with both Margaret and King Louis to restore Henry to his throne.

A few weeks later, Warwick, the Duke of Clarence, John de Vere, Earl of Oxford, and Henry's half-brother Jasper Tudor landed in the West Country with an army. Edward, who had been decoyed to the north, quickly turned back to Doncaster where he expected to be reinforced by the Earl of Salisbury, Warwick's brother. When he discovered Salisbury had defected, taking his forces with him, he had little option but to flee, eventually making his way to Burgundy. On 6 October Warwick visited the no-doubt bemused Henry in the Tower and informed him he was no longer a prisoner, but once more King Henry VI of England.

Warwick's reward for restoring the king was the betrothal and subsequent marriage of his daughter Anne to Prince Edward, but the price of the French treaty now became apparent. Louis of France had demanded and received the promise of English support in a war to finally quash his bitter enemy, Charles of Burgundy. In the late autumn of 1470, while Warwick was urging the swift return of Queen Margaret and the young prince to prop up the feeble rule of the king, Louis refused to allow them to go until practical assistance from England had actually been given for his war. Only in February 1471, when troops from Calais had been directed to move against Burgundy, did Louis permit the English royal family to leave. By that time, outraged that England was supporting his enemy, Charles of Burgundy had thrown his weight behind the alternative English king, Edward IV.

Both Edward and the queen and prince were delayed by the weather in the Channel, but in the event Edward got away first, with his army of 900 English and 300 Flemish troops. An initial attempted landing in Norfolk was thwarted, and so it was that, in an exact replica of the invasion of Henry IV some seventy years earlier, he arrived at Ravenspur on the mouth of the Humber, declaring he had come only to claim his own duchy of York.

Given his forgiving nature, King Henry might even have let him have it, but Warwick was not so gullible. Leaving the king in London with the Duke of Somerset and the archbishop of York, he took a force of some 4,000 men as far as Coventry. Edward, meanwhile, moved to Doncaster gathering support all the way, and now declared his true intention, to take back the crown. Warwick was prepared for a final, decisive battle, but, receiving a message from Clarence that he was coming with a force of men from the West Country to join him, he duly waited for his arrival. While he did so, Edward slipped past and met Clarence, who immediately defected once more and was welcomed back by his brother.

Even before Edward appeared outside London the Duke of Somerset had abandoned his charge and left, allegedly to raise forces for the king. The Warkworth Chronicle contains a bizarre little story that, as Edward approached, the Recorder and aldermen of the city commanded those who were defending it 'to go home to dinner; and during that dinner-time King Edward was let in.' London, as usual, had tested the air and intended to be on the winning side.

Edward arrived in London on Maundy Thursday, the Thursday before Easter Sunday, and by the Saturday evening had marched out again to confront Warwick on the lowland to the north of Barnet. This was one battle where neither side had good intelligence of the other. Edward arrived in the dark and the following morning there was a thick fog, so the opposing forces were misaligned. In the confusion of shifting around the battlefield, Warwick's forces in one place ended up attacking each other. A shout of 'Treason' went up, the battle formation broke, and Warwick, who had been persuaded to fight on foot, was killed while trying to get to his horse.

Even while Edward was enjoying his triumph, Queen Margaret and her son were landing on the south coast at Weymouth. When they heard the news from Barnet, Margaret wanted to return at once to France, but she was persuaded by the Duke of Somerset and Earl of Devon that with the forces they had from the West Country, and the forces Jasper Tudor was raising in Wales, they could still defeat Edward and save the throne for Lancaster. To do that, of course, they first had to meet up with Tudor's forces.

By now Henry was back in the Tower once more, and Edward was powering across the country to intercept the Lancastrians. They needed to cross the Severn, but found Gloucester held against them. The next crossing place was at Tewkesbury, and when they arrived there on 3 May, Edward's army was only a few miles behind.

It was decided to make a stand there, in the boggy ground to the south of the abbey. Prince Edward, now seventeen years old, would take his place in the centre battle, with Somerset to his left and the Earl of Devon to his right. Possibly the prince's presence inhibited Lord Wenlock, accompanying him into his first battle. For whatever reason, when they should have moved to support Somerset's flanking movement they failed to do so. Once more, cries of treachery filled the air, and Wenlock was struck dead by Somerset, whereupon the Lancastrian army broke up again and fled. Prince Edward was killed as he made for the abbey, and while Somerset achieved sanctuary there, two days later he was dragged out, condemned and executed in the market square.

The death of her son seemed finally to break the spirit of the queen. She was discovered in hiding and taken to London, to the Tower, but not apparently to her husband. On the very night she arrived, 21 May 1471, Henry died. The official account declares he died 'of pure displeasure and melancholy', but even at the time there were doubts. Both the Warkworth Chronicle and Croyland Chronicle declare he was put to death by order of the king. With his son dead there was now no reason to keep alive the last frail spark of Lancastrian royalty, and thus the incompetent, infuriating, but equally, gentle, forgiving and even saintly King Henry, was simply removed from the scene, to make way for the new, vibrant Yorkist dynasty.

Henry VII

'What he minded he compassed'

– Bacon

Of all the namesakes that became king of England, Henry VII is the one with the least claim to that title. He was not, like some, the son of a king, and though he could claim with others to be the grandson of a king, it was not a king of England but a king of France, and no-one in France ever contemplated he could claim that crown. Indeed, no-one in England seems to have thought he could claim any crown until he was in his mid-twenties. Then, according to the Croyland Chronicle Continuation, those in the south and west of England, casting around for a plausible leader for their rebellion, 'turned their thought to Henry, earl of Richmond'.

The small spot of English royal blood that Henry possessed came to him through his mother. Margaret Beaufort was the daughter of that Duke of Somerset who, unsuccessful in France in 1443, had come home to his estates and died – possibly killed himself – the following year. Margaret, one year old at the time, thus became a most desirable heiress, not only for the wealth she could bring to a marriage, but also because of her close connection to the Beaufort family, descended from John of Gaunt, and, through him, Edward III. She became a ward of the Duke of Suffolk, favoured counsellor of King Henry VI at the time, and before she was seven was married off to Suffolk's son John.

Suffolk's fall from grace quickly followed, and the marriage was later annulled, both parties being underage.

As part of King Henry's plan to draw his half-brothers closer to the royal family, Margaret now became first the ward, then the betrothed and finally the wife of the elder, Edmund Tudor, Earl of Richmond. They married on 1 November 1455 when he was twenty-five and she twelve. Just over a year later Edmund was dead, possibly dying of the plague while a prisoner in Carmarthen. At the time Margaret was seven months pregnant, and she was immediately taken under the protection of her brother-in-law Jasper Tudor, Earl of Pembroke. Thus it was that her son Henry was born on 28 January 1457 at Pembroke Castle in West Wales.

As the son of the king's half-brother, Henry might call the king his uncle, but he had no claim on the crown. Nor, despite his mother's heritage, would any claim arise through her, for the Beaufort family derived from the mistress of John of Gaunt during the time he was married to Constance of Castile. Though they had been legitimised by Richard II, they had later been specifically barred from any claim to the throne. In the late 1450s, therefore, while the crown sat uneasily on the head of Henry VI, and mighty families jostled for power, there seemed no reason at all to think both crown and power might one day fall to the child born in Pembroke Castle.

By all accounts it was a difficult birth. Margaret was several months short of her fourteenth birthday and small-framed, and though afterwards she spent many years married to two further husbands, she never had another child. Nor did she have long with her son. Within weeks a new marriage was being talked of, and less than a year later she became the wife of Sir Henry Stafford. It was seen as a good marriage despite the fact that he was nearly twenty years older than her. He was the second son of the Duke of Buckingham, and staunchly loyal to the Lancastrian cause in those difficult times. It promised security both for Margaret and for her son, though he remained at Pembroke with his uncle the earl.

All changed for Henry when he was just four years old. The Lancastrian disasters at Mortimer's Cross and Towton saw Jasper Tudor fleeing first to North Wales and later to exile. His title and estates were stripped from him and given to the Yorkist supporter

William Herbert, a descendant of that Davy Gam who was killed fighting beside Henry V at Agincourt. Soon after, Herbert purchased the wardship of young Henry Tudor, who had also lost the title earl of Richmond and the estates he inherited from his father. Transferred from Pembroke to the Herberts' castle at Raglan, the boy was nonetheless well treated. His education was taken seriously as regards both military training and the gentler arts, and over the many years he remained there in the care of Herbert's wife Anne, he came to know a multitude of other children brought up in the household – among them Henry Percy, the future Earl of Northumberland – who would prove useful to his cause in later life.

Fortune's wheel turned again in 1469 when William Herbert was captured and executed along with his brother after the battle of Edgecote. One source places Henry at the battle, though at twelve years of age he would have played no part. By the end of the following year Henry VI had been returned to the throne and Jasper Tudor was back, collecting young Henry and taking him to visit his namesake. According to Polydore Vergil the king then prophesied that Henry would one day wear his crown, but as Vergil was writing this not earlier than 1505, and specifically at the request of Henry Tudor, we are allowed to take this with a pinch of salt.

At around this time Henry was also able to pay a visit to his mother and stepfather. The two weeks he passed with her were the longest time they had spent together since he was a baby. The circumstances of both, however, were about to change again, with the return of Edward IV in the spring of 1471. By then Henry was in Wales with Jasper, so they missed the ill-fated battle of Barnet, but Henry Stafford was not so lucky, receiving a severe wound from which he never recovered. Six months later Margaret Beaufort was a widow for the second time at the age of twenty-eight.

The news of the crushing defeat at Tewkesbury on 4 May reached Henry and Jasper at Chepstow. With all hopes of a Lancastrian revival dead, they disbanded the forces they had gathered and fled westwards to Pembroke once more. There they were briefly besieged in the castle before managing to break out and make their way to the coast at nearby Tenby, then an important port. They were sheltered for several days by a wealthy wine merchant, before slipping through tunnels that led from his cellar down to the harbour and taking ship for France.

They never reached that long-time sanctuary of Lancastrian exiles. A storm in the Channel blew them off course, and they either landed or were shipwrecked on the coast of Brittany. There, however, they were made welcome by Duke Francis II, who, at least initially, treated them as honoured guests. Later they became more or less prisoners, albeit in very comfortable circumstances.

They would remain in Brittany for eleven years, sometimes together and sometimes separated to deter attempts to kidnap or murder two valuable pawns in the power games of Europe. Edward IV in England, Louis XI of France, Charles the Bold of Burgundy, and, indeed, Francis himself, all had an interest in controlling Henry Tudor – now again calling himself Earl of Richmond – and his uncle Jasper. For Edward, Henry represented a potential threat to his throne, though a diminishing one as time passed. Nonetheless, with all the bloodletting of the recent wars, Henry was a last slender thread of Lancastrian 'royalty', and Edward would dearly have loved to control his destiny. Burgundy and Brittany saw the boy as a weapon to use against the ambitions of Louis to unite all the French duchies under his own hand. By threatening to support him in England, or promising to hand him to Edward, the English king could be persuaded to take up arms to defend their cause. Equally, Louis felt he could prevent alliances between England and the duchies if he had custody of Henry Tudor. Edward, indeed, still had ambitions of his own in France. He launched an abortive invasion in 1475 but was quickly bought off by the wily Louis in a treaty which, among other things, allowed for the return of Margaret of Anjou to retirement in France.

While his stay in Brittany was relatively comfortable, therefore, Henry would never have felt secure. This was particularly so after the time in 1476 when Francis was persuaded Edward meant no harm to the nineteen-year-old and delivered him as far as St Malo, before changing his mind and snatching him back. What the young man did receive, however, was a first-class education in the diplomatic manoeuvring of those seeking to achieve or retain power in a world full of enemies.

At this time, too, he had leisure to indulge his interest in the legends of King Arthur. Wales and Brittany shared Celtic traditions, and the stories Henry had heard in his early years were reinforced by those current in Brittany. Perhaps to give himself hope in dark times, Henry strongly identified with Arthur, and also with an ancient Welsh prophecy that one day a Welshman would be crowned king in London, restoring the ancient British race to rule over the Saxons. As the years passed, though, this must have seemed the merest daydreaming as far as Henry Tudor was concerned.

The situation in England was changing, nevertheless. In June 1472 his mother married Thomas, Lord Stanley, a steward of Edward IV, and was drawn closer into Yorkist court circles. She became friendly with Edward's queen, Elizabeth Woodville, and began to hint that Henry could marry one of Elizabeth's daughters. Then, quite unexpectedly, in April 1483 the forty-year-old King Edward died.

His heir was his twelve-year-old son, born at Westminster Abbey when his mother was in sanctuary during Warwick's successful rebellion. The boy was now named as King Edward V, but within months his father's marriage to Queen Elizabeth was declared void on the grounds that the king had previously contracted to marry Lady Eleanor Butler. Young Edward and his younger brother Richard, both residing at the Tower of London prior to Edward's coronation, were now proclaimed to be illegitimate. The crown was then offered to Richard of Gloucester, younger brother of the deceased king, who, on 26 June 1483, became Richard III. The Act of Parliament known as Titulus Regius, which was passed later to confirm this, having recited the 'pretended marriage' of Edward and Elizabeth, and the fact that the children of the second brother, George Duke of Clarence, were barred by their father's treason, then declared to Richard, '... there is no other person living but you alone who may rightly claim the said crown and royal dignity.' There were, of course, others who disagreed.

The picture of events in 1483 has been considerably muddied by the many contradictory accounts written about them, often years later and by people who were not there at the time. Controversy has raged over the intervening centuries, with factions supporting one theory or another, and with few if any solid facts on which to rely. Suffice to say that at some point in the summer or autumn of 1483 the two young princes disappeared from the Tower, with no concrete evidence as to what might have happened to them. At the same time, splits among the Yorkist supporters that were already evident widened considerably. Many of these related to support for, or opposition to, the existing dominance of the Woodville family, which was widely unpopular among the older established nobility. The dowager queen Elizabeth Woodville had already taken herself and her daughters into sanctuary at Westminster Abbey, and it was clear that if Richard was to be king, the role of the entire family would be greatly diminished. In addition, many families that had previously supported the Lancastrian monarchs re-discovered these sympathies at this time.

Margaret Beaufort, wife of Lord Stanley, was still highly favoured at court, carrying the new queen's train at Richard's coronation. Nonetheless, she was still in contact with the former queen, and still urging support for her son Henry and his marriage to King Edward's eldest daughter, Elizabeth of York, which seemed considerably more attractive now than it had a few years before. They were not the only schemers, however. The Croyland Chronicle speaks rather vaguely of 'people in the southern and western parts of the kingdom' beginning to plan together, ostensibly to free the princes from the Tower, 'It soon became known that many things were going on in secret,' for this purpose, 'especially on the part of those who ... had availed themselves of the privilege of sanctuary,' a reference to the former queen, and possibly her son the Earl of Dorset, and brother, the Bishop of Salisbury.

At some point Henry Stafford, Duke of Buckingham, was drawn into this, having apparently 'repented his former conduct' in supporting Richard, again according to the Chronicle. His repentance may have been prompted by John Morton, Bishop of Ely, a man who had changed sides before, and now, seeing no profit in Richard, abruptly returned to the Lancastrian camp. Morton was for a time imprisoned at Brecknock Castle, Buckingham's seat in the Welsh Marches, and may have persuaded the duke to join his proposed rebellion. Buckingham's own father had died fighting for Henry VI at Northampton, and he was a nephew by marriage of Margaret Beaufort.

It is at this point, too, so the chronicle claims, that those looking for a leader for their enterprise first woke up to the potential of Henry Tudor. While it names Buckingham as the chief mover of the enterprise, it quickly adds that, on the advice of Morton, Henry Tudor was sent for to marry Elizabeth of York and take the throne. As Churchill commented, he was 'the nearest thing to royalty the Lancastrian party possessed'.

It may have come as a pleasant surprise to the exile that suddenly people were speaking of him as a realistic challenger for the crown, but co-ordinating the different elements of what was supposed to be a general uprising on 18 October 1483 proved difficult. A campaign of rumours was begun suggesting Richard had murdered the young princes, and it may be these rumours that were faithfully reported by Dominic Mancini in his account of the situation in England in the summer of that year. Thomas Woodville, Marquis of Dorset and eldest son of Queen Elizabeth, escaped from Westminster to raise men around Newbury, and the intention was that he would join with Buckingham and another force from Devon, at the same time as the men of the south-east were expected to attack London. Meanwhile, money had been sent to Henry in Brittany, and with the help of Duke Francis he had assembled men and ships for a landing on the south coast.

They were defeated by bad timing and bad weather. The men of Kent attacked early and were thwarted by John Howard, the newly created Duke of Norfolk. Richard, who with his wife and son was on a progress through northern England, then had time to assemble an army before the others moved. Torrential rain, rising rivers and the desertion of many of his men prevented Buckingham from joining with those from the south and west, and when he abandoned his forces, the uprising crumbled and fell. By the time Henry, delayed by the same storm, arrived off the coast of Plymouth, all was over and Richard was poised with an army at Exeter. Not even risking a landing, Henry sailed straight back to Brittany.

The biggest loser in all this was Buckingham. Betrayed to Richard, he was tried and beheaded in Salisbury. Many others, including Morton and Dorset, escaped, and while the bishop settled in Flanders, Henry's embryo court in Brittany was swelled by numbers of these escapees. Though Richard offered pardons, even to Bishop Morton, his offers were not accepted. Similar leniency, though, was shown to one of the major plotters, Margaret Beaufort. Though she was stripped of her lands, these were simply handed to her husband who was told to keep a closer watch on her activities in future.

The biggest winner was Henry. Bolstered by this new support he made it clear he would not abandon his claims. On Christmas Day, in the cathedral at Rennes, he took a solemn oath that, when he became king of England, he would marry Elizabeth of York. The following year, however, he was once again forced to flee for his life.

On 9 April 1484, Edward, Prince of Wales, the only son of King Richard, died before his eleventh birthday. Now more than ever was the king vulnerable to rival claims, though those closest to the throne, nine-year-old Edward Earl of Warwick, and twenty-four-year-old John de la Pole, Earl of Lincoln, were never seen as a threat. The Earl of Warwick, indeed, was virtually adopted by Richard's wife Anne before she fell ill, and for a while was named as Richard's heir apparent. Anne herself died in the spring of the following year.

It was the Lancastrian Henry Tudor that the king saw as his greatest challenger, and in the autumn of 1484 he nearly succeeded in getting hold of him. During a period when Duke Francis was ill and incapable, his treasurer Pierre Landais agreed, for a price, to hand him over. Forewarned, Henry managed to escape to France dressed as a servant, having previously established he would be welcome there. The devious King Louis XI – known as the Universal Spider for the webs of intrigue he wove – had recently died and been replaced by his thirteen-year-old son, Charles VIII. The policy of Louis was not changed, however. Richard was seen as a far greater threat to France than his brother had been, and every facility was given to Henry in his attempt to overthrow him.

Supplied, therefore, with a generous loan, with ships and with some 2,000 French mercenaries, Henry's enterprise was further bolstered by the arrival of an experienced commander, in the person of John de Vere, Earl of Oxford, who had escaped his long-time imprisonment at Calais. Together with Jasper Tudor, and with a revised battle plan, it was a more hopeful fleet that set sail from Harfleur on 1 August 1485.

Their welcome in England was still uncertain, whereas in Wales, as an embodiment of the ancient prophecy and with established friendships, it was more assured. It was to Wales, then, that they travelled, landing on 7 August at Mill Bay near Dale in the far west. According to Fabyan's Chronicle, Henry immediately 'kneeled down upon the earth, and with meek countenance and pure devotion began this psalm, "Judica me Deus et discerne causam meum".' (Psalm 43: Judge me, O God, and plead my cause.) Then, when he had finished and kissed the ground, 'he commanded such as were about him boldly in the name of God and St George to set forward.'

Richard would have expected his men in the area to resist any such landing. Indeed, his principal lieutenant in south-west Wales, Rhys ap Thomas, is said to have sworn that any invader 'must make his entrance over my belly'. In the event Rhys joined Henry almost immediately, and the story goes that he fulfilled his oath by standing under the nearby Mullock Bridge – which must have been considerably less silted up in those days – while Henry rode over the top.

Henry and Jasper led their men northwards by a coastal route, possibly deliberately visiting Machynlleth where, some eighty years before, Glendower had had himself crowned Prince of Wales. By now Henry had considerably embroidered his Welsh ancestry, claiming descent from such heroes as Cadwaladr, Arthur and even Brutus, the legendary first king of Britain, himself descended from Aeneas, prince of Troy. Cadwaladr's red dragon banner had been added to his own, the more to attract Welshmen to his cause. Meanwhile Rhys ap Thomas travelling by a different route, gathered men as he went, so that by the time the two met up at Welshpool, his force was a good deal larger than Henry's.

Richard was at Nottingham when the Tudor landing took place, anticipating an invasion but unsure where it would occur. Seeing Henry now marching unopposed past Shrewsbury, he summoned his own forces to assemble at Leicester. John Howard of Norfolk was his staunchest supporter, and Henry Percy of Northumberland also answered the call. The Stanleys were a different matter. Thomas, Lord Stanley was technically Henry's stepfather, and when initially summoned had pleaded illness. He was at his Lancashire estates, having left his son, Lord Strange, with Richard as a hostage for his loyalty. Stanley's younger brother William was based in Cheshire, holding office from the king, but he had already let Henry pass unhindered, and it was alleged he was in correspondence with the invader. All his life he had been a staunch Yorkist, and it is unclear why he now chose to change sides.

The forces finally confronted each other on the morning of 22 August 1485 at a place later known as Bosworth Field, south of Market Bosworth. Richard's forces considerably outnumbered Henry's, with Norfolk leading the northern battle, Richard in the centre and Northumberland as rearguard. Numbering some 8-9,000 men, they were supported by archers and cannon. Henry had around 5,000 men, with the main body led by the Earl of Oxford, and Henry himself in the rear surrounded by a small force, more bodyguard than battle. Aloof and at right-angles to the opposing forces, Lord Stanley and his brother had some 3,000 men apiece. It was a more balanced situation than it appeared, despite the mismatch of numbers. Richard had the power but was uncertain as to the loyalty of his men. Henry had the loyalty but was uncertain as to their power.

Few details of the battle were recorded at the time, and even the site of the action has been reassessed in recent years, suggesting a movement away from the traditional placing at Ambion Hill, towards the flatter land around Fenn Lane, nearer Dadlington. It seems clear, though, that Richard drew up his battle lines first on a ridge of higher land, leaving Henry's forces to approach around boggy ground. Fabyan's Chronicle is particularly terse on the events of the day. It was, he said, 'a sharp battle, and sharper should have been if the king's party had been fast to him, but many before the field (i.e. before the battle) refused him and yielded unto the other party, and some stood far off, 'til they saw to which party the victory fell.'

Norfolk could not be accused of such aloofness. A warning had apparently been pinned to his tent the night before. 'Jockey of

Norfolk, be not too bold, for Dickon thy master is bought and sold.'
Nevertheless, he was the first to engage with the enemy following
the opening archery and cannonade. On the other hand, the Stanley
brothers maintained their position, watching from the side, even when
Richard threatened Stanley's son with immediate beheading if he did
not at once joint the fight. In an echo of William Marshal's father
many years before, he sent back the message, 'I have other sons.'

By now, though, the fighting was too urgent to carry out an order
to behead the young man. The Earl of Oxford was more than holding
his own against Norfolk's men, and Norfolk himself was killed
quite early in the struggle. Though ordered in as reinforcements,
Northumberland and his men did not move, possibly aware of the
Stanleys poised to the side and as yet uncommitted. Wary of thinly
spread troops, Oxford ordered his men to close up around their
battle standards, and in doing so probably inadvertently drew them
away from the marsh protecting their flank. Suddenly Richard saw
a gap open up between himself and his prime target, Henry, with
his small protecting force. It was an opportunity to end the matter
quickly and cleanly, and Richard didn't hesitate.

At the forefront of his men, the king's charge took him to
within feet of his enemy, striking down his standard bearer with
one blow. By some accounts Henry fought back manfully, by
others he was so transfixed with fear he was unable to move,
as his attendants closed around to defend him. It was at that
moment, when all hung in the balance, that William Stanley
joined the battle, his men crashing into Richard's forces from the
side, driving them away from Henry, towards the marshy ground
where many were bogged down and slain.

There are many things wrong with Shakespeare's depiction of
Richard III, but in the last speech he gives him on the battlefield,
he may well have read his mind correctly. Urged to flee and save
himself for another day, he replies, 'I have set my life upon a cast,
and I will stand the hazard of the die.' Unhorsed, he was beaten
down by numbers, and it is claimed that Rhys ap Thomas was the
one to finish him with a savage blow to the head.

If in his landing Henry had asked God to judge his cause, he
seemed to have his answer now. Thomas Stanley it was, according

to tradition, who found the royal circlet Richard had worn over his helmet, and placed it on his stepson's head. After twenty-eight years as a penniless pawn in other people's games, Henry Tudor was king of England.

With his instinct for a suitable finale at the end of his play, Shakespeare gives a long speech to the new king, concluding, 'Now civil wounds are stopped; peace lives again.' Similarly, history books looking for clean endings and beginnings, cut off medieval England on 22 August 1485 and begin a new era the next day. Of course, at the time things were nothing like as clear-cut.

As a practical matter Henry was king because there was no other, but the crown had changed hands abruptly three times in the last twenty-five years, and who was to say there would not be another sudden reversal, if not immediately, certainly within the foreseeable future? The one advantage that Henry had was that so much blood had been shed in recent times, so many fathers, sons, brothers of royal and noble families sacrificed for one side or the other, that almost all that were left were women and children.

One child the new king took pains to secure immediately was Edward, the ten-year-old Earl of Warwick, sometime heir to Richard, and at present residing in Richard's castle at Sheriff Hutton in Yorkshire. Within days Edward had changed his residence to the Tower of London, and there he would remain for the rest of his short life. Henry's other potential rival, however, John de la Pole, Earl of Lincoln, had escaped from the battlefield, and he and Richard's chamberlain, Francis, Lord Lovell, would be a threat for some time.

What hadn't changed after the battle was the weakness of Henry's title to the throne. This was to be made good by his marriage to Elizabeth of York, but he had no intention of basing his claim upon his marriage, and, in any case, Elizabeth at that time was still declared to be illegitimate. Parliament could alter that, and indeed he issued writs for his first parliament within a few weeks of Bosworth, but he wasn't going to owe his crown to parliament either. Nor would he claim it by conquest or by right of battle, since he intended to date his reign to the day before Bosworth. He had basically the same problem as Henry IV before him but did even less than that predecessor to justify his right to the throne. A magnificent coronation took place on 30 October, and parliament, meeting a week later at Westminster, simply confirmed the fact that the crown belonged to Henry and his heirs, for 'the avoidance of ambiguities', without ever specifically explaining why.

This same parliament repealed Titulus Regius, all copies of which Henry ordered to be destroyed. The legitimacy of his future bride was thus restored, but since it would also restore the legitimacy of the young princes, Henry must by then have been confident the boys were dead, however that might have come about. Strangely, it is one serious crime he never accused Richard of committing.

There was more disquiet about the Act of Attainder passed early in the parliament. Though the Croyland Chronicle Continuation praises Henry's 'moderation' in only targeting thirty of his opponents, it is less happy with the reason for their attainder. They were labelled traitors because they 'traitorously' assembled men to fight at Bosworth, and then 'traitorously levied war against our sovereign lord and his true servants'. Thus, without any election, hereditary right, coronation or consecration, Henry claimed he was the true king at Bosworth, and Richard and those lawfully fighting for him were therefore rebels and traitors, whose persons, lands and property were now all forfeit, and whose heirs were disinherited. 'Oh God,' cries the chronicle, 'What assurance from this time forth are our kings to have,' if all those lawfully supporting them can be treated thus afterwards.

What it did achieve, however, was to bring into the king's hands prosperous estates spread throughout the country, while weakening further the power base of noble families. Some rewards, of course, were now due to his faithful followers, but the king was relatively frugal in what he gave away. Uncle Jasper was immediately reinstated as Earl of Pembroke, with an additional promotion to Duke of Bedford. He now married Buckingham's widow, Catherine Woodville, the dowager queen's sister, and was given the wardship of her seven-year-old son Edward, who was also restored to his father's dukedom as 3rd Duke of Buckingham.

For his inaction, Thomas Stanley became Earl of Derby. Henry's mother thus became Countess of Richmond and Derby, although she took to signing herself 'Margaret R' as though she was in fact a royal queen. She'd had very little input into her son's childhood, but would be a major influence from now on, being referred to as 'my lady the King's mother'. All her estates were returned to her, and she was given the unusual right of holding them as a 'sole person', that is, quite independently from her husband. It is probably as well that she and her son shared many characteristics, among them piety and love of learning.

Between Bosworth and the king's coronation a mystery illness known as the 'sweating sickness' swept the land, causing severe fever and carrying off its victims within twenty-four hours. Fabyan's Chronicle says most people saw this as an omen that Henry's reign would be harsh, but the chronicler himself, with the benefit of hindsight, declares it predicted that the king 'would never draw a peaceful or idle breath'. Certainly, he would have a fair share of troubles during his reign.

Under medieval laws of consanguinity Henry needed a papal dispensation to marry Elizabeth of York, since they shared an ancestor in John of Gaunt. This did not arrive before January 1486 – indeed the full confirmation came later – so it was on 18 January 1486 that the two were married at Westminster, with the new queen promised a coronation when she had done her duty and produced a son. It is possible the couple lived together before this date, as the son was duly born on 20 September, a mere eight months after the wedding. Described as strong and healthy, it is unlikely he would have been so, especially at that time, if a whole month premature. He was born at Winchester, ancient capital of kings of Britain and, true to his father's ideology, was christened Arthur. Further sons would follow: Henry on 28 June 1491, and Edmund on 21 February 1499.

Between the wedding and Arthur's birth Henry had been on a progress to the northern parts of his kingdom and had suffered the first of many attempts to unseat him. Fabyan notes he was the first king of England to have his own bodyguard – the Yeomen of the Guard – and no doubt it was they who saved him from attempts to seize or assassinate him at York on St George's Day. Francis, Lord Lovell is credited with the attack, having slipped out of sanctuary at Colchester where he had been since escaping Bosworth. At the same time the Stafford brothers, Humphrey and Thomas, distant relations of the dukes of Buckingham, tried to raise a rebellion in the Midlands, which also failed. Lovell escaped to the continent, to the court of Margaret of Burgundy, sister of the Yorkist kings Edward and Richard. The Staffords were not so lucky, fleeing to sanctuary again, this time at Culham in Oxfordshire, and being forcibly dragged out and imprisoned by the king's officers. Sanctuary, it was declared, did not apply to traitors. Humphrey was executed as an example to others, but Thomas was later pardoned.

A sterner challenge came the following year in the form of a boy known as Lambert Simnel. Simnel – which may not have been his real name – came of humble though obscure origins. His father has been variously described as a shoemaker, an organ-maker, a baker or a joiner. What the boy did have, though was a strong resemblance to the children of Edward IV. An unscrupulous Oxfordshire priest, Richard, or possibly William, Symonds, took him in hand and taught him courtly manners. The intention was to pass him off as Richard, the younger of the princes in the Tower, with Symonds aiming to become archbishop of Canterbury. Then in the autumn of 1486 it was rumoured that Edward Earl of Warwick had escaped from the Tower, and Simnel, closer in age to Warwick, took on that identity instead. In truth it didn't matter what name he took since he was merely a figurehead for the remaining Yorkists. Had they succeeded in toppling Henry, either the real Warwick, or more likely the Earl of Lincoln, would have stepped in at once. Lincoln, in fact, played along. From the safety of Burgundy he claimed he had helped Warwick escape – despite the fact that in February 1487 Henry displayed the boy alive in London.

Simnel was taken to Ireland where the Earl of Kildare, already snubbed by Henry, claimed to be convinced by the boy, and staged a lavish coronation in Dublin on 24 May 1487. An army was raised for him under the earl's younger brother Thomas, joined by the Earl of Lincoln and Lord Lovell, and by 2,000 Flemish mercenaries hired by Margaret of Burgundy under the leadership of the German mercenary Martin Schwartz.

What began well with a bold landing in the Furness area of Lancashire on 5 June came to a sorry end a little over a week later at the battle of Stoke Field, south of Newark in Nottinghamshire.

Very few English had joined as the army marched to York, and they were refused entry there. Turning south as Henry's army came north, they met the vanguard of that army led by the Earl of Oxford near the village of East Stoke. The rebels were not only outnumbered but also, apart from the mercenary element, poorly armed and armoured. While the Irish were vulnerable to the royal archers, however, the Flemings fought fiercely, and it was only weight of numbers that finally defeated them as the rest of the royal forces arrived. Schwartz was killed, as was the Earl of Lincoln and Kildare's brother. Lord Lovell disappeared, never to be seen again, possibly drowned in an attempt to swim his horse across the nearby River Trent. Centuries later, however, a skeleton that some claimed to be the missing lord was found in a secret room at his former manor in Oxfordshire.

Recognising that Simnel had only been a pawn in the hands of others, Henry pardoned him and set him to work in the royal kitchens, from whence he eventually rose to become a royal falconer. The priest Symonds was imprisoned for life. Another apparently implicated in some way, the dowager queen Elizabeth Woodville, had already been forcibly retired to a convent at Bermondsey, her estates being given to her daughter, the new queen.

The battle of Stoke is generally regarded as the last battle of the Wars of the Roses, and it ushered in a period of greater peace and stability, at least in England. Unfortunately, Henry was now about to find himself drawn into other people's conflicts on the continent.

Louis the Universal Spider had already taken chunks of the extensive lands of the Duchy of Burgundy in his policy of absorbing all the semi-independent dukedoms into a greater France. He had been checked by the marriage in 1477 of Charles the Bold's heiress Mary to Maximilian, son and heir of the Holy Roman Emperor, but Mary's death in 1482 allowed him to go further, particularly as Maximilian was then engaged in conflict with Hungary. Mary left a three-year-old son, Philip, and a two-year-old daughter, Margaret. Under the Treaty of Arras, Margaret was betrothed to Louis's heir Charles, with further chunks of Burgundy as a dowry, and the child was taken away to be brought up at the French court.

Charles VIII of France was thirteen when his father died in 1483, with his sister Anne appointed as Regent, but within a few years he, too, was seeking to expand his domain, this time looking west to Brittany, ruled by the ailing Duke Francis II. Now the English King Henry had a dilemma. Charles and his sister had generously supported his invasion of England, and he had a peace treaty with France, but Francis had sheltered him for many years. Initially, when Francis asked for help against a French invasion Henry prevaricated, while negotiating with both sides to try and achieve a settlement. Edward Woodville, the queen's uncle, was not so hesitant, however, launching his own poorly planned expedition and getting himself and most of his small band of followers killed. A few weeks later Francis was forced to sign the Treaty of Sablé, acknowledging himself to be a vassal of the French king, and promising his daughter and heiress Anne would not marry without Charles's consent. A matter of weeks after that he himself died, and the eleven-year-old Anne became Duchess of Brittany.

For centuries there had been close links between England and Brittany, and Henry was also anxious there should be a friendly coast across the Channel. In January 1489, therefore, he asked parliament for money for an army to confront 'the ancient enemies of the realm'. The vast sum demanded was only reluctantly granted, and collecting it was another matter. Resistance in Yorkshire resulted in Henry Percy, newly restored to his earldom of Northumberland, being killed by a mob. The king, meanwhile, promised help for Brittany, though at the Bretons' expense, and persisted in his diplomacy, in particular trying to put together a coalition of countries to defend Brittany against French expansion.

Before his death, Francis had been trying to arrange for the marriage of Anne to Maximilian, now titled King of the Romans. As he had checked French ambitions before, he might do so again with the forces of the Holy Roman Empire. Maximilian was not a natural ally for Henry, having repeatedly allowed Margaret of Burgundy, the Dowager Duchess, to shelter his enemies at her court in the Low Countries. Nonetheless, in February 1489 a treaty was signed for the defence of the Bretons.

Henry was also negotiating with a new rising power in Europe. Spain was moving towards unification following the marriage in 1469 of Ferdinand of Aragon and Isabella of Castile, and they were looking for links, especially by marriages for their five children, with countries capable of checking the power of France. A marriage was proposed between Henry's son Arthur and their youngest daughter Catherine, and though the Spanish initially regarded Henry's bargaining position as weaker than their own, he refused to be bullied. The treaty finally signed by Ferdinand and Isabella in March 1489 not only provided for the marriage and for a dowry of 200,000 crowns, but for mutual support in action against the French. Henry later realised the terms of the treaty could bind him to war with France indefinitely at Spain's request, as neither was permitted to make a separate peace until his territorial demands were met, and Henry's – comprising Normandy and Aquitaine – were considerably larger than Spain's. He only ratified the treaty in 1490, and then with amendments, and it was only ever partially implemented. In the meantime he sent some 6,000 men to Brittany, and in May 1489 English forces from Calais defeated French ambitions in the Burgundian Netherlands. In spite of this, in July of that year Maximilian made a separate peace with Charles, apparently abandoning his aim of marrying Anne of Brittany. Indeed, he advised her to get rid of the foreign troops in her lands and give in to France.

Henry persisted with his diplomacy, however, and though Spanish troops only briefly visited Brittany, he was determined to achieve something in return for his efforts. Maximilian, though still pre-occupied with affairs in the east of Europe, was persuaded to return to his marriage plan, and at the end of 1490 was married by proxy to Anne, who began calling herself Queen of the Romans. There were factions within Brittany, however, opposed to a Burgundian 'takeover', and, with mutinies among Breton forces over a lack of pay, the French invasion when it came in the spring of 1491 met little resistance. Once again appealed to for help, Henry sent some men, but he was not yet ready for a full-scale war, and no assistance was provided by Maximilian or the Spanish.

The matter was finally settled by Charles storming into the Breton capital Rennes, and offering marriage to the beleaguered duchess, who, with little other option, was forced to accept him. There was a small matter of her existing proxy marriage to Maximilian, and Charles's legally binding betrothal to the eleven-year-old Margaret of Burgundy, both of which needed papal dispensations to annul, but these were readily forthcoming, albeit a few weeks after the actual wedding, which took place on 6 December 1491. Pope Innocent was anxious to clear all obstacles from the path of Charles so he could invade the kingdom of Naples in support of the pope's war against its Aragonese ruler.

With the loss both of Brittany and of his allies, Henry stood to come off badly from his continental entanglements, and he really could not afford to lose face at this time. He had spent some £124,000 on supporting the Bretons already. Instead, he proposed to the parliament called for October 1491 that he would himself lead an army to France, not in support of someone else's rights but to claim his own. To some this meant nothing less than the re-opening of the Hundred Years War, and parliament was generous in its response. Henry's ambitions, however, were considerably more limited. Through most of the following year, therefore, while men, ships and supplies were being assembled on a larger scale than for many years, he was still negotiating with Charles, persuading him it would be in everyone's interests to settle matters peacefully.

In October 1492 Henry and his army finally sailed for France. On 18 October Boulogne was put under siege, and nine days later Charles, anxious to leave for Italy, asked for a truce. The resulting Treaty of Étaples, signed on 3 November, gave Henry all and more than he had wanted, payment of all his expenses in Brittany, plus all the arrears of a pension that had been owed to Edward IV under the old treaty of Picquigny, the whole amounting to some 50,000 crowns a year, payable over a considerable period. Returning to England in mid-December, Henry felt well able to ignore the dissatisfaction of those who had wanted to reconquer Normandy, which had never been a realistic prospect. Besides, he now had further challenges at home to deal with.

The name of this latest challenger has come down to history as Perkin Warbeck. By his own later confession, freely given or otherwise, he was the son of John Osbeck, otherwise Jehan de Warbecque, of Tournai in Flanders, and he must certainly have known the place, as many he referred to appear in the town archives. Polydore Vergil is emphatic that it was Margaret of Burgundy who, noticing the boy's resemblance to her nephew Richard, younger of the princes in the Tower, set about coaching him in secret in all the ways of the York family and English court, so he could impersonate the prince. Other chronicles disagree and say Warbeck was appearing as Richard before he met Margaret. There may have been a strong family resemblance, but it is not clear that Margaret ever met her young nephew. It is also interesting that no pretender to the throne ever claimed to be the older prince, suggesting it was clear he was dead but the younger boy's fate was less certain.

Apart from Vergil's claim, Warbeck seems first to have been identified as Richard in Cork, Ireland, where he had travelled in 1491 in the employ of a Breton merchant of fine textiles. This time the Earl of Kildare, pardoned for his assistance to Simnel, would have nothing to do with him, but the rival Earl of Desmond gave him support. Next, he was passed on to Charles VIII of France who treated him as the 'duke of York' but was forced to expel him in 1492 under the terms of the Treaty of Étaples.

Now he came – or returned – to the Netherlands and the court of Margaret of Burgundy, who purported to examine him carefully before acknowledging him as her nephew. The story was that Richard had been spared his brother's death because of his youth and innocence, and had been smuggled abroad and brought up by those sympathetic to the Yorkist family. Margaret in turn convinced her step-son-in-law Maximilian, who invited Warbeck, as Richard IV of England, to his father's funeral in 1493.

Henry didn't believe a word of it, dispatching spies to the Netherlands, and claiming to have uncovered the boy's humble origins. When young Duke Philip of Burgundy refused to expel him, the king imposed a two-year trade embargo between England and the Netherlands, despite Philip – who was only fourteen and still subject to a regency – assuring him he had no powers to limit Margaret's activities.

Unsurprisingly, there was talk among some of the lesser English lords about the claims of Warbeck, and Sir Robert Clifford either volunteered or was sent to the Netherlands to find out the truth.

It has been suggested that Clifford was also one of Henry's agents, as his report, suggesting Warbeck really was Richard, was quickly followed in England by the arrest of a number of these lords, most prominently Sir William Stanley the Lord Chamberlain. The only involvement proved against Stanley was the comment that, if Warbeck really was Richard, he would not fight against him, but that was enough. Notwithstanding his role in winning the crown for Henry, he was beheaded in February 1495 as a traitor to that crown. Clifford, by contrast, was given a full pardon and a gift of £500 from the king.

In July 1495, with the backing of Margaret and Maximilian, Warbeck finally prepared to invade England. Before he left the Netherlands, he promised that Maximilian and Duke Philip would inherit his rights in England, France, Wales and Ireland in the event of his death, but it is likely they welcomed his departure as the trade embargo was already damaging the interests of Flemish merchants. The 'invasion', however, was a complete failure. Warbeck himself never set foot on land, and his advance party, landing near Deal in Kent, far from being welcomed as they expected by a county notorious for rebellions, were set upon and killed or captured by the local inhabitants.

Trying his luck next in Ireland he fared little better. A short siege of Waterford by his ships in the harbour and Desmond's forces on land was seen off by Henry's Lord Deputy of Ireland, Sir Edward Poynings. By November 1495 Warbeck had moved on to Scotland, where he was given a warm welcome by King James IV.

As a general policy James was inclined towards peace with England, so it may well be that he believed Warbeck's claims. He certainly encouraged his marriage to James's kinswoman, Lady Catherine Gordon, in January 1496, though as Lady Catherine was only a distant cousin he may have been hedging his bets. By the summer, however, he was prepared to back him to the extent of a joint invasion of England.

Once again, Henry had a spy in the right place. One John Ramsey warned the king that the invasion would be small and poorly provisioned, and it would only need a small force to defeat it, and so it proved. Crossing the border at Coldstream on 20 September

1496 with an army of no more than 1,400 men, the self-proclaimed King Richard found no support at all in 'his' kingdom, and with the threat of Lord Neville advancing towards him with some 4,000 men, very rapidly retreated to Scotland. There were, however, some serious consequences for Henry.

James IV had broken a peace treaty by taking part in the invasion and the English king decided to retaliate with force. The parliament that met in January 1497 was reluctantly persuaded to vote an enormous sum for a war with Scotland. While there was some resistance to paying this new tax throughout the country, it was in Cornwall that open rebellion broke out. Why, they demanded, should poverty-stricken Cornwall have to pay for a skirmish in far-off Scotland? Then, armed only with bows and farming tools, they set out in May to march to London. Along the way they swelled to some 15,000 men, and acquired a commander in Lord Audley, adopting the old excuse that they only wanted to free the king from his evil advisors.

Whatever their intentions, Henry was taking no chances. As they marched unhindered through Taunton, Wells and Winchester, he sent his wife and six-year-old son Henry to the Tower for safety, set guards on all the bridges over the Thames, and called up the army being prepared for Scotland under Lord Daubeney. To the great disappointment of the Cornish, the men of Kent refused once again to join a rebellion, and by the time the rebels were camped at Blackheath south of Greenwich, many were repenting their rashness. Some slipped away. Others offered to trade Audley and the Cornish leader Flamank for a general pardon. Instead, early in the morning on 17 June Henry sent in the army, and within hours some 2,000 of the Cornish were dead and many more captured, including the leaders Audley and Flamank, who were rapidly tried, condemned and put to death. As so often, the rank and file were pardoned, but only on payment of heavy fines that in fact brought in more than the tax they had complained of.

While still preparing for war with Scotland, Henry had not given up on diplomacy, sending his trusted negotiator Richard Foxe, Bishop of Durham, to persuade James to hand over Warbeck and pay compensation as the price of peace. By the time Foxe arrived, however, Warbeck had already left, sailing with his new wife and a few supporters from Ayr on 7 July. There is a suggestion that James had planned an invasion of England on two fronts, himself from the north and Warbeck from the already unsettled West Country. He certainly made a raid across the border on the bishop's castle at Norham but was quickly driven back. If Warbeck was supposed to co-ordinate, however, he spoiled the plan by calling at Ireland on the way, and not landing at Whitesand Bay near Land's End until 7 September.

Leaving his wife at St Michael's Mount, he progressed to Bodmin gathering men on the way, and there proclaimed himself King Richard IV of England. An attempted siege of Exeter was a failure, however, and by the time he reached Taunton it was clear Henry's forces were closing around him. On the night of 21 September, with Lord Daubeney little more than twenty miles away at Glastonbury, Warbeck slipped away from his army and fled towards Southampton, no doubt hoping to find a ship for the continent. Pursued and in danger of being overtaken, he could only reach Beaulieu Abbey where he claimed sanctuary, but then, realising his cause was hopeless, he surrendered and threw himself on the king's mercy.

Henry was merciful. Once his full confession was written and read in public, the pretender, still only twenty-three years old, was permitted to reside at court, while his wife became a member of the queen's household. Clearly, though, Warbeck was a prisoner rather than a guest, and on 9 June 1498 he escaped. Quickly recaptured, this time he was imprisoned in the Tower, where in November 1499 a plot to release both him and the Earl of Warwick was discovered. Whether fully involved or not, both were condemned to death. On 23 November Warbeck was hanged at Tyburn, and six days later Warwick, a prisoner for fourteen years, was finally beheaded on Tower Hill.

There was clearly some urgency at the time for the king to rid himself of challenges for his throne – another pretender, Ralph Wilford, had been hanged in February of that year – for he was about to achieve a major alliance with Spain. The marriage between his son Arthur and Catherine of Aragon, initially proposed a decade before, was about to become a reality. It was probably the rapid success of Charles VIII of France in driving all before him in Italy in 1494, that convinced Ferdinand of Aragon of the need for an alliance of the enemies of France, and though Charles had been driven back the following year, the Spanish confirmed the marriage treaty in 1497. Under its terms Catherine was to come to England when Arthur reached the age of fourteen, which would be in 1500, and each applied to the pope for permission to marry under the legal age. Her dowry of 200,000 gold crowns would be payable in instalments, half immediately after the wedding, and the other half in equal parts over the following two years. It was also stipulated that Catherine would have no right to inherit Spain unless all the other children of Ferdinand and Isabella died without heirs.

In 1499 there were two proxy marriages between Arthur and Catherine, but her father would not send her to England until he was satisfied Henry had achieved a settled peace. His ambassador, indeed, helped Bishop Foxe to negotiate a long-term peace treaty with Scotland. Finally, in October 1501, Catherine arrived to meet her bridegroom, who declared that no woman in the world could be more agreeable to him. They were married a few weeks later on 14 November at St Paul's Cathedral, with the bride escorted to the altar by Arthur's ten-year-old brother Henry.

Arthur had been brought up from babyhood as a future king of England and was clearly the joy of his father's heart. He had been instructed well in the art of government, and, following his wedding and the month of feasting and revelry that celebrated it, he departed for Ludlow Castle with his bride to gain practical experience in governing his principality of Wales.

At that point Henry must have felt well pleased with life in general and his position as monarch in particular. After sixteen years on the throne he was unshakeably secure, and recognised and courted by the leading powers of Europe. Always more inclined to peace than war, his diplomacy meant that, although he had signed up to Ferdinand's Holy League against France in 1496, he was never more than a sleeping partner. He placed more value on the Treaty of Étaples made in 1492, and when Charles VIII died suddenly in

1498, hitting his head on the lintel of a door, he renewed the treaty with his successor Louis XII.

He had a treaty, too, with Archduke Philip of Burgundy, now running his own affairs and seeming likely to inherit not only his father's empire but, through his marriage to Joanna of Aragon, Catherine's sister, at least a part of Spain as well. The treaty, known in the Netherlands as Magnus Intercursus, had put an end to the trade embargo that was harming both countries, enabling the English Merchant Adventurers company, which had a monopoly in trading English cloth, to move its business back from Calais to Antwerp.

Trade was important to Henry, as shown by his many treaties with countries like Denmark and the city states of Northern Italy. It would also have been the prospect of opening new trade routes to the spices of the east that led him to sponsor John Cabot and his sons to sail under an English flag to 'all parts of the eastern, western and northern seas', to discover unknown lands to be claimed for the English crown. Cautious as always, Henry put none of his own money into the venture but was to receive a fifth of any profit from the voyage. Cabot sailed from Bristol on 2 May 1497, and, like Columbus before him, found not the west coast of Asia but the east coast of present-day Canada and America, returning to report to Henry in August of that year. Though there was no profit from the original voyages, these discoveries would have a profound effect on the later history of England, while at the time adding to the prestige of the English king. If the Spanish could discover a New World in the west, well, so could he.

Perhaps more than most, Henry was aware of the steady rise in importance of the middle class, the merchants, craftsmen and manufacturers, at the expense of the established nobility. The latter had been much thinned by years of war, and now were to be restricted by his own laws against the giving of liveries and maintenance of huge retinues. He could not abolish retinues entirely since, when needed, they formed the basis of his army, but it was certainly his intention that no-one should have the power that Richard, Duke of York and the Earl of Warwick had wielded in bringing down monarchs. The court later to be called the Star

Chamber, which was originally a committee of his council, was particularly given the task of dealing with over-mighty subjects who could coerce lesser tribunals.

There were probably very few people that Henry trusted absolutely and almost all of them had been with him for at least part of his exile in Brittany and France. Uncle Jasper Tudor would have been the chief of his confidants until his death in 1495. For military matters the Earl of Oxford and Giles Daubeney were relied on, and for general wisdom and diplomacy, John Morton and Richard Foxe. Morton became Archbishop of Canterbury in 1486 and chancellor in 1487, holding that office until his death in 1500, while Foxe was successively Bishop of Exeter, Bishop of Bath & Wells (none of which places he ever visited), Bishop of Durham, and finally Bishop of Winchester. These men, together with Reginald Bray, a most trusted servant of his mother and afterwards chancellor of the Duchy of Lancaster, made up the core of Henry's royal council through which he largely ruled the country. He had a rather old-fashioned view of parliament, calling it only when he needed money and increasingly rarely later in his reign.

Though Henry has come down to us as a rather grim, cold figure, this was clearly not the case, at least to this point in his reign. His accounts are full of payments to morris dancers, actors, clowns and jugglers, while he was especially fond of music. Although pious and conventionally religious, he did not think it necessary to dress in dark and dowdy robes. Indeed, he felt that magnificent clothes, jewels and pageantry were necessary to a king in order to inspire awe in his subjects. He was generous in almsgiving, and in spending on the various royal palaces, refacing the Palace of Placentia in red brick and re-naming it Greenwich, and completely rebuilding the palace at Sheen, which he then called after his first title, Richmond Palace.

Although no great scholar, like his mother he was fond of books and learning, patronising the new technology of Caxton's printing press, and encouraging writers and learned men to gather at his court. These men, such as John Colet, William Grocin, Thomas Linacre, Thomas More and Erasmus, were bringing new ideas, new debates to England, and adding newly translated Greek philosophers to their previously studied Roman equivalents.

Thus far then, King Henry had achieved all and more than he had set out to achieve when bidding for a crown. And then it all began to go wrong.

In March 1502, first Catherine and then Arthur fell ill. It may well have been a return of the sweating sickness that had attended Henry's first weeks as king. Whatever the cause, Catherine recovered but Arthur did not, passing away on 2 April 1502. When the news was brought to the king, his first thought was to send for the queen and break it to her himself. Then the royal couple took turns in comforting each other, both distraught with grief at the loss of a favourite child.

In among his personal grief, though, the king must also have felt a pang of fear for his dynasty. Of the three sons Elizabeth had given him, two had now died in the last two years, young Edmund being only around a year old when he died in 1500. All now depended on Henry, who, until this moment, despite being loaded with titles such as Lord Lieutenant of Ireland and Warden of the Scots Marches, had probably been intended for a career in the church. Even as Elizabeth reassured her husband that they were both young enough to have more sons, another thought might have gone to the Spanish alliance, and possibly another to the enormous dowry Catherine had brought with her.

It has been said that Henry was never the same after the death of his son, but fate had further blows in store. True to her word, Elizabeth was pregnant again within weeks, but the birth of a daughter in February of the following year was quickly followed by the deaths of both mother and child – perhaps unsurprising at the time, as Elizabeth died on her thirty-seventh birthday. We are told that Henry shut himself away for days, refusing to speak to anyone. Though their marriage had been purely political, it seems that a true affection had grown up between them. The king would become even more isolated when, a few months later, his eldest daughter, Margaret, departed to marry King James of Scotland. Perhaps some of Henry's wilder suggestions at the time might be put down to the distraction of his grief.

At one point, for example, he proposed that he himself might marry Catherine of Aragon, a suggestion firmly vetoed by her mother Isabella of Castile. Much more conventionally, on 25 June 1503, the twelve-year-old Prince Henry was formally betrothed to the seventeen-year-old widow. He was much too young to marry, so this might perhaps be seen as an insurance policy by the king, since Ferdinand had already asked for Catherine's dowry back and Henry in return had demanded the other half of the money.

Papal dispensation was needed for such a match, and this issue was complicated by disagreements as to whether Catherine's marriage to Arthur had been consummated. Catherine and her mother insisted it had not, but Henry declared it had, his own mother having devised an unprecedented 'bedding' ritual. The death of the pope in August delayed matters, and the issue was still unresolved, at least to Henry's satisfaction, when Isabella herself died in November 1504.

Now the situation was changed, and it was Ferdinand who was most anxious to preserve the English connection. Without his wife he had no claim to rule Castile, which Isabella willed to her daughter Joanna, and then to Joanna's son Charles. Ferdinand was only named as regent until Joanna returned to Spain from the Netherlands, or if she proved unfit to rule. With these internal divisions Spain did not seem quite such a desirable ally for Henry, and in 1505 Prince Henry was told to formally protest his doubts about marriage to Catherine, despite the fact that the papal dispensation had now been delivered. Catherine, meanwhile, was living in fairly frugal conditions and protesting her poverty to her father.

Henry began to look closer to home for a bride for his son. The Netherlands had always been an important trading partner for England, and with Joanna's husband Duke Philip looking set to control at least Castile, as well as the Netherlands and Holy Roman Empire, Philip's six-year-old daughter Eleanor was a possibility. Ferdinand, however, was determined to hold on to power. In an abrupt change of policy he signed a treaty with his long-time enemy France, and married the niece of the French king. If he could have another son, Joanna and Philip's hopes could be thwarted. Meanwhile he declared that Joanna was mad and unfit to rule.

In January 1506 Philip and Joanna set off for Spain, to take Castile by force if Ferdinand would not give it up. A storm in the Channel, however, saw them shipwrecked on the coast of England near Weymouth. With a great show of friendship, Henry welcomed them to Windsor with feasting and revelry, but behind the scenes some hard bargaining was going on. The outcome was very much to Henry's advantage. He would support Philip against Ferdinand and watch over the Netherlands for him. In exchange Philip must hand over Edward Earl of Suffolk, who, living in Burgundy and calling himself the White Rose, had been representing himself as the last hope of the Yorkist cause. In addition, a new trade agreement was made which gave every advantage to English traders. Three marriages were also proposed – Henry himself to Philip's sister Margaret, Prince Henry to Philip's daughter Eleanor, and Mary Tudor, Henry's youngest daughter, to Philip's son Charles.

Most of these agreements came to nothing. The White Rose was duly handed over and imprisoned in the Tower, but the trade agreement was never ratified. Margaret flatly refused to marry Henry, and though Mary Tudor was later married by proxy to Charles, the match was eventually called off. As for Prince Henry, as soon as Philip had left, the marriage with Catherine was again being promoted, with the king demanding the rest of her dowry before it could go ahead. This appeared a wise move when Philip died a few months later. Ferdinand promptly declared Joanna was mad and locked her up, thereby enabling himself to rule as regent in her place. The stories of her madness have generally been discounted in recent times. Henry had certainly not found her so during her stay in England. He offered to marry her himself, but again this came to nothing.

The king cuts rather a sad and isolated figure at this time. He seems never to have been close to his younger son. Though Prince Henry was now in his mid-teens and living at court, he had received none of the training in kingship lavished on his brother. He was not present at council meetings and rarely at audiences with foreign representatives. He had no household of his own, and his friends were chosen by his father. The king's obsession seemed to be to keep him from the world lest he should die like his brother, a fate which seemed perilously close in 1508 when the sweating sickness returned and carried off three of those serving the prince.

It is at this time, too, that Henry is accused of avarice. He had always been careful in money matters, like Henry V before him, scrupulously checking and signing off his accounts, and managing to turn a profit even on his wars. Now, however, he is accused of making money his passion. This is probably an overstatement. As a penniless exile he would have been well aware of the value of money, and that, while it could not always buy power of itself, certainly power would be unattainable without it. By the same token, reducing the wealth of the nobility would be a way of keeping them in their place. It is noticeable that in later years he drew his money not from income voted by parliament, but mainly from fines, dues and benevolences or gifts from the wealthy.

In 1495 a committee of the king's council was established known as the Council Learned in Law. Under the direction of Reginald Bray its function was to explore and enforce the king's feudal rights. It was this council that became most associated with Henry's accumulation of wealth, particularly after Bray's death in 1503, when his work was taken over by Edmund Dudley and Sir Richard Empson. Thereafter the accusation was made of invented dues and extortionate fines, though Polydore Vergil claims the king tempered his severity with mercy, so that 'their plucked feathers grew back.' Nonetheless, many ended up with large debts to the king, which again gave him mastery over them.

This grasping for money seems not to have been an inborn characteristic of the king, who had certainly been generous enough before. Such as it was, it probably came from greater insecurity as the king grew older and became increasingly ill. Fear for the succession was a constant with Tudor monarchs, and Henry probably wished his son to have sufficient resources to defend his throne. Possibly, he also had a poor opinion of Henry's ability to raise money for himself.

From 1507 the king was repeatedly ill, probably already suffering from tuberculosis, and with failing eyesight. He was still firmly in control, however, and still demanding the remainder of Catherine's dowry before her marriage to Henry could go ahead. Even when a new Spanish ambassador brought bills of exchange for the dowry the following year, the king quibbled. By the end of 1508 Ferdinand was demanding either his daughter back or the marriage, but by then it was clear that Henry's illness was such that it would only be a matter of time before his reign came to an end.

On 21 April 1509 King Henry died at Richmond Palace. At his bedside were his mother and the children Henry and Mary, and some accounts say his last instruction to his son was that he was to marry Catherine. He had asked for a plain but dignified funeral, 'avoiding damnable pomp and outrageous superfluities', but it was a magnificent affair – though, in accordance with tradition, it was not attended by his son. Some half a dozen years before he had begun to add a splendid chapel to Westminster Abbey, intending it as a shrine for Henry VI. Instead, it had become the resting place of his beloved wife, and now Henry joined her, their tomb later to be adorned with remarkable, life-like effigies.

As a usurper he was considerably more successful than most. Though history has not always been kind to him, overshadowed as he was by the charisma (or infamy) of his son, still those at the time appreciated his gifts. The Fabyan Chronicle declares 'sufficient laud and praise cannot be put into writing, considering the continual peace and tranquillity which he kept this his land and commons in ... subduing his outward enemies ... by his great policy and wisdom, more than by shedding of Christian blood or cruel war'. Furthermore, it adds, his noble acts exceeded those of all his predecessors back to the Conquest. He was, it claims, nothing less than a second Solomon.

Henry VIII

'How soon this mightiness meets misery'

– Shakespeare

When we think of Henry VIII we tend to picture a burly, defiant, magnificent figure, a man in his middle years, the Holbein portrait, perhaps. So it comes as something of a shock to find that when Henry became king of England in April 1509 he was still two months short of his eighteenth birthday. Nor do we look for his likeness anywhere else, yet there is a close parallel, and one that was clear to those at the time, not burdened with our willingness to divide history at 1485.

Henry's maternal grandfather was King Edward IV, tall, handsome, auburn-haired and affable. Only a year or so older than Henry when he took the throne, he loved magnificence, followed his own way, married for love rather than policy, and indulged all his pleasures to the full. It seems fairly clear that, though his upbringing and passage to the throne were markedly different, it is Henry's swashbuckling Yorkist grandfather that he took after, rather than his cautious, rather dour father.

This likeness may have been encouraged by his mother, Edward's daughter Elizabeth, who had charge of his upbringing for the first eleven years. She chose his brilliant but not always conventional tutors, and rising stars in the new learning spreading through Europe were also welcomed at Henry's childhood home, Eltham Palace. Indeed, one day in 1499, Thomas More and Erasmus were entertained in the royal nursery by an eight-year-old Henry and his younger sister.

What Henry didn't have, of course, was Grandfather Edward's turbulent and militarily successful teenage years. Instead, the loss of his brother and, more devastatingly, his mother, brought Henry under the sterner guidance of his father, and the suffocating over-protection of his life at court. Even his own chamber could only be accessed through that of his father, who, in his late forties, must have seemed ancient to his teenaged son. Indulged in everything but freedom, young Henry thus grew up intelligent, athletic, full of theoretical knowledge gleaned from a classical education, but with an insecurity born, at least partly, from his own father's fears for him, and a hypochondria that would last a lifetime.

On the rare occasions when Henry was allowed a moment in the spotlight he had revealed an exuberant personality, and becoming king after the long dark years of his father's decline must have seemed like emerging into the sunshine. There was some caution, though, in handing over power to so young an heir, and it was agreed the old king's council would be retained, with Lady Margaret Beaufort acting as regent until Henry reached his eighteenth birthday.

It is unclear whether the first two decisive acts of the new reign were prompted by the old king's dying wishes, by the council or by Henry's own initiative. A general pardon for all crimes except treason, murder and serious felonies was certainly traditional for a dying king, and this was formally confirmed by Henry immediately afterwards. Whether the old king had added a wish to recompense all those wrongly fined by Empson and Dudley is more controversial. What is certain is that these two were quickly made the scapegoats for all the extortion of the last few years. Promptly arrested and imprisoned in the Tower, they would later be attainted on trumped-up charges of treason, and beheaded.

Again, while some accounts say Henry VII directed his son to marry Catherine of Aragon, Hall's Chronicle says the suggestion came from the council, to avoid her taking her enormous dowry elsewhere. Hall also declares that this was 'much murmured against in the beginning, and ever more and more', though this may be with the benefit of hindsight. In other accounts it is Henry himself who impulsively proposed to the lady, causing surprise and some shock after all the shilly-shallying of recent years. The quietness of the wedding that took place at Greenwich on 11 June 1509 may well argue for the latter, and for a residual fear that, even now, someone would try and prevent it.

In marked contrast was the coronation of king and queen that took place on midsummer day, 24 June. Hall devotes pages to descriptions of the clothes, the processions, the streets hung with tapestries and cloth of gold, the ceremonial and the feasting that followed. As for the king himself, he declares, 'I cannot express the gifts of grace and nature that God hath endowed him withal.'

One gift that was missing, however, seems to have been a disposition towards hard work. Though Henry would happily wear himself out with hours of hunting, jousting, games of tennis and other athletic pursuits, he showed a marked reluctance to appear in the council chamber and attend to the affairs of state. Even Polydore Vergil is moved to remark that, like a calf baulking at the yoke, the young king seemed to baulk at taking on his responsibilities.

It may be that the council was happy to continue running things on his behalf. Lady Margaret Beaufort died the day after Henry's eighteenth birthday, but the core of the council still reflected her son's cautious rule. Chief among the councillors were William Warham, Archbishop of Canterbury and chancellor, Richard Foxe, Bishop of Winchester and keeper of the privy seal, and Thomas Howard, Earl of Surrey and treasurer. It was tedious, however, to have to run after the king wherever he was to be found in order to obtain his instructions or his signature on some document, and when a younger man was found who would happily do so, he quickly obtained a position of prominence among these older established councillors.

Thomas Wolsey was thirty-six years old when Henry came to power. The son of an Ipswich butcher, he had boundless ambition and almost equally boundless energy and ability. He had entered the church because that was the only way a man from common stock could achieve power at the time, and by serving as chaplain to various people had come to be secretary to Richard Foxe. Foxe saw him as an ally against the more military-minded faction led by Thomas Howard, and in 1509 secured for him the relatively lowly position of King's Almoner, with a seat on the council. The Almoner, responsible for distributing alms on behalf of the king, had constant contact with Henry. Nor did Wolsey see it as in any way beneath his dignity to act as messenger boy for the council. It was a situation that gave a clever man unparalleled possibilities for influence at the highest level, and Wolsey was certainly a clever man.

Within a short time, Wolsey had become indispensable to the king and popular with the young – and not so young – courtiers who were the king's friends. An excellent reader of character, he knew the king was idle rather than stupid or gullible, and began sifting the information presented to him and offering a range of options for the king to choose from, rather than laying before him an open book. The king's policies became Wolsey's policies and vice versa. Thus, when in 1511 the king decided he wanted to go to war, war, and how to succeed at it, also became the policy of Thomas Wolsey, no doubt to the infinite regret of his patron Richard Foxe.

At the beginning of that year there had been great national rejoicing. After producing a premature stillborn daughter the previous year, on 1 January 1511 Queen Catherine had given birth to a son. Named Henry after his proud father, the child had been christened with great pomp on 6 January, but the rejoicing was cut short just a few weeks later when on 22 February young Henry died. At just over seven weeks, he would be the longest lived of any son born to Catherine.

It may have been this loss that turned Henry's mind towards proving himself in other ways. He had grown up with a head full of stories of King Arthur, Alexander and Henry V. He was young and strong and brave, and longed to emulate their deeds and win glory for himself. After all, was he not descended from Arthur himself, and, more certainly, from the widow of that same King Henry?

After his brief successful foray to Boulogne, Henry VII had stayed well clear of the ongoing continental struggles, but Henry had already shown a willingness to abandon his father's policies. When in 1511 Pope Julius proposed a Holy League against the

French, including Ferdinand of Spain and Holy Roman Emperor Maximilian, the English king was quick to join. Wolsey had recommended this, against the wishes of the more conservative members of the council, and he was involved in the Treaty of Westminster which followed, whereby Henry agreed with his father-in-law Ferdinand to assist him against their common enemies.

A less than successful expedition to help Ferdinand in Navarre in 1512 was discouraging, but Henry took little persuading by his queen and by Wolsey to plan for a greater attack on France to be led by himself in 1513. The papal offer of the kingdom of France and the title 'Most Christian King' was a further incentive, though that seems to have died with the pope himself in February of that year. War with France, of course, always threatened to bring in Scotland on his northern border, so while Wolsey was meticulously organising an army to attack from Calais, Thomas Howard, Earl of Surrey, and his son Edmund were dispatched with another force to the north of England. Another of Howard's sons, Edward, had been appointed Admiral, and was already having success against French ships in the Channel, clearing the way for the army to embark for France. Henry had inherited the nucleus of a navy consisting of seven warships and had added to this, so that Howard had command of eighteen vessels. In the spring of 1513, however, they met a French fleet reinforced by ships from the Mediterranean bearing heavy guns known as basilisks. In the ensuing action one English vessel was sunk by cannon fire, and the admiral, leading an assault on the French flagship, drowned after being forced overboard in full armour.

The vanguard of Henry's army nevertheless crossed in safety to France that summer and proceeded to besiege the town of Thérouanne to the south of Calais. Henry himself arrived with the main army of some 11,000 men in July, ignoring a warning from James of Scotland that if he did not leave France, James would invade England. Before he left, Henry had secured his realm from other challenges by executing without trial the Duke of Suffolk – the White Rose – who had spent the last half a dozen years in the Tower.

On 16 August the French attempted to relieve the siege of Thérouanne and were seen off in what the English referred to as the Battle of the Spurs, the name relating to the speed with which the French spurred their horses away when they saw the size of the English army. There has been a suggestion, however, that this was a sham, staged by agreement between Maximilian and Louis of France, who wanted to give Henry a small victory before they came to terms with each other, which they were already negotiating to do. Be that as it may, Thérouanne fell to the English on 24 August, and in September the army moved on to another successful siege at Tournai.

In the meantime, James of Scotland had been as good as his word, crossing the border into England on 22 August and taking Norham and three smaller castles before establishing a strong camp at the top of Flodden Edge, He anticipated an English army would approach from the south and be forced to fight uphill, giving him a major advantage. In fact, three English armies were mustered. The men of the north rallied to the aged Earl of Surrey, while his son Thomas, the new admiral, brought men and guns from the English fleet at Newcastle. A second army, to assemble in the Midlands, was commissioned by Queen Catherine as regent for her husband, while Catherine herself raised the men of the south and marched with them as far as Buckingham.

They were not needed. Though Surrey was seventy, crippled with arthritis and often transported in a wheeled conveyance – the Scots jibed at the 'old crooked earl in a cart' – he was an experienced and wily commander and knew the lie of the land well. Apparently withdrawing his army from its initial contact with James, he marched them around to the north of the Scots, to the gentler slopes of Branxton Hill. There, on 9 September in pouring rain, was fought the battle of Flodden.

The English artillery quickly neutralised the Scottish guns, and though the initial Scots charge against Edmund Howard on the English right wing was successful, the impact of the gunfire on the massed Scots ranks of the main army brought them down from their commanding position on the hill to be cut to pieces in hand-to-hand fighting below. By the end of the day, among many thousands of Scottish dead, lay the flower of Scotland: some thirteen earls, fourteen lords, three bishops and the king of Scotland himself. Though Wolsey had sought to sideline Surrey in England, denying him the honours expected to be won in France, in fact he had achieved a much more significant victory, leaving Scotland with an infant king and a long regency, initially in the hands of Henry's sister, Margaret Tudor.

King Henry, returning to England in October, felt satisfied with his gains. He had not conquered France but he had been true to his alliance, which his allies had not. When Louis was forced to make peace with the pope at that time, Henry could claim at least some of the credit. The following year, those who had served him well got their rewards. Wolsey became first Bishop of Lincoln, and then later in the year Archbishop of York. Thomas Howard became Duke of Norfolk, with the title earl of Surrey passing to his eldest son, another Thomas. Also benefitting was Charles Brandon, the son of the standard bearer of Henry VII who had been killed at Bosworth. Brandon had been brought up at court with Henry and was his closest friend. He had distinguished himself in France and was now created Duke of Suffolk – a title perhaps a little lacking in good taste as its previous holder had only been executed the year before.

The year 1514 also saw a change in policy towards France. Annoyed at the machinations of Ferdinand and Maximilian, Henry signed a peace treaty with Louis. Negotiated by Wolsey, it provided for generous 'pensions' to be paid by the French, which Henry interpreted as 'tributes'. More controversially it also provided for Henry's sister, the eighteen-year-old Mary Tudor, to marry fifty-two-year-old Louis, whose wife had recently died. Mary would later insist she only agreed to this on condition that, after Louis's death, she might marry the man of her choice. Be that as it may, later in the year she was escorted to France by the dukes of Norfolk and Suffolk. On 9 October she was married to Louis, and on 5 November she was crowned Queen of France. Mary would not be queen for long, however. King Louis died on 1 January 1515, worn out, according to the French, by the attentions of his young English wife. Within a few months Mary was married again, this time to Charles Brandon, who had been sent to bring her home.

It was Wolsey who managed to calm the fury of Henry when he heard of his sister's remarriage. Years later, when he himself was in disgrace, he would remind the duke that it was only by his pleading that Brandon still had a head on his shoulders. For the time being, however, Wolsey could do no wrong. Made chancellor in 1515, he was particularly adept in handling the king's foreign policy, which now tended towards peace. The highlight of his achievement was the Treaty of London, also known as the Treaty of Universal Peace, signed in 1518 by representatives of twenty nations including France, the Netherlands, Spain, the Holy Roman Empire and the pope. By this time Wolsey himself had been appointed cardinal and papal legate for life in England, ranking him higher than the archbishop of Canterbury.

The death of Louis, however, had begun a major change in the balance of power in Europe. He was succeeded by his twenty-year-old second cousin, Francis I, and over the next few years the deaths of Ferdinand of Aragon in January 1516, and the Holy Roman Emperor Maximilian in January 1519, saw both those territories come into the hands of the equally young Emperor Charles V. From being the youngest ruler, at twenty-seven Henry was now the oldest, three years older than Francis and nine years older than Charles. These three young men, all of them proud and ambitious, were to dominate Western Europe for decades to come.

The post of Emperor was an elective one and both Francis and Charles had paid considerable bribes to the electors, with Francis coming off second best. There was, thus, bad feeling between them from the start, while each feared the power of the other. Charles anticipated his far-flung empire – Germany, the Low Countries and Spain – being cut in two by the intervention of France, while Francis feared encirclement by that very empire. Both looked to England for guarantees of security.

In 1520 a face-to-face meeting between Henry and Francis was arranged. Taking place on the edge of English territory around Calais and masterminded by Wolsey, it became known as the Field of the Cloth of Gold, as each monarch tried to out-do the other in terms of the splendour of their pavilions and their retinues. Wolsey alone took three hundred servants. Over a period of ten days in June, in the midst of banquets, masques and tournaments, the two kings met and spoke together, though no new treaty resulted.

Just before this meeting, however, Henry had entertained Charles in England where they had celebrated Whitsun together at Canterbury. Immediately after the Field of the Cloth of Gold, Charles was invited to Calais, and there an agreement *was* signed, to the effect that neither would make a new alliance with Francis. Henry, of course, valued the trade connection with Charles's Netherlands, but it is likely that Wolsey was more swayed by the new emperor's promise to support him when next there should be a vacancy for pope.

For, of course, there was another power in Europe, that of the papacy, and perhaps if recent popes had spent more time on the needs of the church and less on their accumulation of land, wealth and glory, the challenge that now confronted them might have been avoided. Well over a century before, John Wycliffe had criticised the church for its wealth and worldliness, and nothing had changed in the interim. As well as costly wars in Italy, Popes Julius and Leo had taken on vast expense in the rebuilding and decoration of St. Peter's Basilica in Rome. When we admire the magnificent Renaissance buildings and the glorious works of Michelangelo and Raphael, perhaps we should remember that they were largely paid for by the sale of indulgences, and it was this outright exploitation, as well as the scandal of absentee bishops and pastors, that sparked the challenge of Martin Luther.

Luther was a German priest and scholar, and it was his particular study of New Testament writings that led him to publish, in 1517, the 'Disputation of Martin Luther on the Power and Efficacy of Indulgences' – the so-called 95 Theses. The story that he nailed this to the church door in Wittenburg is probably untrue, but he certainly sent it to his bishop who, instead of replying and opening a debate as Luther had probably intended, passed it on to Pope Leo. The following year it was translated into German and by the power of the printing press Luther's ideas were soon spread over Germany and beyond, finding a ready audience in others critical of current church practices.

Other writings followed, crystallising the ideas of what was to become a new religious movement. Chief among them was the idea of 'justification', that man is saved by faith in Christ alone which is a gift from God, and that good works are not essential. Furthermore, it was claimed every man should be able to read and interpret the Bible for himself in his own language, rendering the pope, bishops, monasteries and all the apparatus of the church unnecessary, while only three sacraments – baptism, penance and the eucharist –were rooted in the Bible, and nowhere did it say that relics of saints should be venerated, or that priests should not marry.

There was little there that Wycliffe and his followers had not said before, but it was new to its time and the result was the same. In 1521, instead of engaging in scholarly debate the pope excommunicated Luther and banned his writings. Wolsey in England had bonfires made of all copies that could be found, but it is quite likely that descendants of the original Lollards, having laid low for a century or so, now welcomed this new champion for the cause of reform.

A number of learned men, Thomas More and Erasmus among them, did take issue with Luther, writing refutations of his ideas and affirming the basic teachings of the church, albeit with a need for some reform. King Henry himself wrote a book, 'Assertio Septem Sacramentum' – In Defence of the Seven Sacraments – with the assistance of More. When More suggested Henry's wholehearted support of papal power might be moderated a little, however, in case the king himself should ever quarrel with the pope, Henry refused, clearly regarding such an eventuality as unthinkable. An expensively bound copy of this work was presented to Pope Leo, personally signed by the king. In return the pope bestowed on Henry, not the title he wanted 'Most Christian King', but a reasonable substitute, 'Fidei Defensor,' Defender of the Faith, which in its abbreviated form, 'Fid. Def.' or 'F.D.' has been inscribed on English coins ever since.

By this time, however, Henry was becoming preoccupied with his lack of a male heir. He had been married for twelve years, and in that time Queen Catherine had had at least six pregnancies that we know of, resulting in only one child still living, a daughter, Mary, born in 1516. There had been at least three sons, all either stillborn or dying shortly after birth. For a long time Henry had accepted the situation, but an affair with Bessie Blount had resulted in a healthy son, born in the summer of 1519, acknowledged by the king and christened Henry. If he could get a healthy son with a mistress, why could he not get one with his lawful wife?

Henry's paranoia was also growing, to the extent that anyone suggesting his kingship or his dynasty might not last was seen as a threat, particularly if they had any Plantagenet blood. One such, Edward Stafford, Duke of Buckingham, was thrown into the Tower in April 1521 accused of listening to prophecies concerning the king's death and having designs on the throne. He had made an enemy of Wolsey, which gave him little chance, and the witnesses from his household were apparently coached in what they had to say. Found guilty of treason on 16 May, he was beheaded the next day.

By now Henry had a new mistress and the rise of the Boleyn family was underway. This family had steadily married itself up the social scale. Sir Geoffrey Boleyn in the early 15th century had been a member of the mercer's guild in London, made a fortune, became Lord Mayor and married a knight's daughter. His son William married the daughter of an earl, albeit an Irish one, and William's son Thomas married the eldest daughter of Thomas Howard, then Earl of Surrey and later Duke of Norfolk. Thomas Boleyn was a man of learning and languages and for a time was ambassador to the French court. Both his daughters, Mary and Anne, had served Mary Tudor when she was briefly queen of France, and had remained in France to serve the new Queen Claude.

The eldest daughter, Mary, was sent home to England in 1519 after reputedly having an affair with King Francis I. She was quickly married off to a favoured courtier of Henry's, William Carey, but equally quickly began an affair with Henry himself. There is a suggestion that the son and daughter born to her in the 1520s were both Henry's children, though he never acknowledged them as such.

In 1522 Mary's sister Anne also returned to England. She was meant to marry James Butler, an Irish relation, in order to settle a property dispute. Instead, she fell in love with Henry Percy, son of the earl of Northumberland, and a page in Wolsey's household. How far they went with this is uncertain. Both had been promised to other partners, and in 1523 they were split up by Wolsey, probably on the orders of the king, and each sent home. Whereas Percy was quickly married off to his betrothed, Catherine Talbot, however, Anne soon reappeared at court in the queen's household. But she never forgave Wolsey for his actions.

It soon became apparent Henry had fallen for Anne. Unlike her sister, however, she flatly refused to become his mistress, possibly the first time in many years Henry had been refused anything. His pursuit of Anne became an obsession, but there must always have been a number of factors involved. True she was young, attractive and lively, and her refusal must have piqued him, but Anne was in her early twenties and Henry's wife had turned forty and was clearly not going to give him the legitimate male heir he craved. In 1525 he created his six-year-old illegitimate son, Henry Fitzroy, Duke of Richmond and Somerset, and there were strong rumours he meant to make him his heir, though nothing came of this.

Steadily through the 1520s the king grew a conscience, although of a rather selective kind. In the Bible, Chapter 20, verse 21 of the book of Leviticus declares that a man who marries his brother's wife shall remain childless. Henry now claimed this meant his lack of a legitimate son showed his marriage was sinful. He must have talked of this openly, for when envoys from France came in 1527 to discuss a marriage for the Princess Mary, they picked up on the point and queried the validity of the king's marriage, and thus the legitimacy of the princess. Wolsey was now told Henry intended to marry Anne and a way must be found to free him from his existing marriage.

There seemed to be three possibilities. First, the dispensation granted by Pope Julius in 1504 might be proved technically invalid, for instance if the wording depended on whether Catherine's first marriage had or had not been consummated. Secondly, it might be argued the pope had no power to grant a dispensation overriding the clear rule in Leviticus. Thirdly, Catherine might be persuaded to go quietly, retiring to a convent and leaving Henry free to marry again. This third would be by far the simplest, but unfortunately Catherine refused to co-operate. With not only her own status but that of her eleven-year-old daughter to consider, she insisted she was queen of England, lawfully married, and intending to remain so.

Wolsey's next idea was that he, as papal legate, should convene an ecclesiastical court at which Henry would be charged with the sin of living with his brother's wife. On 17 May 1527 Henry appeared before the court and pleaded guilty. Catherine, however, insisted her marriage with Arthur had not been consummated and that the dispensation given by Pope Julius was perfectly valid. To Wolsey's horror, the court decided the matter was so serious it must be sent to Rome for a decision.

In theory, this should not have presented a problem. Marriages were often annulled and divorces given on very flimsy grounds, especially if, as in this case, there was an urgent need for an heir. Matters in Europe had moved on, however, since the short-lived peace of 1520. In 1525 Francis I had crossed the Alps to challenge Emperor Charles V in Italy. Utter defeat at the battle of Pavia resulted, with the king himself becoming the emperor's prisoner. Charles showed no inclination, however, to divide up France with his ally Henry, and the English king had no resources to pursue the matter, especially as Wolsey's money-raising proposal, the 'Amicable Grant' – in effect a forced loan from laymen and clergy alike – was so widely unpopular it had to be abandoned. Instead, Henry changed sides. Wolsey and the mother of Francis negotiated the Treaty of the More, which Henry signed, undertaking to support France and work for the release of its king, in return for an increased 'pension'. Pope Clement, too, offered his support against Charles. Then, just when Henry needed him, in May 1527 Rome was sacked by some of Charles's troops and the pope was forced to take refuge in Castel Sant'Angelo. Though he disclaimed responsibility for the attack, Charles made no move to release him – and Charles was the nephew of Catherine of Aragon.

In July, Wolsey, at the king's request, travelled to Avignon to meet other cardinals in the hope he might be given powers to decide Henry's case himself while Clement was incapacitated. This came to nothing, however. Catherine, meanwhile, had written to Charles asking for his help, and though he released Clement later that year, he made it clear he would not look kindly on anything that threatened his aunt's position.

The pope now had a seemingly insoluble dilemma. He dared not defy Charles, but on the other hand he badly needed Henry's support against the Lutherans winning ever increasing numbers of followers in northern Europe. Wolsey, too, had been a stalwart against the new religion, and Clement may well have been aware of the cardinal's plummeting popularity, both with his king and in England in general. Even while he had been in France, the Boleyns and their Norfolk connections had been doing all they could to undermine him.

In the end, the pope played for time. He gave Wolsey a commission to try the case in England, but the judgement could only be given with the aid of a second papal legate, Cardinal Lorenzo Campeggio, who was also commissioned for this purpose. This must have given Wolsey some hope, as Campeggio was an absentee Bishop of Salisbury and might be expected to have some sympathy for the political practicalities in England. On the other hand, Clement also told Campeggio to delay the matter as much as possible.

When he finally arrived in England in the autumn of 1528, Campeggio's initial approach was to try and reconcile Henry with Catherine, and when this failed, to persuade her to retire to a convent. By now Wolsey's stock with the king was so low that, when jibes were made about his lavish lifestyle, he tried to placate Henry by giving him Hampton Court, the magnificent riverside residence he had spent ten years perfecting for himself. If this grand gesture had any effect, it was only temporary.

In May 1529 the court presided over by Wolsey and Campeggio was finally opened. Despite Catherine's protestations that it had no authority and only the pope could rule on such a matter, she had appointed Archbishop Warham and Bishop John Fisher among others to present her case, and Fisher especially spoke up boldly on her behalf. Henry's case was that the wording of the original dispensation could not cover a situation where Catherine's marriage to Arthur had been consummated, and that it had been. In vain did Catherine's team produce a further dispensation sent by Pope Julius to Catherine's mother Isabella in 1503, providing for just such a situation. In any case, Catherine insisted the marriage had never been consummated. Her dignity was impressive. At one point she crossed to where Henry was seated, knelt before him, and put it to his conscience to say whether or not she spoke the truth. It made no difference. In July Campeggio declared the court would be adjourned until October, and before then Pope Clement, having made his peace with Emperor Charles, cancelled the commissions he had given and withdrew the case to Rome for his decision.

For Wolsey, it was the end. On 9 October he was charged with misusing his legatine powers to hear matters without the king's permission. He pleaded guilty and surrendered lands and goods to the king, including York Place in Westminster, which was re-named Whitehall. On 24 October he was stripped of the chancellorship. This was then offered to Thomas More, who accepted it only on condition he should not be involved in matters relating to the king's divorce. Wolsey was allowed to remain archbishop, and initially it seemed he would be allowed to retire quietly to his seat at York, which he had never yet visited. He even planned for a formal enthronement there as archbishop on 7 November 1530, but before that date certain unwise letters had come to light, letters he had sent to France, to the emperor and to the pope. On 4 November he was arrested by Henry Percy on a charge of treason. Brought south by easy stages with the Tower as his destination, he fell ill and died at Leicester on 29 November 1530. On his deathbed he is said to have declared, 'If I had served my God as diligently as I have done the king, He would not have given me over in my grey hairs.'

The fall of Wolsey, though a mighty event, had little impact on the king's Great Matter, that of his divorce. Even before the cardinal's death a new line was being pursued, suggested by one Thomas Cranmer. Cranmer was a Cambridge scholar and priest who by 1529 had carried out some minor missions for Wolsey.

In the summer of that year, in a chance conversation with his friend Stephen Gardiner and Bishop Edward Foxe of Hereford, he suggested that it was in universities that fine theological points were debated, and that the opinions of these skilled theologians ought to be more accurate than that of the pope in deciding whether or not the king's marriage was valid. He was rapidly introduced to the king to whom the idea appealed greatly, and much of 1530 was spent in canvassing the opinions, not only of English universities, but also of all the great universities of Western Europe. The result – with a little selectivity in questions asked and people consulted – came out solidly in favour of the view that the marriage was unlawful. While useful in itself, this did not really settle the matter, particularly as Catherine still refused to retire gracefully. Now Henry was urged to take matters into his own hands.

The so-called 'Reformation Parliament' had been summoned on 3 November 1529 and would sit in a total of seven sessions until April 1536. Closely associated with it is the name of Thomas Cromwell. Cromwell, after an adventurous early life, had been Wolsey's secretary but avoided the crash when the cardinal fell from favour, instead increasing in power as Wolsey sank. He was sympathetic to the religious reforms taking place on the continent – as indeed was Cranmer – and has been accused of packing the parliament with fellow sympathisers in order to undermine the power of the church. Probably very little packing was needed, as many in England also craved reform of some sort.

Initially, it was local abuses that were tackled, in areas such as the use of sanctuary, jurisdiction over wills, and absentee clergy. A hint of things to come, however, was Henry's sudden revival of the old law of praemunire, forbidding foreign, particularly papal, interference with English affairs. The whole convocation of the clergy was charged with this offence and had to buy expensive pardons from the king. Then in February 1531 they were compelled to acknowledge that Henry himself was their 'singular protector, only and Supreme Lord and ... Supreme Head', though they insisted on inserting the words, 'as far as the Law of Christ allows'.

This was not necessarily the decisive step it may appear. In Henry's own mind he was merely taking back power he felt should never have been given away in the first place. At his coronation was he not anointed as God's chosen protector of the church in England? He was probably aware of the attempts of Henry II to delineate royal and ecclesiastical power, and the concessions made after the death of Thomas Becket. It is perhaps ironic that papal power in England should be book-ended by two kings called Henry and the deaths of two saints called Thomas, though that was still some way in the future. At present, Thomas More was still a faithful royal chancellor, announcing to parliament in March 1531 the decision of the universities, though not himself agreeing with that decision.

If Henry hoped his action might put pressure on the pope by threatening a final split, he was disappointed. Nor were relations with Anne Boleyn entirely smooth. Her rather tasteless masque, 'Of the Cardinal's Going to Hell', to celebrate the death of Wolsey had offended him, and by the summer of 1531 she was clearly becoming impatient with the slowness of his divorce proceedings. It was, after all, more than four years since he had proposed and she had accepted him, and neither was getting any younger. By now, she told him, they might have been married and she could have given him an heir.

In 1532, further church reforms followed. In May the 'Submission of the Clergy' gave up the right of Convocation to make canon law (church law) without the consent of the king, while parliament enacted that traditional payments made to the pope would be reduced, and new arrangements made for the appointment of bishops and archbishops. The fact that these last were held over for the king to decide whether or not they should become law indicated that Henry still hoped to pressure the pope into granting his divorce. The only concession he received, however, was papal approval for his nomination of Thomas Cranmer to be Archbishop of Canterbury on the death of Archbishop Warham. Clearly, Pope Clement was also trying to avoid a final breach.

By now, though, Henry had come too far to turn back. When Thomas More resigned as chancellor, ostensibly for health reasons, he was replaced by another non-clerical appointment, that of Thomas Audley. Then, in October, Henry travelled to Calais to meet Francis and ratify a new treaty, and it was Anne Boleyn who accompanied him, boldly dancing with the French king in the masque that followed. With the end of Henry's marriage now, hopefully, in sight, she had finally given in and was living openly with the king, who gave her the title Marquess of Pembroke; a most significant title for the Tudor dynasty.

On 25 January 1533, Henry and Anne were secretly married, and either before or soon afterwards, she was pregnant. In the eyes of most, of course, the marriage was bigamous, and for any heir to be legitimate that situation must be quickly remedied. As soon as parliament re-convened in February, a bill drafted by Cromwell was presented finally to end the power of the pope to decide appeals from England. Passed in April, the Act in Restraint of Appeals declared that English law and the English king were no longer to be subject to any foreign power. Convocation duly ruled that the pope had no authority to decide on the king's divorce, and that the archbishop of Canterbury was the proper person to give judgement. On 23 May Cranmer therefore came to a decision that the marriage between Henry and Catherine of Aragon was barred by church law and thus void, and that the Princess Mary was illegitimate. On 28 May his further ruling proclaimed that Henry's secret marriage to Anne Boleyn was completely valid.

A magnificent coronation was planned for Anne on 1 June. Everything was done to enhance the glory of the new and pregnant queen, but the crowd would not cheer, and she rode through the London streets to a ringing silence. Catherine was well loved, and though the king might cast her off, she still ruled in people's hearts. Nor was there the expected jubilation when Anne's child was born on 7 September. She had promised the king a son but gave him a daughter instead. He made the best of it, calling the child Elizabeth after his beloved mother, but it would not have escaped his notice that Anne was now in her early thirties and her child-bearing days were running out. At about this time, too, as Catherine's household contracted, Jane Seymour, a remote relation of the king, was transferred to the service of her successor.

In March 1534, Pope Clement finally ended his prevarication and declared Henry's marriage to Catherine to be fully valid. Henry must take her back, he said, or be excommunicated. Henry's reply was to push through parliament a series of Acts, carefully prepared by Cromwell, confirming the actions he had already taken against papal 'interference' and adding to them. In particular an Act of Succession, having recited Cranmer's judgement and the reasons for it, confirmed Henry's lawful marriage to Anne and provided that only the children of that marriage could be heirs to the throne. Failure to accept this on oath when required to do so – the wording being laid down in another Act – would lead to imprisonment and forfeiture of property. Before the end of April both Thomas More and Bishop John Fisher had been committed to the Tower for refusing this oath.

Later in the year an Act of Supremacy declared, 'Albeit the king's majesty justly and rightfully is and ought to be the supreme head of the Church of England,' for the purposes of confirmation and by the authority of parliament, 'the king, our sovereign lord, his heirs and successors ... shall be taken, accepted and reputed the only supreme head in earth of the Church of England, called Anglicana Ecclesia.' This was followed by a Treasons Act whose stormy passage through parliament succeeded only in adding the word 'maliciously' to a wide-ranging offence committed verbally or in writing, denying the king's dignity or title, or applying to the king the words 'heretic, schismatic, tyrant, infidel or usurper of the crown'.

It is to be noted that all these things were done 'by the authority of parliament'. For a man who reputedly disliked the institution and had only called it out of necessity, Henry's need had given it at least an appearance of great power. In order not to be seen as a tyrant, he had used a compliant parliament as a screen, acting with the 'approval' of the lords and especially the commons. This weapon wielded by the king would later be turned on his successors with dramatic effect. The immediate result, though, was the trial and beheading of two former friends, More and Fisher, and a revolt in Ireland triggered by this decisive break with Rome.

Henry's Lord Deputy in Ireland at the time was Gerald, 9th Earl of Kildare. It soon became apparent that he was plotting against the English, removing much of the royal arsenal from Dublin to his own castle. In February 1534 he was summoned to England and reluctantly went, leaving his son Thomas, Lord Offaly (known as Silken Thomas) in charge in Ireland. When Kildare was imprisoned in the Tower – not for the first time – Thomas declared for the pope, denounced Henry as a heretic and raised Ireland against the English. Hoped-for support from Spain never materialised, however, and the rebellion was crushed in less than a year, with Thomas and five of his uncles executed at Tyburn. It led, though, to major changes in Ireland. English rule was extended by offering Irish chieftains the opportunity to surrender their lands and have them granted back, often enhanced with lands taken from suppressed monasteries, complete with an English title and English protection. In return they had to learn English and adopt English dress, laws and religion. In 1541, Henry was offered and accepted the title King of Ireland to complete this Anglicanisation of the whole country.

In a similar way, disorder in Wales which had followed the death of Sir Rhys ap Thomas was ended by the re-organisation of the principality into shires on the English model, and the imposition of English laws, religion and government. The so-called Acts of Union of 1536 and 1543 allowed Welsh representation at parliament, but also required that all court officials, MPs and those administering justice had to use English rather than Welsh. Though these moves might appear as a war on native cultures, Henry's policy in Wales and in Ireland was mainly concerned to prevent any Catholic challenge after his break with Rome.

Two days after the beheading of Bishop John Fisher on 22 June 1535, Anne Boleyn gave birth to a premature stillborn child. The matter was hushed up lest people should think it was God's judgement for the death of a bishop. By the end of the year she was pregnant again, but now it was noticeable that Henry had begun paying attention to her maid Jane Seymour, and their usual summer progress had paid a visit to the Seymour home, Wolf Hall in Wiltshire.

Now in his mid-forties, Henry had always been athletic, engaging in day long hunting expeditions and regularly taking part in the jousts that had been forbidden him before he became king. In January 1536, however, he had an accident that would end his jousting career. Riding in full armour against an opponent, he was unseated and fell heavily, with his horse falling on top of him. By one account the king was unconscious for two hours, and an old wound in his leg was re-opened, which would later turn ulcerous. Five days later, Anne miscarried a male foetus. It is a mark of how far she had fallen in the king's favour that he gave her no comfort, merely remarking that clearly God did not wish him to have male children.

A few weeks earlier, Catherine of Aragon had died – she was in fact buried on the day Anne miscarried – and king and queen had dressed themselves in yellow, apparently to celebrate. But Catherine had been his queen for more than twenty years, and Anne's gloating may have jarred with the king. She had cost the lives of other friends, too, Wolsey and More. The latter he had known since he was a boy, and she had reputedly gloated then as well. Her liveliness had often of late become sharpness, and there was a quieter companion, Jane Seymour, whose company the king favoured more and more.

There was, too, a religious flavour to all factions at court now. Henry had displaced the pope but made no other changes to religious life, and while there were some who were happy with this, others wanted to go back, and still others, Cromwell among them, wanted to go much further. In January, Cromwell had been named Vice-Regent and Vicar-General in Spiritual Matters, and had already suggested to the king how the wealth of religious foundations in the country might be brought into the royal treasury. An investigation was begun into the moral, religious and financial aspects of the hundreds of monastic houses scattered throughout the land. Many of these were in sad decline, with few occupants and sometimes little show of piety. In March

1536, parliament passed the Suppression of Religious Houses Act, providing for the closure of any religious house having an income of less than £200 per year, their property then to be passed to the king. Anne Boleyn, by no means a religious conservative, immediately challenged this, not opposing the closures but saying the money should go to educational or charitable causes rather than to the treasury. It was a very bad time to fall out with Cromwell.

The man who had done so much to put her on the throne now began to work to remove her, having in this at least the tacit approval of the king. Nor did Anne help her own cause. A sermon she approved to be preached before the king practically accused him of robbing the church, while her own flirtatious behaviour with young men of the king's household gave ample opportunity for probably innocent words to be given a more sinister meaning.

The end, when it came, came suddenly. On 30 April Mark Smeaton, a musician in the queen's household, was arrested and – almost certainly under torture – confessed that he and other named men of the king's household had committed adultery with Anne. This seemed to back up statements Cromwell had already received from the queen's ladies. All those named, Henry Norris, Francis Weston, William Brereton, and, most shockingly, George Boleyn the queen's brother, were opponents of Cromwell. Thomas Wyatt, who wrote love poems to the queen, was also accused but escaped the fate of the others, probably because his father was Cromwell's friend.

During the May Day festivities, as Henry sat with his wife watching a joust, he was handed a note. When he read it, he immediately left, and shortly afterwards Norris was arrested. Anne herself was arrested the next day, as was her brother, with Weston and Brereton taken the day after. Famously Anne refused to enter the Tower through Traitor's Gate, declaring she was no traitor. It did her no good. She was charged with adultery, incest and high treason, and put on trial on 15 May, three days after Norris, Weston and Brereton had been found guilty of adultery with her. Among the jury that unanimously found her guilty was Henry

Percy, who collapsed and had to be carried out when the verdict was announced. A few hours later her brother was also found guilty of the same charges.

On 17 May Anne watched from a window as the convicted men, including her brother, were executed, but she seems to have become reconciled to her own death. The poem 'O Death, Rock Me Asleep' is attributed to her in her last days. It opens, 'O death! Rock me asleep/Bring me on quiet rest/Yet pass my guiltless ghost/Out of my careful breast.' She was beheaded on 19 May by a swordsman specially brought from France for his skill at quick executions.

The day before the execution, Cranmer had solemnly declared Anne Boleyn's marriage to Henry to be null and void and on 30 May at Whitehall Henry married Jane Seymour. She was proclaimed queen of England on 4 June, but no great coronation was planned. That would have to wait until she had given Henry his longed-for heir.

It could have been a turning point in English history. With both Catherine and Anne dead, Henry, who in his own mind was still a good Catholic, could have turned back to Rome and been welcomed by the pope. It was even a new pope, Paul III, who was prepared to acknowledge the church had faults and to try and reconcile with the Protestants of northern Europe. Instead, Henry allowed Cromwell and Cranmer to move half a step towards the Lutheran doctrines now widely adopted in many German states.

The Ten Articles issued in July 1536 were an attempt to define the core beliefs of the new Church of England. In a preface apparently written by the king himself, it declared the intention 'that unity and concord in opinion may increase ... and all occasion of dissent and discord ... be repressed and utterly extinguished.' In fact, it pleased no-one. The conservatives disliked the way the articles were divided into two groups – those grounded in holy scripture and therefore essential to salvation, and those based on tradition – with only three of the recognised seven sacraments falling into the first group. The more progressive reformers rejected the idea that good works were still linked with faith as necessary to salvation, and that prayers for the dead could still be said and relics and images were still allowed.

Meanwhile the dissolution of the lesser monasteries continued apace, with some inhabitants moved to larger houses and others becoming secular clergy. Lands and property, including monastic treasures sometimes accumulated over centuries, came to the Crown, with everything possible being sold off to increase the royal windfall. The original intention, to stamp out waste, corruption and superstition, was only occasionally remembered. One enforcer commented that they must 'sweep away all the rotten bones that are called relics ... lest it be thought we came more for the treasure than for the avoidance of idolatry.'

Through most of the country this passed off peacefully enough, with local farmers and others buying up lands, taking over buildings and scavenging materials from those too ruinous to be otherwise useful. In October 1536, however, a short-lived protest in Lincolnshire grew into a larger, more serious rebellion further north that became known as the Pilgrimage of Grace. Under the leadership of Robert Aske, a London lawyer who originated from Selby, the men of Yorkshire, Northumberland and Cumberland rallied to protest on a litany of causes, among them the taxes, the enclosure of common land and loss of traditional liberties. The dissolution of their beloved monasteries was simply the last straw, and it gave them a degree of righteousness when Aske christened them pilgrims. Nor were they just a common rabble. Many of the lesser nobility of the area joined them. Lord Darcy surrendered Pontefract, and the Archbishop of York, Edward Lee, also supported their claims. On 16 October, York was occupied and between thirty and forty thousand men, many of them mounted and armed, assembled near Doncaster to meet whatever the king might throw at them.

Henry sent the dukes of Norfolk and Suffolk, together with George Talbot, Earl of Shrewsbury, but between them they could muster only around 12,000 men. Many, in fact, sympathised with the demands of the 'pilgrims'. Forced to negotiate, at meetings between October and December the demands to be put to the king were finalised. These included a new parliament, free of the influence of the king's servants, to be held somewhere in the north within a year, suspension of the dissolution of the monasteries until then, and, of course, a general pardon. A written pardon was received, along with Norfolk's word that their demands would be put to the king – a promise he never intended to keep – and in early December Aske persuaded his followers to disband.

The danger had been real while it lasted. Pope Paul had been encouraging France and Spain to send troops to support the pilgrims, though neither had responded. Reginald Pole, a newly made English cardinal in exile who had already defied Henry, was also sent to the Netherlands to encourage assistance for the pilgrims. Clearly, Henry recognised the seriousness of the threat, as shown by his reaction when early the following year the men of Cumberland and Westmoreland rose again in rebellion under the leader 'Captain Poverty'. Despatching Norfolk to impose order, he directed him to 'cause such dreadful execution to be done upon a good number of the inhabitants of every town, village and hamlet that have offended, as they may be a fearful spectacle to all others hereafter.' Norfolk did just that, raising the king's banner at Carlisle and imposing martial law on the area. In all, some 216 persons are recorded as suffering the death penalty, but that does not include those summarily executed or dying in prison. Aske himself was hung in chains at York and left to die of exposure and starvation.

The Pilgrimage of Grace marks the only occasion when Jane Seymour is known to have interceded with her husband. Throwing herself upon her knees, she is said to have begged him to reverse his policy on closing the monasteries. His reply was to tell her not to meddle, since meddling had cost the life of her predecessor. Not that Jane was likely to meddle. Less lively, less learned, less sophisticated than Anne Boleyn, she is described as a quiet, gentle creature, whose motto was 'Bound to obey and serve'. Altogether a more suitable companion for a middle-aged king, she spread her peace everywhere, even to the extent of reconciling Henry to his eldest daughter, albeit at the cost of Mary reluctantly signing the Act of Supremacy.

When in the spring of 1537 Jane announced she was pregnant, the king was overjoyed, and even more so when on 12 October she gave birth to a healthy boy. He was christened Edward, possibly because he was born on the eve of the feast day of the great English saint Edward the Confessor. As so often before, however, the joy of a birth was quickly followed by sorrow, though not this time for the death of the baby. By all accounts it had been a difficult birth, and the day after the christening Jane fell ill with a fever. Eight days later, on 24 October, she died. Henry was distraught, shutting himself away for days and wearing black for months, even through the Christmas season. With a tradition of kings not attending their wives' funerals, it seems ironic that when Jane was buried in St George's Chapel at Windsor on 8 November, the chief mourner was Henry's daughter Mary.

At last Henry had his longed-for son and heir, but far from making him more secure, if anything it increased his paranoia. It would be at least eighteen years before the child had a hope of ruling successfully and Henry was increasingly aware of his own mortality. With ulcers on both legs now, he was often in severe pain, and while his mobility was reduced his appetite was not, resulting in a steady gain of weight. He had headaches, too, probably another legacy of the jousting accident, and none of this helped his temper, which had always been volcanic. Now anyone with a challenge, or even potential to challenge, might end up in the Tower – or worse.

By now almost all with Plantagenet blood had been eliminated, but the Pole family, descended from George, Duke of Clarence, remained. Cardinal Reginald Pole was a focus for Catholic hopes, but he was on the continent, beyond Henry's reach. His family, though – his mother Margaret, Countess of Salisbury, brothers Henry, Lord Montague, and Geoffrey, and their kinsman Henry Courtney, Marquis of Exeter –were all arrested in 1538 for little more than their family connection. Geoffrey admitted treasonable communication with Reginald, implicated the others, attempted suicide and was pardoned. His brother and Henry Courtney, however, were convicted and executed. The countess was held in the Tower until 1541 when she was finally, clumsily beheaded at the age of sixty-seven.

The biggest potential challenge, of course, might come from the Catholic rulers of France and Spain, and, nearer to home, France's long-time ally Scotland. So far Henry had been lucky in that Charles V and Francis I had been too busy fighting each other and dealing with religious troubles in their own lands, while James V of Scotland had been a minor until 1528, and then took time to assert his rule over Scotland. In 1538, however, Charles and Francis signed a peace treaty, and James married Mary of Guise, a French duchess with close links to the royal family.

In England the fledgling church still lacked a definite direction. Some, such as Stephen Gardiner, Bishop of Winchester, and the Duke of Norfolk, inclined toward the Catholic side, with others, particularly Cromwell and Archbishop Cranmer pushing for more radical changes. Initially, the radicals held sway. Through 1538 and 1539 the dissolution of the monasteries continued apace, no longer confined to lesser houses, but involving even the most prestigious in the land. Abbots and priors who surrendered their houses voluntarily were rewarded with fairly generous pensions, and some support was also given to the monks provided they maintained their vows of celibacy. In other cases, including at the mighty foundations of Glastonbury and Reading, the abbots were hanged. In March 1540 Waltham Abbey was the last to be closed, and a by-product of this activity was that in parliament the church was now only represented by the bishops, who were well outnumbered by the temporal lords and by the commons.

Hand in hand with the closure of religious houses went the destruction of the shrines of saints, ostensibly to prevent the superstitious idolatry of the common people, but also yielding substantial quantities of gold and jewels, which went, of course, to the king. Some of the most ancient and revered shrines in the land were utterly destroyed, including that of Our Lady at Walsingham and of St Swithin at Winchester. At Canterbury, Wriothesley records that 'the bones of St. Thomas of Canterbury were burnt in the same church by my lord Cromwell,' in addition to which his image was torn down, and even a stained-glass window recording his story was removed, 'so that there shall no more mention be made of him never.' They had rather more difficulty at Durham where the body of St Cuthbert was found still intact and uncorrupted in his ancient tomb. After two years of dithering, it was quietly buried beneath the site of his former shrine.

All of this, together with the introduction of an English Bible based on the translations of William Tynedale and Myles Coverdale, was part of Cromwell's project to guide the country ever closer to the Protestantism currently being adopted in many German states. It was his suggestion, too, that the king might form an alliance by marriage with one such state. He had, after all, been without a wife for two years. Henry's own idea, that he might have acted as arbitrator between Protestants and Catholics, had fallen flat, but he found similar 'middle way' sentiments in the duchy of Cleves, the ruler of which had two marriageable daughters. Hans Holbein, Henry's court painter, was dispatched to paint portraits of Anne and her younger sister Amalia, and in October 1539 Henry contracted to marry Anne.

The wedding was set for 4 January 1540, but, delayed by bad weather, Anne only reached England on 26 December. Henry planned a surprise meeting with her at Rochester a few days later, and by most accounts was horrified by what he found. Anne appeared older and plainer than her portrait, was reportedly 'large and loud' and spoke no English. The wedding was postponed to 6 January, but Henry could find no way out of it, and married the lady among much pre-planned festivity.

Almost at once he tried to find ways to dispose of this cheerful but unwanted wife. He declared he could not consummate the marriage through repugnance, though it is hard to believe one account that suggests Anne had no idea what consummation involved. Nor had the alliance with Cleves proved particularly useful. It is probable, incidentally, that Holbein paid a lengthy visit to his wife in Basel at about this time. He certainly never received another commission from Henry.

It was Cromwell who suffered the backlash for this failure. He had already taken the king further along the road to Protestantism than his conscience approved, as evidenced by the Six Articles enshrined in law in June 1539 and enforceable by the death penalty. These returned the church to a more conservative religious position, with all seven sacraments recognised equally, celibate clergy, and holy images permitted for purposes of inspiration to prayer. Then when it was discovered that Cromwell had concealed from the king the exact circumstances of a pre-contract by which Anne was to marry the son of the duke of Lorraine, the end was in sight.

Despite being created Earl of Essex in April 1540, less than two months later Cromwell was arrested and taken to the Tower. The charges read as though cobbled together – protecting Protestants guilty of heresy, corruption, failing to enforce the Six Articles, and plotting to marry Henry's daughter Mary – but the real offence was failing his king and making him a laughing stock. He was not even given a trial, and though pleading with the king in a letter that ended, 'Most Gracious Prince, I cry for mercy, mercy, mercy,' he was beheaded on 28 July 1540 before a large crowd on Tower Hill.

His fall was probably hastened by long-term enemies such as the Duke of Norfolk who, playing on the king's susceptibilities, had already brought to his notice another of his nieces, Catherine Howard, daughter of his ne'er-do-well brother Edmund. Reputedly it was love at first sight, at least on the part of the king. They were married on the very day of Cromwell's execution, the inconvenient marriage to Anne of Cleves having been declared null and void by Cranmer a few weeks before. Very sensibly, Anne had accepted the position of 'King's Sister' and a large pension, though Wriothesley was probably not alone in lamenting that it 'was a great pity that so good a lady as she is should so soon have lost her joy.'

It is perhaps a shame Norfolk had not enquired a little more closely into the upbringing of his niece before pushing her into the arms of the king. For more than a year they were blissfully happy, Catherine adopting as a motto, 'No other wish but his.' By the autumn of 1541, however, her past had begun to catch up with her. Born around 1520, her mother's death when she was about ten years old had resulted in her being placed in the large and ill-disciplined household of her step-grandmother, the Dowager Duchess of Norfolk. There, attempts to keep the young men from the 'Maidens' Chamber', effectively the girls' dormitory, had been regularly thwarted, with Catherine apparently a leader in what was probably at the time seen as nothing more than mischief. A young gentleman, Francis Dereham, was reported as a regular visitor, though whether they were actually lovers is not clear. They referred to each other as 'husband' and 'wife' and may have hoped to make this reality if Catherine had not been whisked away to higher things.

In the autumn of 1541, some of this story began to emerge, probably originating with Mary Lascelles, another of the girls in the household. Mary told her brother, who told Cranmer, who in turn passed it on to the king. Henry flatly refused to believe it – but then told Cranmer to investigate further. On being pressed, possibly tortured, Dereham admitted he had lain with the queen before her marriage, but claimed another, Thomas Culpepper, had replaced him in her affections since. Culpepper, it appeared, had secretly met Catherine several times at night on a recent expedition to the north, at the connivance of Catherine herself and one of her ladies, Lady Rochford. She – the widow of George Boleyn – corroborated this, though was clearly terrified at the questioning. She put the responsibility solely on Catherine, while Catherine claimed Rochford had encouraged her. It is just possible the king's constant desire for another child had led the misguided young girl to believe any child would do. If so, it was to be her undoing.

On 5 November Henry abruptly left Hampton Court for Whitehall. Dereham and Culpepper were arrested, put on trial for treason and executed on 10 December. Meanwhile Catherine was held at Syon House and stripped of her title. Early in the New Year both she and Lady Rochford were condemned for treason, Lady Rochford becoming so frantic with terror she was declared literally insane. It didn't save her from the block. Catherine took her punishment with more courage, being beheaded early in the morning of 13 February 1542.

Henry may well have felt himself duped over his last two marriages, but the old lion was not done yet, and soon the world would hear him roar again. England had seemed uniquely vulnerable in 1538 but already action had been taken to improve its defensive position. A series of fortifications had been built, mainly along the Channel coast, but some as far west as the Milford Haven waterway in Wales, and one as far north as the Humber. Some were merely reinforced earth banks, but others, as at Deal and Pendennis, were strongly built castles, bristling with guns. Money had also been spent on building or re-building ships, while in 1540 An Act for the Maintenance of the Navy of England was passed. Some famous names appear in the list of the fleet, among them the *Mary Rose* and the *Henry Grace à Dieu*, known as the Great Harry, but the English fleet still generally lagged behind that of the Scots and the French in terms of modern design and armaments. Indeed, it was piratical attacks by the Scots, along with Scottish Catholicism, that turned Henry's mind to Scotland, when he began once again to go on the offensive.

Henry and Catherine had travelled to York in 1541 for a meeting with King James V of Scotland but James did not appear. Immediately Henry prepared an invasion force, and in November 1542 the Scots army, without a properly appointed commander, was soundly beaten at the battle of Solway Moss. When James heard of this he took to his bed. The birth of a daughter, his only heir, on 8 December failed to rouse him, and on 14 December he died.

Scotland, too, was divided between Catholic and Protestant factions, and for a time it seemed Henry might succeed in uniting the countries by a treaty for the marriage of Prince Edward and the Scots Princess Mary. Then the French offered assistance to Scotland, the Catholic Cardinal Beaton got the upper hand, and the treaty was overthrown. In retaliation Henry began the series of violent attacks on Scotland that continued over a period of years and became known as the 'Rough Wooing'.

In 1543, in the space of three weeks in the summer, Henry had declared war on France and obtained for himself another wife. The French war was declared on 22 June in pursuance of a new arrangement with the ever-unreliable Charles V and, to most people's horror, Henry committed himself to lead his army personally the following year. The wife was acquired entirely on Henry's own initiative and ostensibly greatly against the inclination of the lady in question.

She was Katherine Parr, a thirty-year-old, twice married, childless widow. Her last husband Lord Latimer, twenty years older than her, had been dead a matter of months, and Katherine was in love with Thomas Seymour, one of Jane's brothers. The king's proposal, however, was equivalent to a command. Seymour was sent as permanent ambassador to the Netherlands, and Katherine overcame her reluctance and settled down to be a good wife to the over-sized, unattractive king, now in his early fifties. She made such a good job of it, gathering his children to court and overseeing their education, that when Henry left for France on 14 July 1544, Katherine was left as regent.

Some 40,000 men accompanied Henry to Calais, and though command of the army was left to Charles Brandon, Duke of Suffolk, the king in full armour rode with them on 25 July to put Boulogne under siege. The town fell on 13 September, and, says Wriothesley, 'the King's Majesty entered the said town the 18 September with great triumph.' Te Deum was sung in St Paul's in London, and it might have been Henry V all over again – except that, on the same day, Charles V signed a peace treaty with Francis. Henry refused to sign if it meant giving up Boulogne, and returned to England with his victory intact at the end of September.

The following year the French made determined attempts to re-take Boulogne, and then in mid-July set out with a fleet of some 200 ships – considerably larger than the later Spanish Armada – to invade England. The English fleet was based in the Solent, with Henry, a seemingly rejuvenated Henry, on hand at Portsmouth to direct matters. On 19 July the French were sighted rounding the Isle of Wight, and as the English retreated to the more confined spaces of Portsmouth harbour, all seemed set for a mighty naval battle. In fact, it was indecisive, with ships in both fleets struggling to manoeuvre effectively. The greatest English loss was the *Mary Rose*, sunk not by cannon fire but by a stray gust of wind as she went about, flooding her gun ports and turning her over.

The French briefly landed troops on the Isle of Wight but were driven off by the local militia, and after another naval skirmish off Shoreham Bay, by the end of July they had returned to France. There was more fierce fighting around Boulogne, but in the spring of 1546 peace negotiations got underway. The resulting treaty, signed in May, provided for Francis to pay arrears of pensions owed at a rate of 90,000 crowns per year, while Henry would keep Boulogne for the next eight years, after which Francis could effectively buy it back for two million crowns. It was also agreed that no further French help should be given to Scotland.

Though this sounded like a good deal, Henry's military actions in France and in Scotland had actually cost him in the region of £3 million, and the French money barely scratched the surface. To pay for this he had to sell off some two-thirds of the property he had obtained from the dissolution of the monasteries, impose heavy taxes, and even debase the silver coinage. In the end so much copper was mixed with the silver that Henry was (privately) referred to as 'old coppernose', from the colour produced when his profile on the coins became worn.

Henry's wartime rejuvenation proved to be very temporary. From late 1545 he was regularly ill, in great pain from the ulcers on his legs, and increasingly immobile. As 1546 progressed it was clear the king was deteriorating rapidly, and court factions began jockeying for position in the regency that was sure to follow. The latest Act of Succession in 1544 had named Edward as heir, but he was only nine years old and his minority would be a long one. Religious differences fuelled the fire, and though Katherine nursed her husband devotedly, more than one attempt was made to undermine her on the grounds she was urging Henry to more radical Protestantism. She in turn declared she only discussed religion with him to keep his mind off the pain in his legs.

In this feverish, factional atmosphere, on 12 December the Duke of Norfolk and his son the Earl of Surrey were abruptly arrested. Various allegations were made against them, but when Surrey was put on trial on 7 January 1547 the only charge was that he had treasonably added the arms of Edward the Confessor to his coat of arms, having pretensions to usurp the crown. Surrey denied the charge, but his father confessed to concealing his son's wrongdoing and both were condemned to death.

Even before this trial it was clear the king was dying. On 30 December he had dictated his will. This did not prevent Surrey from being beheaded on 19 January, and Norfolk himself was due to suffer the same fate nine days later. Early in the morning on that day, 28 January, Henry died. By tradition prisoners in the Tower were pardoned on the death of a king, and Norfolk's sentence was never carried out, though he remained in the Tower through the whole of the next reign.

Most earlier kings were lavishly praised at their deaths by the various chronicles of their times. By contrast, it is hard to find anything said about Henry VIII beyond the fact that he died and was buried. After all the youthful hopes and promise, and in spite of the pomp and magnificence, his reign hosted more conflict than achievement. Certainly, no other English king is recorded as killing so many former dear friends. There were no doubt many people who rejoiced to hear of the death of Henry VIII – though probably none more so than Thomas Howard, Duke of Norfolk.

Epilogue

In nearly 500 years since 1547 no other English king has borne the name Henry, though there might have been two more. The offspring of Henry VIII notoriously failed to produce offspring of their own, but when James VI of Scotland became James I of England in 1603, his seven-year-old son and heir was named Henry. Called after his grandfather, Henry, Lord Darnley, rather than Henry Tudor, he became at once Duke of Cornwall, and when he reached sixteen he became Prince of Wales and Earl of Chester, his investiture celebrated with great pageantry. Handsome, educated, athletic, he was an immensely popular prince, not always on good terms with his father, but a far more exciting prospect as future king than his weakly, backward little brother Charles. His death from typhoid in November 1612 caused an outpouring of grief, his chaplain, Daniel Price, proclaiming in a sermon, 'the Sun is gone out of our firmament, the joy, the beauty, the glory of Israel is departed.'

Some thirty years later Charles I named his third son Henry. At the end of the Civil War, when his mother and brothers had escaped to the continent, Henry, aged eight, was captured by the Roundheads, and there was talk of putting him on the throne as a puppet king in place of his father. Allowed a last visit to Charles the day before his execution, the king solemnly told him, 'Thou must not be a king as long as thy brothers Charles and James do live.' Henry's response was, 'I will be torn in pieces first.' By the time he was released by Cromwell in 1652, Henry had become a staunch

Protestant, and he later gained a reputation as a fine soldier in the Franco-Spanish wars. Returning to England with his brothers at the Restoration in May 1660, he died of smallpox a few months later.

Thereafter, the name of Henry went completely out of fashion for royalty, appearing only for illegitimate sons of James II and William IV. In the twentieth century, however, it has made a limited comeback, chosen as the name for the third son of George V and, in our own time, the second son of Prince Charles, though he is generally known as Harry.

Nevertheless, when we look at the contribution made by the eight kings of that name, we find it underpins almost every aspect of our nation and its institutions. To the first two we owe our legal system and department of finance, to the third, intentionally or otherwise, the origins of our parliament. The fifth decreed the widespread use of English in official documents, leading to dramatic developments in that language. The seventh began a transatlantic link that has endured, with greater and lesser friendliness, over the centuries. The eighth, again arguably unintentionally, brought into being the Church of England.

Through the five hundred or so years spanned by the eight Henrys certain threads are constant. The relationship with the nobility is one, and the relationship with the church, particularly with Rome, another. In the times of strong kings – the first, second and fifth – these relationships were by and large peacefully settled. In times of weak kings – the third, sixth and eighth – it was a rockier ride.

Only two of the eight were born to be kings, and these – the third and sixth – proved to be the weakest. The rest owed their kingship to fate or their own actions. For some, family was the greatest support, for others the greatest challenge.

Among their number we find national heroes, the saintly and the murderous, the most dynamic and the least effective. Some are household names, some not known at all, or only through Shakespearean dramas playing fast and loose with the facts. Some should be much better known, some could well be forgotten. Between them they represent every possible shade of kingship, and each in his own time was 'Harry of England'.

A Note on Sources

History would indeed be dull if we only had a list of dates and facts. Instead, a whole pageant of life and personality is laid before us in the writings of those who lived through these times. Some diligently check sources and cross-reference, while others are happy to throw in anecdote and hearsay, which, if not strictly, provably accurate, gives us a flavour of the ideas, fancies and prejudices current at the time.

For the earliest records we are heavily indebted to monks, working away in the scriptoria of their monasteries and gathering news from those passing through their guest halls, the hotels of their time. In particular, Orderic Vitalis and William of Malmesbury, both Anglo-Norman, one in Normandy and one in England, give us a vivid picture of the events of the 11th and early 12th centuries. Also contemporary, though less detailed, are the various versions of the Anglo-Saxon Chronicle, compiled in monasteries around the country at Peterborough, Winchester and Canterbury, while other viewpoints are found in the writings of John of Worcester, Henry of Huntingdon and Symeon of Durham.

The Augustinian canon William of Newburgh, writing in the 12th century, aimed for a serious, accurate history of past and present times to counter the romantic fictions of Geoffrey of Monmouth, popular at the time. Roger of Hoveden covers roughly the same period with extensive inside knowledge, being a clerk connected to the court of Henry II. He even accompanied Richard I on his crusade. Another eyewitness, William fitzStephen, gives a detailed, though biased, account of the dispute between Henry II and Thomas Becket, being Becket's clerk. Similar detailed knowledge of the times is displayed in the Brut Chronicle, ranging, with various extensions, from the 13th to the 15th centuries, and possibly written at least in part by clerks of the royal chancery.

St Albans Abbey provides a string of chroniclers, most of whom borrowed from previous writers for parts of their chronicles, but they were impressively well informed on their own times. Roger of Wendover called his work 'Flowers of History', comparing it to gathering flowers from different fields, but he is contemporary with the period 1216 to 1235. His chronicle is then continued by Matthew Paris, who gathered many eye-witness accounts through his friendship with Henry III and Richard of Cornwall. Later, Thomas Walsingham, from the same abbey, gives detailed contemporary accounts of the reigns of Richard II, Henry IV and Henry V.

Two Augustinian canons, Henry Knighton and John Capgrave, cover the latter part of the 14th century, while Adam of Usk is particularly detailed on the fall of Richard II, having worked for both Henry IV and Archbishop Arundel. He also gives a Welshman's view of Glendower's wars, and reports much of the career of Henry V. The latter's reign is covered in detail by the anonymous royal chaplain who wrote the *Gesta Henrici Quinti* (Deeds of Henry V), having observed the battle of Agincourt from the dubious safety of the baggage train.

The Chronicle of Croyland Abbey, often referred to as Ingulph's Chronicle after an early abbot, is particularly useful in its continuations covering the Wars of the Roses and the Yorkist kings. By now, though, London citizens have become prominent chroniclers of their times. The so-called Gregory's Chronicle is more of a scrapbook than a chronicle, and there is no agreement about its author. William Gregory was an alderman and later Lord Mayor of London in the fifteenth century, and was originally, rather dubiously, identified as the man who recorded details of London life and times. Since it continues after his death, however, some at least must have been written by another. Whoever it was witnessed many important events, including Cade's rebellion, ending with the deposition of Edward IV.

Another London alderman was Robert Fabyan, contemporary with events at the end of the 15th and beginning of the 16th centuries. Not only did he witness the coming of the Tudors, but he also records the arrival of three men from the New Found Land across the Atlantic. Fabyan's son was apprenticed as a grocer to the father of Edward Hall, which may have inspired Hall to take up his own pen and write about recent and contemporary events. Though he was a child during the latter days of Henry VII, he no doubt had access to many who had witnessed those times, but he would have seen for himself the dramatic events of the reign of Henry VIII. The final part of his chronicle was written by the printer Richard Grafton from notes made by Hall.

Two men very close to the events they chronicled were Charles Wriothesley and Polydore Vergil. Wriothesley, a trained lawyer, came from a dynasty of heralds, and himself became a member of the college of arms and ultimately Windsor Herald, though not reaching the heights of other members of his family. Unsurprisingly, his chronicle is richly detailed on the pageantry of the time, though also full of beheadings, burnings, and suppression of heretics, continuing as it does up to the first year of the reign of Elizabeth I.

Polydore Vergil, on the other hand, was a priest, a scholar and a diplomat. Italian-born, he arrived in England in 1502 representing Cardinal Castellesi who had been appointed Bishop of Bath & Wells. He stayed on as Archdeacon of Wells and became an English citizen in 1510. Commissioned by Henry VII in 1505 to write his *Anglica Historia*, he must be regarded as unreliable in relation to the deeds of Yorkists before Bosworth, but in general was careful to gather materials from a range of sources. Later his implied criticism of Wolsey and Henry VIII landed him in the Tower for a period of months in 1515. Initially covering the period from early times to the beginning of the reign of Henry VIII, a later revised version extended this to the year 1537.

Select Bibliography

Primary Printed Sources

A Chronicle of England During the Reigns of the Tudors, Charles Wriothesley, ed. William Douglas Hamilton (London: Camden Society, 1875-77)

An English Chronicle of the Reigns of Richard II, Henry IV, Henry V and Henry VI, ed. Rev. John Silvester Davies (London: Camden Society, 1856)

Anglica Historia, Polydore Vergil, ed. & trans. Dana F. Sutton (The Philological Museum of the University of Birmingham))

Anglo-Saxon Chronicle, ed. & trans. J.A. Giles (London: G. Bell & Sons, 1914)

Annals of Roger of Hoveden, trans. Henry T. Riley (London: Henry G. Bohn, 1853)

Brut, or the Chronicles of England, ed. F.W.D. Brie, (London: Keegan Paul, Trench, Trübner & Co., 1906)

Chronicle of England, John Capgrave, ed. Rev. Francis Charles Hingeston (London: Longman, Brown, Green et al., 1858)

Chronicle of Henry of Huntingdon, ed. & trans. Thomas Forester (London: Henry G. Bohn, 1853)

Chronicle of John of Worcester, trans. Thomas Forester (London: Henry G. Bohn, 1854)

Chronicle of John Streeche for the Reign of Henry V (1414-1422), ed. F. Taylor (Bulletin of the John Rylands Library xvi, 1932)

Chronicle of the Kings of England, William of Malmesbury, ed. & trans. J.A. Giles (London: Henry G. Bohn, 1847)

Chronicon Adae de Usk AD1377-1421, ed. & trans. Sir Edward Maunde Thompson (London: Henry Frowde, 1904)

Chronicles of Enguerrand de Monstrelet, Vols 1-4 ed. & trans. Thomas Johnes (London: Longman, Hurst, et al. 1810)

Chronique de la Traison et Mort de Richart Deux, Roy Dengleterre, ed. & trans. Benjamin Williams (London: Aux depens de la Société, 1846)

Ecclesiastical History of England & Normandy, Vols. 2, 3 & 4, Orderic Vitalis, ed. & trans. Thomas Forester (London: Henry G. Bohn, 1854 & 1856)

English Historical Documents 1042-1189, Ed. David C. Douglas & George W. Greenaway (Oxford: Routledge, 2001)

English Historical Documents 1189-1327, David C. Douglas, ed. Harry Rothwell (London: Eyre & Spottiswoode, 1975)

English Historical Documents 1327-1485, David C. Douglas, ed. A.R. Myers (London: Eyre & Spottiswoode, 1969)

Gregory's Chronicle, The Historical Collections of a Citizen of London in the 15th Century, ed. J. Gairdner (London: Camden Society, 1876)

Hall's Chronicle, containing the History of England, Henry IV to Henry VIII, ed. Henry Ellis (London: J. Johnson, F.C. & J. Rivington et al, 1809)

Historia Anglicana, 1381-1422, Thomas Walsingham, ed. H.T. Riley (London: Rolls Series, 1864)

Historical Works of Simeon of Durham, trans. Rev. Joseph Stevenson (London: Seeleys, 1855)

History of William of Newburgh, trans. Rev. Joseph Stevenson (London: Seeleys, 1856)

Ingulph's Chronicle/Chronicle of the Abbey of Croyland, with Continuations by Peter of Blois and others, trans. Henry T. Riley (London: George Bell & Sons., 1908)

Knighton's Chronicle, Henry Knighton, ed. J.R. Lumby (London: Rolls Series 1889-95)

L'Histoire de Guillaume Le Maréchal, ed. Paul Meyer (Paris: Société de l'Histoire de France, 1901)

Matthew Paris's English History, 1235-1273, trans. J.A. Giles (London: Henry G. Bohn, 1852-1854)

Roger of Wendover's Flowers of History, trans. J.A. Giles (London: Henry G. Bohn, 1849)

The Life and Death of Thomas Becket, William fitzStephen, ed. & trans. George Greenaway (London: Folio Society, 1961)

The New Chronicles of England & France in Two Parts, Robert Fabyan, ed. Henry Ellis (London: F.C. & J. Rivington et al, 1811)

The Reign of Henry VII from Contemporary Sources, sel. & arr. Pollard, A.F., (London: Longmans, Green & Co., 1914)

The Song of Lewes, ed. C.L. Kingsford (Oxford: Clarendon Press, 1890)

Secondary Sources

Allmand, C., *Henry V* (New Haven and London: Yale University Press, 1997)

Ashley, M., *Mammoth Book of British Kings & Queen*, (London: Robinson Publishing, 1999)

Barratt, Nick, *The Restless Kings, Henry II and His Sons and the War for the Plantagenet Crown* (London: Faber & Faber, 2018)

Barber, Richard, *Henry II: A Prince Among Princes* (London: Penguin Books, 2015)

Bennett, M., Bradbury, J., DeVries, K., Dickie, I., Jestice, P.G., *Fighting Techniques of the Medieval World AD500-AD1500: Equipment, Combat Skills and Tactics* (Staplehurst: Spellmount, 2005)

Bevan, Bryan, *Henry VII, The First Tudor King* (London: Rubicon Press, 2000)

Bindoff, S.T., *The Pelican History of England – Tudor England* (Harmondsworth: Penguin Books, 1950)

Borman, Tracy, *Henry VIII and the Men Who Made Him* (London: Hodder & Stoughton, 2018)

Breverton, Terry, *Henry VII, The Maligned Tudor King* (Stroud: Amberley, 2019)

Carpenter, David, *The Struggle for Mastery – The Penguin History of Britain 1066-1284* (London: Penguin, 2004)

Chibnall, Marjorie, *Anglo-Norman England* (Oxford: Blackwell, 1986)

Churchill, Winston, *A History of the English-Speaking Peoples*, Vols 1 & 2 (London: Cassell, 1968)

Crouch, David, *Normans – The History of a Dynasty* (London: Hambledon Continuum, 2002)

Davis, H. W. C., *England Under the Normans & Angevins 1066-1272* (London: Methuen, 1921)

Davis, John Paul, *The Gothic King: A Biography of Henry III* (London: Peter Owen, 2013)

Dockray, K., *Warrior King: The Life of Henry V* (Stroud: The History Press, 2006)

Delouche, Frédéric, *Illustrated History of Europe* (London: Cassell Paperbacks, 2001)

Green, J.A., *Henry I, King of England and Duke of Normandy* (Cambridge: Cambridge University Press, 2009)

Guest, Ken & Denise, *British Battles* (London: Harper Collins, 2002)

Guy, John, *Henry VIII, The Quest for Fame* (London: Allen Lane, 2014)

Hollister, C. Warren, *Henry I* (New Haven & London: Yale University Press, 2003)

Hutchinson, Robert, *Henry VIII, The Decline & Fall of a Tyrant,* (London: Weidenfeld & Nicholson, 2019)

Jacob, E. F., *The Fifteenth Century 1399-1485* (Oxford: Clarendon Press, 1961)

Johnson, Lauren, *Shadow King, The Life and Death of Henry VI* (London: Head of Zeus, 2020)

Kinross, John, *Discovering Battlefields of England & Scotland* (Princes Risborough: Shire Publications, 1998)

Kiralfy, A.K.R., *Potter's Historical Introduction to English Law* (London: Sweet & Maxwell, 1958)

Lewis, Matthew, *Henry III, Son of Magna Carta* (Stroud: Amberley, 2018)

Maurois, A., trans. Henry L. Binsse, *A History of France* (London: Jonathan Cape, 1949)

Mackie, J.D., *The Earlier Tudors 1485-1558* (Oxford: Clarendon Press, 1952)

McKisack, M., *The Fourteenth Century 1307-1399* (Oxford: Clarendon Press, 1959)

Mortimer, Ian, *The Fears of Henry IV, The Life of England's Self-Made King* (London: Jonathan Cape, 2007)

Oman, C., *The History of England: From the Accession of Richard II to the Death of Richard III 1377-1485* (London: Longmans, Green & Co., 1906)

Poole, A.L., *Domesday Book to Magna Carta, 1087-1216* (Oxford: Oxford University Press, 1955)

Powicke, Sir Maurice, *The Thirteenth Century 1216-1307* (Oxford: Clarendon Press, 1962)

Ramsay, J. H., *Lancaster and York: A Century of English History AD1399-1485 Volume 1* (Oxford: Clarendon Press, 1892)

Rodger, N. A. M., *The Safeguard of the Sea: A Naval History of Britain 660-1649* (London: Penguin, 2004)

Ross, James, *Henry VI, A Good, Simple & Innocent Man* (London: Penguin Books, 2016

Seward, Desmond, *The Demon's Brood, The Plantagenet Dynasty that Forged the English Nation* (London: Constable, 2014)

Starkey, David, *Six Wives, The Queens of Henry VIII* (London: Chatto & Windus, 2003)

Warren, W.L., *Henry II* (Newhaven & London: Yale University Press, 2000)

Williams, Neville, *The Life & Times of Henry VII* (London: Weidenfeld & Nicholson, 1973)

Woolf, Alex, *The Tudor Kings & Queens, The Dynasty that Forged a Nation* (London: Arcturus Publications, 2017)

Index